Professing to Learn

Professing to Learn

*Creating Tenured Lives and Careers
in the American Research University*

ANNA NEUMANN

The Johns Hopkins University Press

Baltimore

The Johns Hopkins University Press
2715 North Charles Street
Baltimore, Maryland 21218-4363
www.press.jhu.edu

Library of Congress Cataloging-in-Publication Data

Neumann, Anna.
    Professing to learn : creating tenured lives and careers in the American research university / Anna
Neumann.
        p.   cm.
    Includes bibliographical references and index.
    ISBN-13: 978-0-8018-9131-1 (hardcover : alk. paper)
    ISBN-10: 0-8018-9131-0 (hardcover : alk. paper)
    1. College teachers—Vocational guidance—United States. 2. Scholars—Vocational guidance—United
States. 3. College teachers—Tenure—United States. I. Title.
    LB1778.2.N478 2009
    378.1′2—dc22   2008027264

A catalog record for this book is available from the British Library.

Chapter 2 includes revised versions of two previously published articles: Anna Neumann, "Professing Passion: Emotion in the Scholarship of Professors in Research Universities," *American Educational Research Journal* 43, no. 3 (2006): 381–424; and "To Glimpse Beauty and Awaken Meaning: Scholarly Learning as Aesthetic Experience," *Journal of Aesthetic Education* 39, no. 4 (2005): 68–88. © 2005 by the Board of Trustees of the University of Illinois. Used with permission of the University of Illinois Press.

Chapter 4 includes revised material from an article previously published as: Anna Neumann and Aimee LaPointe Terosky, "To Give and to Receive: Recently Tenured Professors' Experiences of Service in Major Research Universities," *Journal of Higher Education* 78, no. 3 (2007): 282–310. © 2007 The Ohio State University. Reprinted with permission.

Appendix C is a revised version of a paper previously published as: Anna Neumann, "Observations: Taking Seriously the Topic of Learning in Studies of Faculty Work and Careers," in *Advancing Faculty Learning through Interdisciplinary Collaboration,* edited by Elizabeth G. Creamer and Lisa Lattuca, 63–83, in New Directions for Teaching and Learning series, no. 102, Marilla D. Svinicki, editor-in-chief, and R. Eugene Rice, consulting editor (San Francisco: Jossey-Bass, 2005).

CONTENTS

ACKNOWLEDGMENTS

This volume reflects my own learning with and among others. My experience would not have been as deep, rich, or varied without the many individuals and communities whose contributions mark every page. I am indebted to all.

First and foremost, I express profound gratitude to the forty newly tenured scholars participating in the *Four Universities Project* and the thirty-eight in the *People's State University Project* for the time, thought, and trust they gave me. They, more than anyone else, taught me what it means to learn and to be a learner in a major American research university. My thanks as well to the eight university administrators and senior faculty leaders who oriented me to the campus cultures; to the top-level university officers who welcomed me onto their campuses, and to the several "institutional contact persons" who helped me acquire faculty lists and related campus data.

I also am very grateful to those who funded this work, thereby making it possible for me to bring it into being. The *Four Universities Project* was generously supported, over three years, by the Major Grants Program of the Spencer Foundation. Although I thank the many fine individuals at the foundation who had a role in the project, I single out former president Patricia Albjerg Graham and senior program officer Catherine Lacey for the confidence they expressed over many years. A most special thanks to Lauren Jones Young, senior program officer, for incomparable thoughtfulness, intellectual inspiration, and friendship. The earlier *People's State University Project* was funded by a series of small grants from the College of Education and central administration of Michigan State University and by a sabbatical fellowship at the University of Michigan's Center for Education of Women and Institute for Research on Women and Gender. My thanks to Charles Thompson, Robert Floden, and Mary Kennedy at Michigan State University and to Carol Hollenshead and Abigail Stewart at the University of Michigan for this direct support and for many helpful conversations. My writing of this book, as the culmination of a long line of my scholarly work, was made possible by a generous Dean's Grant for Tenured Faculty Research at Teachers College, Columbia University. I extend great appreciation also to Jacqueline Wehmueller, executive editor at the Johns Hopkins University Press, for her faith in this work and for incomparable writing advice. Special thanks as well to the "blind" peer reviewers whose comments enriched this book. Although I have benefited in many ways from these many sources of support, I claim full responsibility for the content and quality of this work, including the data presented, statements made, and views expressed. All quirks or errors are purely my own.

This volume draws broadly and deeply from my ten years on the faculty of the College of Education at Michigan State University (MSU), especially from my participation in a community of scholars of educational psychology (learning and development) and teacher education. I credit my learning—about learning itself, about teaching, and about intellectual lives and careers—to my work with many MSU colleagues who lived so much of what they professed. My personal thanks to Penelope L. Peterson, who introduced me to the intrigues of subject matter learning; Steven Weiland, who opened doors to intellectual autobiography; Suzanne Wilson, who inspired my work on learning in teaching; Deborah Ball, for clarifying teaching's contributions to countless professions; David Labaree, for modeling excellence in all lines of faculty work; Lynn Paine and Brian Delany, for upholding the value of critique; and not least, Dick Prawat, for representing an incomparable blending of learning and leadership. I thank Dick especially, along with Dean Carole Ames, for letting me craft a space in which my learning could flourish.

Still more directly, I thank the following colleagues at Teachers College and around the country for generous critiques that strengthened my thinking and writing. Estela Bensimon, Kevin Dougherty, Judith Glazer-Raymo, Joseph Hermanowicz, Penelope Peterson, and Carolyn Riehl read between four and eight chapters of an earlier draft and provided insightful and helpful comments. Gregory Anderson, Elizabeth Creamer, Lori Custodero, David Hansen, Lisa Lattuca, Dan McAdams, and Kerry-Ann O'Meara provided thoughtful reviews of discrete writings over the years. My colleague Jane Monroe has shown unceasing interest and encouragement. My friend Maxine Greene was and is a source of unremitting inspiration.

I also want to thank the amazing doctoral students at Teachers College and MSU who assisted me in my research over the years. At MSU Susan Blake, Porntip Chaichanapanich, Diane Hamm, and Yonghee Suh served as project assistants, helping me get both projects off the ground. At Teachers College Macy Lenox and Aimee LaPointe Terosky, both research assistants, made core contributions to my work, and I am grateful to them both. Macy's synthetic talents made the five campus descriptions (chap. 6 and app. A) possible. Aimee's intellectual fingerprints are on almost every page of this volume; I will say more shortly about her contribution to my work. My thanks, too, to Kimberley B. Pereira for assistance in data analysis and helpful textual commentary; she is a coauthor of chapter 5 on professors' agency for scholarly learning. Kerry Charron, Katie Conway, Negar Farakish, Jennifer Hong-Silwany, Riva Kadar, Frances Magee, Anabella Martinez, Tamsyn Phifer, and Julie Schell gave freely of their ideas, creativity, and energy, reviewing drafts of the emerging work and sharing in the writing of several conference papers and articles. The *Four Universities Project* would not have been possible without the excellent administrative assistance I received from Lisa Payne, Jeff Sun, and especially Eda (Dolly) Sankar, along with outstanding interview transcription from Karla Bellingar. My sincere appreciation to all.

I close with heartfelt thanks to those, some of whom I mentioned already, who have been closest to me and, by extension, to my work: Susan Kraemer, for helping me understand distinctions between passion and profession, learning and life; Aimee LaPointe Terosky, for "taking seriously" the teaching and learning in which she so readily engages and shares with others; Penelope Peterson, for promoting learning as a way to live and for extending a friendship and collegueship that informed this book to its core; and Aaron Pallas, for sharing invaluable observations about the life course and about the conduct of educational research, for questioning me at every turn while communicating steadfast belief in me and my work, for making me laugh when I most needed to, and for showing me that love is what matters most of all.

Professing to Learn

Introduction

Most people imagine university professors lecturing in front of large auditorium-style classes or probing students' understandings in small advanced seminars. In other words, teaching. Others think of university professors as researchers—puzzling over laboratory experiments, leafing through texts in far-off archives, intently revising manuscripts behind closed office doors. Academics themselves see much more. Not only do they and their colleagues teach and conduct research; they also advise students on course selection, mentor master's theses, guide doctoral dissertations, and sit on university committees. Professors' work involves teaching, including student advising and mentoring; research, including artistic creation and disciplinary or interdisciplinary scholarship; and service, including institutional maintenance, upkeep of the discipline or field, and outreach to publics near and far.

Popular images of university professors reflect two assumptions: first, that the professors are in full professional maturity—they are tenured and probably midcareer; and second, that what infuses the full span of their work is deep content knowledge and equally deep expertise in research. But the popular view covers up a reality that only professors experience firsthand: professors develop over time, and professional maturity is itself an unfolding process. Maturity "feels" different at different points of the advanced career. Professors themselves also know that just as they grow, develop, and change, so does their subject matter expertise—sometimes in exciting and forward-moving ways and at other times more slowly, in ways that can feel more like loss than gain. Different professors experience their stature, sense of intellectual-professional self, and expertise in different ways at different times, even within tenured careers.

Although professors' work has been discussed in detail in numerous research studies—as has professors' development and the challenges and opportunities they face in the mature, tenured career—rarely is it talked about in relation to their *scholarly learning*. We know very little about what happens to professors' scholarly learning as they proceed in their careers: what happens to their sense of engagement with a subject that means a great deal to them or to which they have committed themselves deeply throughout their lives. Yet without that subject, and the scholarly learning that it implies, the professor has little to profess—to teach, learn, research, and serve. Although central to their work and careers, professors' scholarly learning is a "black box" in the public's understanding of what it means to be a professor and to engage in academic work. It is similarly an enigma to policy makers, university leaders, and many educational researchers.

Viewing that gap as a serious impediment to the improvement of American higher education, I designed this volume to address it at a critical career point: the years immediately following the awarding of tenure. I refer to this period as the "early post-tenure career." Why this career phase in a book that is deeply concerned with professors' scholarly learning? An underlying assumption of American higher education is that once a professor gains tenure, she is professionally and intellectually self-sufficient. Because the professor has passed through a tenure review—arguably the most challenging evaluation of scholarly learning in the academic career—this feature of her career no longer needs attention. I see it differently. Drawing on two three-year studies of newly tenured university professors' learning and development, I contend that the early post-tenure years merit close attention, that they may serve as a critical pivot point in the contemporary university-based faculty career, and that the changes that professors experience in their work through this period can bear on their learning, their scholarly learning in particular.

Why We Need to Pay Attention to Newly Tenured Professors' Learning

The work of a university professor changes through the early post-tenure career. My research confirms a pattern familiar to many professors but rarely addressed in higher education research: that at this career stage professors' responsibilities expand, sometimes in overwhelming ways. As these professors carry out this growing workload, they encounter a faculty and administrative culture that has been largely invisible to them in the past. They teach larger, increasingly diverse classes. Their advisement and student mentoring go up. They also begin to mentor junior colleagues. Not least, they take on new research obligations that are sometimes more important to others than to themselves. Newly tenured university professors often find that they are doing more work than ever before. They also find that their work becomes more diversified and more complex: a single research project is suddenly multiple, disparate research projects. Students are no longer traditional-age majors; they vary in age, experience, major interests, and degree of commitment. Colleagues are more than coworkers and senior mentors; many are now players with lives and agendas of their own. What could be time for reading and study becomes time for committee work.

And not only does the work of newly tenured professors expand and grow more complex. So does their learning. I contend that this second change—largely undiscussed in higher education—is critical. It explains why as university professors learn more and more so they can carry out the expanding new work that "comes at them" at this career stage, they must set some of their scholarly learning aside. Human attention and energy stretch only so far, and it is challenging to learn many complex activities, some interesting and others not, all at once. For newly tenured professors it is hard to learn the new responsibilities of midcareer while continuing to learn their core subject matters. Thus, in the early post-tenure career professors may find that they cannot commit as much time and energy to their scholarly learning as, years earlier, they thought they would at this career point. They may instead be engaged in learning their newly inherited post-tenure duties while carrying them out. Many at this career stage experience surprise. Some of them adjust quickly, shifting into new modes of thinking, acting, and learning. Others cope as best they can, searching for ways to improve their lot. A few seek ways out of careers they had long struggled to build.

Despite challenges such as these, a good number of the newly tenured professors I interviewed persisted, responsively and responsibly, through the learning challenges of the early post-tenure career while also promoting their core substantive learning. They did this by carefully orchestrating their work, becoming strategic about their careers, and remaining attentive to their scholarly learning. In the following chapters, I draw on these professors' experiences to make a case for the meaning and importance of scholarly learning in the academic career. I argue that scholarly learning must have a place in conversations about professors' development and academic affairs. I also define the challenges that newly tenured professors often experience as they strive to pursue their scholarly learning. Not least, I present strategies that newly tenured professors can use to hold on to or advance their scholarly learning, along with organizational strategies that leaders may invoke to help them do so. This storyline assumes the significance—and power—of the early post-tenure career and of learning, especially scholarly learning, within it.

SIGNIFICANCE OF THE EARLY POST-TENURE CAREER

Little scholarship exists on academic midcareer, from the awarding of tenure through retirement, a period of up to twenty-five years. (Exceptions are Roger Baldwin, Christina J. Lunceford, and Kim E. Vanderlinden's analyses of data collected through the National Study of Postsecondary Faculty, NSOPF-99.) Faculty at this career stage constitute the large majority of the American professoriate. As its "senior members," "productive corps," and "full citizens," midcareer faculty shoulder core institutional responsibilities: research, teaching, service, and outreach. Aside from studies of the tenure review itself,[1] successful applicants' experiences of the pre- to post-tenure transition have not been studied. I refer to this period as the "early post-tenure career" and at times as "early midcareer." This phase of the academic career is largely unstudied, though myths about it abound (consider the post-tenure myth of unlimited freedom, irresponsibility, or guilt and depression).[2]

The lack of attention to the early post-tenure career is not surprising. Research on higher education is often framed in response to perceived problems. There is not much that is openly troublesome in this career phase. After all, recently tenured professors have just gone through the roughest review of the academic career, and if they have "made it," they must be fine: their research record is likely to be more developed than it has been at any other time in their careers. And their teaching evaluations are also likely to be up to par. Moreover, the majority of their external reviewers have attested to the value and quality of these professors' past accomplishments and future promise. Right after getting tenure, problems of professional performance and commitment are not likely to be in sight. Further, professors at this stage sometimes go on sabbatical, so they may fall off their university's "radar screen" for a brief period of time. Given their career positioning, they may be viewed as having just passed through the rigors of early career socialization and thus as being far from advanced- or end-career burnout. They are in the "young adulthood" of their careers—at their prime, the future before them. What's to worry about?

Yet a problem lurks just beneath the surface of this career stage: how to position recently tenured university professors, as a central intellectual resource of this nation, on tracks of work that will keep them intellectually and pedagogically alive for the full duration of their careers. The costs of ignoring this problem are potentially great, given the up-front institutional investment that tenure represents. Much has been said about the costs of tenure weighed against a career incumbent's lifetime return to a college or university.[3] We must consider also the broader social costs of faculty preparation: the resources devoted to identifying, preparing, and otherwise supporting promising students, then junior scholars, through tenure. Institutions bear these costs. Families and individuals also invest deeply in the making of an academic career, whether in terms of rising university tuitions or forgone salaries. And the public also pays to support universities in their faculty development endeavors. The question "What's the return?" must be targeted at employing institutions and the public at large.

The question must also be targeted at professors. Behind the institutional and social investment is the personal investment that large numbers of individuals, aspiring to scholarly lives, make over many years prior to earning tenure: the years of crafting subjects of expertise, learning to engage in inquiry or creative endeavor, starting up a career and mobilizing the resources of a university workplace, building a personal and family life that accommodates academic work, developing collegial networks and mentoring relationships, and learning to teach, advise, and do service. At the point of the "test" that tenure represents, professors are likely to be at an apex of accomplishment and promise—as prepared, supported, and polished in their scholarly work as many ever will be. Given the alignment of the early post-tenure career with early midlife, many professors also are at an age of heightened potential for productivity, engagement, and contribution. This is as good as it may get for some, and the challenge now is how to keep it that way for as long as possible and build on it.

We are faced with this challenge: how to position university professors, all at a career high, to hold on to their learning and to advance it, to become better learners than they already are, and to help their students learn as they themselves have. This is a relatively unspoken problem of the early post-tenure career—admittedly, one that simmers rather than boils and one that professors and institutional leaders could work on prior to its becoming a manifest problem. Addressing such issues proactively early in the post-tenure career may yield bolder and more positive results than can faculty development, in the form of remediation, applied later on. But doing so requires better understanding than we have now of what goes on through this career period and why it matters.

THE IMPORTANCE OF LEARNING IN THE PROFESSORIAL CAREER

To understand scholars' personal investments in higher education, we must understand their scholarly learning, especially *what* they learn in it and how that "what" changes over time. We also need to know what else they learn, besides knowledge deemed scholarly, and how these various learning experiences interact.

But what is learning? I define *learning* as the construction of knowledge, scholarly and otherwise, that a person experiences through mental processes that involve realization, surprising juxtapositions of thought, contextualization of ideas within other ideas or building bridges between them, and so on. Mental experiences such as these can yield new understandings of problems, puzzles, and images. Such knowledge construction requires the presence of a subject (a problem, puzzle, or image) to be explored and known. It assumes a thinker's inner engagement with it. Learning as inner experience often draws on knowledge from within the learner's life. How, and what, one knows from living one's life can shape and shade one's learning—what one knows. Professors are no exception. Their work has personal roots of this sort. But despite its personal sources, learning is social and interpersonal, occurring through minds that interact in considering a subject of study. The early post-tenure career poses numerous opportunities for such knowledge interchange. It also poses challenges to scholarly learning.[4]

But why should we care about what professors learn after tenure? We should care so that we can assess, first, whether professors are positioned, after earning tenure, to continue in their study of the subject matter knowledge that drives their teaching and research. We should care also so that we can gauge the adequacy of professors' learning of practices and topics they will need to progress meaningfully through their careers—for example, how to teach increasingly diverse students, how to exert departmental and collegiate leadership, and how to write major grant proposals. We should care further so that we can promote professors' efforts to continue to learn and develop the content that they share with the public that relies on and supports their work.

If we view the primary function of the professoriate, and of higher education, to be the construction, sharing, and application of disciplinary and professional subject matter knowledge, lack of understanding about what keeps professors vital in the long run, in these subjects, is problematic. Without a solid understanding of how professors create and share their subject matter knowledge through their careers, we cannot address larger questions of academic relevance and effectiveness—notably, why higher education teaching, learning, research, and scholarship are not as meaningful or effective as they might be and why institutional, state, and federal policies directed toward improving these activities often fail. More pointedly, if we do not know what contributes to the making of a generative teacher or thoughtful researcher, then it is hard to know what kind of leadership or policy to invoke in the name of fostering such development. And if we do not know what contributes to some professors' thriving as scholars and teachers, we have little beyond the anecdotal to draw on to promote constructive growth. Without clear understanding of how professors experience their scholarly learning, including the personal and professional conditions that facilitate and inhibit it, institutional and policy structures aimed at improving knowledge production and dissemination are unlikely to be usefully directed toward academic improvement. Scholarly learning is in many ways at the heart of the academic enterprise.

What Context Contributes: Professors' Learning in Tenured Positions in Research Universities

This book explores the learning experiences of a select portion of contemporary postsecondary faculty in the United States: tenured professors in major research universities who have just recently acquired tenure. Because universities strive to lead scholarly endeavor in society and because tenured faculty are those university's scholarly leaders, these individuals' career-long learning must be viewed as a prized resource. Increasing demands for scientific knowledge, for policies and practices that advance the social and political-economic good, and for understanding that contributes to the flourishing of humanity all hinge on the learning that thoughtful learners can help to advance. That said, scholarly learning is a concern for *all* faculty regardless of appointment status and institutional type. Although reflecting only the experiences of newly tenured university professors, the studies I conducted have meaning for all who pursue scholarly learning. To appreciate the opening that this book provides into scholarly learning in this broader sense requires acknowledging the broad range of learners, in faculty positions and institutions, to whom it applies.

Appointment Status

The contingent workforce is less prominent in research universities and selective liberal arts colleges than in other institutions, but increasing numbers of academics, based in research universities, work off the tenure track.[5] Because the work of these faculty members contributes substantively to core university missions—especially teaching and research—we must understand that scholarly learning matters to them as well. Although I was not able to explore the scholarly learning of contingent faculty in the two studies I report on here, I hope that future research will do so. Recent writings on higher education portray massive and transforming changes in faculty appointments (toward increased contingency), faculty work (toward intensified teaching or research), academic careers (toward decline in stature of the profession), and institutions (toward diversification),[6] along with mounting workplace challenges: expanding and fragmenting faculty workload marked by decreasing professional autonomy; and concomitant concerns about equity, academic freedom, autonomy, flexibility, collegiality, and opportunities for growth.[7] Such changes are likely to affect the work of all faculty, directly or indirectly. The changes will in all likelihood also affect the faculty's learning amid the new work and changed work contexts that they create.

Institutional Type

In addition to reaching across the tenure track, scholarly learning reaches across diverse types of higher education institutions. It is not the sole property of faculty in major research universities. It also matters to professors and instructors in community colleges, liberal arts colleges, and comprehensive colleges and universities as well as to knowledge workers in a variety of other modern-day educating institutions—from software development firms and purveyors of distance education to public television, museums, and art galleries. Scholarly learning matters, too, to K–12 teachers and students attuned to subject matter learning.

This is not an irrelevant point. Speaking from the perspective of higher education, Jack Schuster and Martin Finkelstein refer to a "steady" yet major "rerouting of faculty from the research and doctoral universities to other institutional types" (43), especially to community colleges and public comprehensive institutions, mostly over the past twenty-five years. Doctoral students increasingly take their degrees, and their passions and energies for subject matter learning, to jobs outside academe—or at least they try. Schuster and Finkelstein discuss numerous new work options for the academic of the twenty-first century: proprietary institutions, distance-learning enterprises, commercial coursework companies, and corporate universities.[8] These days scholarly learning can grow well outside the major research university. But even for aspiring scholars who succeed in acquiring full-time tenure-track appointments in major research universities, change is on the horizon. Noting that faculty work "has increased in all types of institutions," Schuster and Finkelstein emphasize that "it has increased most dramatically at the research universities, where faculty have been subjected to increasing instructional demands *and* increasing research demands" (81). Such changes in professors' work may also imply changes in professors' learning. For example, as some of the intellectual resources they need for their learning dissipate (autonomy, time to think), others materialize anew (increased connection to external communities that may benefit from academic research)—in either case, reshaping those professors' learning.

One additional wrinkle on the topic of faculty work and workplaces needs ironing out: whereas historic changes to professors' work may help explain what it means, and what it is like, to learn as a professor today, the content and structure of the higher education system—its design, so to speak—contributes as well. In other words, to appreciate faculty work and faculty learning for what they are at any point in time requires attention to social-evolutionary changes and variation purposefully built into the system. I refer here to cross-institutional differences that arise from institutions' unique social purposes and identities—namely, their missions, the power of institutional type in American higher education.

What do differences in institutional mission (and thereby institutional type) imply for professors' scholarly learning? This question demands attention in light of my concern in this book with what and how professors working in a particular type of institution, the major research university, learn: the kinds of knowledge they pursue, encounter, and take into themselves as real and meaningful within an institution committed, through its core mission, to the production of academic knowledge—that is, to scholarly learning. One must then ask: how is it that the unique mission of the major American research university, and the unique missions of other types of institutions, may palpably touch professors' learning? Through what features of organizational design might this occur?

Classical theories of organization, drawn from organizational psychology, help to explain why and how this may happen: an organization's overarching, socially chartered aim—its mission—is fulfilled by the internal transforming mechanisms and processes established, and funded recurrently, to fulfill that aim. These central mechanisms and processes are instrumental to an organization's achievement of its mission. In higher education this transforming organizational core includes teaching, research, and other academic activities. The individuals hired to activate those internal processes (in higher education, professors and instructors) must learn how to carry them out in ways that will realize their employing organization's unique aim. [9]

The application of this view to higher education in its diverse forms is fairly direct: community college instructors, tied to a mission to teach and otherwise respond to community needs, are socialized to the conduct of instruction and service. The faculties of comprehensive colleges become engaged in large-scale teaching, advisement, and service in response to regional or state imperatives also in line with their employing organization's mission. Liberal arts college professors, socialized to a mission of liberal education, usually are held to teaching, advisement, and other campus work directed at this collegiate aim. University professors, linked to a mission of research (e.g., in support of societal progress or human development), are pulled toward research and to preparing researchers. In sum, what professors are urged to do on the job in a distinctive higher education organization is framed by the organization's equally distinctive mission. Their work is critical to the realization of that mission.

Two implications surface for the faculty's learning. First, what professors learn as they carry out their particular college or university jobs and what campus administrators and faculty leaders value and reward vary by campus in reference to the work activities (teaching, research, outreach, and service) that the institution's mission values. This is not to say that professors in community colleges, liberal arts colleges, and state institutions do not engage in scholarly learning. They no doubt do, and they should. Yet the nature of professors' scholarly learning—and how it relates to research, teaching, outreach, and service—is likely to vary by institutional type, as reflected in the kinds of work that professors do to carry out core institutional activities aimed at realizing a college or university mission. In other words, scholarly learning may take diverse forms (e.g., it may be manifest in research, teaching, outreach, or service), but a particular institutional mission may value some forms of scholarly learning over others, providing resources toward the more valued forms, and constraining access to those less valued.[10]

Second, faculty work that is central to a university's mission (e.g., research) is likely to figure prominently in the pre-tenure careers of an institution's faculty, such that pre-tenure faculty will have to learn that work and establish records of doing it well to warrant tenure. This suggests, of course, that after earning tenure, university professors need to engage in catch-up learning to round out the many things, less central to their campus's mission but nonetheless relevant to organizational existence, that they did not learn earlier in their careers (e.g., university administration and service or large-scale teaching). Professors in other kinds of institutions may experience fewer discrepancies between their pre- and post-tenure work. Professors in community colleges or state universities, for example, well socialized in extensive teaching and service before earning tenure (given the demands of their campus missions), are likely to be less surprised with new or increased teaching and service demands after getting tenure than will university professors who, because of their campus's emphases on research and researcher development, learned little about their university's teaching, advising, mentoring, service, and administrative responsibilities through their pre-tenure careers. These activities arrive, post-tenure, sometimes by surprise. How university professors respond to them must be considered in conceptualizations of their career development and their learning specifically.

Foregrounding Scholarly Learning

Professors' scholarly learning demands attention through the full faculty career. But to study the totality of that career thoroughly and in its multiple forms would require a much more complex design than my research projects allowed. I chose to hone in on a sample, a microcosm of study—a reflection of the academic universe in a grain of the many sands that constitute it.[11] I chose the university-based post-tenure career as my study location for three reasons. First, as I have already noted, the early post-tenure career promised me access to professors at "high points" in their careers. Professors might be more accessible through it than they would be later on as they accumulate senior-level responsibilities. This period, I thought, would also lend itself to self-reflection in ways that others might not. Pre-tenure professors might be caught up in others' expectations, for example, and be less attentive to their own desires; professors in more advanced career might be well set in their ways and less attuned to the exploration that scholarly learning assumes. Second, the location—the major research university—offered an assemblage of resources fitting to the substance of the problem at issue: the research university's mission-driven interests in knowledge production guaranteed me access to professors who would be engaged in the construction of disciplinary and field-based subject matters through research. Thus, the research university gave me ready access to the phenomenon I most wanted to study: scholarly learning. And third, in "being there" myself—in the university and at early post-tenure—at the very time I initiated this line of study, I was personally motivated to understand it, given the questions I was asking about my own work and career at the time. My standpoint at the time, combined with my perspective now, have let me see features of scholarly learning that a narrower and less personally grounded time frame might not have allowed.[12]

The story of scholarly learning in this book reflects a unique setting (the major research university as place, the early post-tenure career as time) and a unique role (that of the tenured university professor). But as the preceding discussion indicates, the book is not fully about these things. To be about them would require that I explore both the university and the early post-tenure career in far greater detail—attending not just to professors' scholarly learning but also to the systems of institutional and disciplinary rewards and assessments through which professors proceed, elements of professors' socialization and their own later contributions to the socializing systems into which they enter, professors' contributions to and their experiences of the multiple faculty cultures of which they are a part, their responses to power and politics in the university, the extent to which professors' jobs are framed by the changing mix of permanent and contingent faculty on their campuses, institutional support in the management of personal and professional lives, and patterns of programmatic support, among other elements. Although important—even urgent at times—none of these features of professors' work elucidate professors' scholarly learning; they may, in fact, distract attention from it. Despite their centrality to other research, and in the higher education enterprise at large, I set them aside in this book in order to stay tuned to my central concern: scholarly learning. It is relevant that I am more attentive to the person in the role, job, career, and institution—and to her experiences of scholarly learning—than to the organizational rubrics that identify her socially as a certain kind of worker.[13]

For much the same reason, I depart from an established convention in higher education research: namely, describing organizational context before discussing something of interest (such as professors' learning) that goes on in it. Detailed presentations of organizational context first can filter out features that have little to do with the organization as such. Studies of faculty that begin with discussion of governance, evaluation, rewards, and institutional improvement, for example, "color" their topics with organizational meaning in ways that can cover up other equally important meanings stemming from other sources. Such studies, which privilege the organizational stance, typically do not give equal voice to the personal origins and meanings of career as situated in a personal life, also a context.[14] Life as context portrays scholarly learning differently than does professional organization as context. To stay focused on scholarly learning, I delay discussion of the organizational locations of professors' scholarly learning until late in the volume and then do so as part of a learning-anchored organizational analysis (see chap. 6 and app. A).

Organization of the Book

Chapter 1 defines scholarly learning as a central experience in recently tenured university professors' careers and lives. Drawing on the experiences of three recently tenured professors—a physicist, literary scholar, and public health researcher—I define scholarly learning as professors' continuous learning in subject matters that are deeply meaningful to them. The chapter also summarizes the two research projects on which the book is based, the *People's State University Project* and the *Four Universities Project*.

Drawing on data collected through the *Four Universities Project,* chapter 2 delves into the personal and emotional features of professors' scholarly learning. Drawing on the experiences of the forty professors participating in the *Four Universities Project,* and especially the experiences of a musician and astronomer, I introduce the concept of "passionate thought" as a high point in professors' scholarly learning. Passionate thought encompasses professors' goals, immediate feelings, and memories; it propels professors' scholarly pursuits amid their daily academic work.

Whereas in chapter 2 I accent the passionate aspects of passionate thought, in chapter 3 I emphasize the nature of the thinking involved in it. I provide a professor-as-learner's eye view of the kinds of knowledge changes that professors experience in their scholarly learning. Chapter 3 also documents changes in professors' instrumental learning—their gaining of knowledge relevant to their professorial work but not focused on scholarly learning, such as learning to address the political dynamics of colleagueship, learning to navigate bureaucratic cultures of the university, gaining facility in the procedural tools and artifacts of organizational life, and so on.

Chapters 4 and 5 explore how newly tenured university professors respond to calls for instrumental endeavor, required by the university or others beyond it, while "holding true" to their scholarly learning and advancing it. Rather than choosing one kind of learning to the detriment of the other, how might professors orchestrate both in useful and generative ways? In response, chapter 4 presents the range of contexts in which newly tenured university professors may experience their scholarly learning—where in their lives it happens—and then explores more fully two of those sites: their teaching first and foremost (graduate and undergraduate) and their service (outreach and institutional). Building on that discussion, chapter 5, coauthored with Kimberley B. Pereira and informed by my previous work with Aimee LaPointe Terosky and Julie Schell, discusses how newly tenured university professors may position themselves as agents of their scholarly learning amid growing calls to engage in other endeavors. The chapter presents several work-management strategies for doing so.

Drawing on the realization that newly tenured professors simply "can't do it all," chapter 6 considers how the university supports and impedes their scholarly learning. In this chapter I document campus sites that professors, representing diverse disciplines, genders, and institutional forms, associate with growth and challenge for their scholarly learning.

Chapter 7 summarizes the book's key points, restates the meaning and importance of professors' scholarly learning, and offers insights and suggestions to professors, university leaders, and researchers who strive to strengthen it.

I view professors' scholarly learning as animating—and humanizing— higher education's mission of knowledge production for the social good. Scholarly learning converts the abstract concept of "knowledge production" into a human event, a living person's experience that, at its best, is a search for personal meaning. To understand such learning requires understanding how its most central learners— professors—feel, know, and otherwise experience it. That is what I have sought to learn and to profess.

CHAPTER ONE

Into the Middle

Mapping the Early Post-Tenure Career in the Research University

What happens to university professors after getting tenure? What happens to their desires and commitments to study and create the subjects, ideas, and practices they teach and write about and otherwise share? What happens to their learning as scholars? Drawing on interviews with seventy-eight recently tenured professors working in five leading American research universities, I show that professors at this career stage are facing unique challenges. Many struggle to keep up the learning required to teach and conduct research in the areas in which they have been trained—not for lack of ability and clearly not for lack of direction or interest.[1]

Quite the contrary, with tenure in hand, most university professors want to contribute to their disciplines and fields of study, campuses, society, and humanity. The professors I interviewed cared a great deal about their students and classes; they cared about the work they did to advance the good of others, on and off campus. They spoke, often eloquently and with feeling, about the subjects, questions, and ideas they pursue in their research, teaching, service, and outreach. They spoke of sharing their learning with others and of crafting jobs and careers that allow them to do so. Many counted on the tenure they had just earned to do so, viewing it as a sign that the community values their work. Tenure promises continuous employment. For the newly tenured scholar it also marks heightened stature, professional freedom, and opportunities to learn freely within the academic community.

Upon entering their post-tenure careers, most of the newly tenured university professors I interviewed found that two things had changed: their workloads, as higher education administrators and policy makers often call it; and significantly, their learning loads.[2] To do the work—much of it new to them—they had to learn how to do it. Both the doing and learning to do absorbed a great deal of their time and energy.

My research highlighted workload and learning load increases in the following academic job domains: research, research management, teaching, advisement and mentoring of students and colleagues, department or program administration, committee leadership and other forms of institutional service, university outreach, and disciplinary/professional service.[3] Such changes in doing and learning caught many of the newly tenured professors I interviewed off-guard, and they struggled to respond. Protected from a fair amount of institutional duty pre-tenure, many university professors experience their new post-tenure work—appearing in the form of service, teaching, and research unrelated to their interests—as a surprise that distracts them from the learning of subjects that mean a great deal to them. These newly tenured professors may feel caught between work that advances their academic passions—their scholarly learning—and other work that is necessary to the academic enterprise but of lesser personal meaning to them. I will occasionally refer to the latter work as "instrumental."[4] Instrumental work also entails learning.

How does scholarly learning differ from learning that is more instrumental? A professor who engages in scholarly learning engages with subject matter that means a great deal to her. This is work that she loves or that for nameless reasons she feels compelled to pursue: consider the committed scholar who actively studies themes of *wanting* in the poetry of Emily Dickinson. The scholar organizes her days (though with some struggle) around close readings of Dickinson's poems and critical commentary on them. She makes it a priority to stick with the Dickinson she loves and desires to understand, even when rewarded for doing something different—for example, to study the writings of Dickinson's contemporary Walt Whitman or to pursue the impact of their combined voices in the shaping of twentieth-century American poetry. In contrast, a professor who engages in learning deemed more instrumental engages with subject matters of lesser meaning to her, sometimes to the detriment of the learning that she loves: consider the committed Dickinson scholar who agrees to write a book about the poetry of John Keats, literature to which Dickinson herself was drawn, yet framed as a project that requires her to set aside her own pursuits, which she loves, for extended time. Or this scholar might take on an absorbing project that reflects little or no literary content at all, as in the case of the committed Dickinson scholar who takes on an administrative job or vast committee responsibilities that remove her from virtually all study of literature for long stretches of time. The balance between scholarly and instrumental learning matters a great deal in how professors view themselves, their work, and their careers.

But this is not how most policy makers, university leaders, and writers in higher education think about university professors' work. They attend more to the amount of teaching, research, and service that professors produce rather than to balancing their scholarly and instrumental work and learning. Drawing on data collected through two studies of the university-based early post-tenure career, I argue for a revised view in which professors' work and learning, scholarly and instrumental, surges through all elements of their teaching, research, service, and outreach. In this view it is not enough to think about the amount of teaching and service in which professors engage. One must also assess the kinds of learning that go on in each of these work activities, and across them, especially the extent to which these activities lend themselves to professors' scholarly learning.

Before pursuing this point further, I must deepen the view of scholarly learning. What does it mean and feel like for a professor to engage in scholarly learning—to be in its grasp? What does that professor see and sense, and what does she derive from within experiences of scholarly learning? Given my initial, distanced introduction, I turn now to "up-close" views of professors' scholarly learning, exploring how they experience it inside.

RICHARD MARIN: "BY LOOKING OUT THERE, I'M LOOKING IN HERE"

Richard Marin, a theoretical physicist newly tenured at Hope State University, spoke with vivid excitement about his pursuits of "individuality and identity . . . [in] the subatomic world" of quantum mechanics and microphysics.[5] He described a newly opened angle in his continuing research. I asked him if he thought that he had changed as a researcher over the past few years.

"To a certain degree," he said, "I don't know if it's a fundamental change, but it's a noticeable change . . . It may end up being a fundamental change when all is said and done."

I puzzled over Marin's comment, then asked him to elaborate. "It's even subtle to me," he explained.

It's not that I have a new set [of] techniques. I use the same old techniques . . . I think the class of problems I'm drawn to are still . . . the same. It's really changed in the degree to what I'm looking to get out of [that] class of problems . . . A problem is like . . . a big building . . . and you can look at it from a bunch of different angles. And some angles you always find more interesting than others. And so [the new class of problems has] rearranged what angles I find pretty . . . the things I found pretty before, I still find beautiful. But certain things that before I just passed over quickly . . . I'm paying more attention to. But . . . more importantly, I see new views that I never thought were there before. It's like . . . a whole new side has opened up to a problem that I never knew was there.

Early in our talk Richard Marin introduced me to his latest work in physics, describing its content and what it is like for him to experience moments of "revelation," as he calls them. Marin says that his newest subject matter project is the primary "space" of his scholarly learning. In that space he glimpses beauty, a view of his subject that he had previously overlooked but that now grips his attention—a set of problems, new to his thought, that lead him to see "a whole new side . . . open[ing] up." Yet Marin does far more than "glimpse" this beauty. In working it, exploring it, he engages it in terms all its own. That beauty touches him deeply, and when it escapes him, he struggles to find it again.

I asked Marin to tell me what it is like for him personally—what it feels like—when things are going well in his research.

I'm not so sure how common this is, [but] when things are going well, what happens is first of all, it affects me physically, not just intellectually . . . My body kicks into a higher gear . . . I shake, and I can't stop moving . . . I'm restless . . . I barely sleep as it is, and I sleep even less. It just really affects my whole rhythms. Although it might sound like it's distracting, it's not. It's wonderful, it really is. My students [say] that I'm talking to the muses. I start channeling things. I start spewing forth conjectures or mathematical ideas without really knowing where they're coming from. And it's an interesting process. Obviously your subconscious is doing the information processing . . . when you're in . . . this agitated state . . . giving you the results of it while hiding the reasoning. And so then you have to go back and reconstruct where it came from and then try to use it. It's a wonderful feeling of . . . channeling. It's . . . like you're not creating it . . . It's being revealed to you. That's part of the reason I'm so interested in scripture . . . The notion of revelation in my work . . . I just love when I get these feelings—that I'm not creating physics or mathematics, but it's being revealed to me. And it's a fascinating feeling. And this difference between creation and revelation, to me, has always been fascinating. And so this revelatory experience is certainly a part of the great times . . . that's something I really, really, really enjoy. Yeah.

I asked him about his feelings when things go less well. "The bad times," he answered, "sometimes you just don't know why they're occurring."

I've been tired lately . . . It's midterms and my teaching, so . . . you're not completely focused . . . But other times, you're feeling sharp . . . you're thinking clearly, you're focusing and you're not distracted, and you still can't get anything done. It's a very frustrating feeling. I think a lot of physics . . . is about 95 percent failure, but you learn to live with that. But when that 95 goes to 99, you really do start saying, "What's going on?" And it really is . . . banging your head against the wall. And it's not a terrible feeling, but it's certainly something that you want to get past, and what [that] requires is . . . this tenaciousness. I mean, you just can't give up. I mean . . . you don't have to be aggressive . . . A lot of what I do . . . is really very passive work. I . . . soak in a mathematical tub . . . it's very passive . . . but you just gotta keep soaking. You just can't divert your attention. You have to keep focusing when things aren't going well, when you're not getting somewhere, you have to keep focusing. And it'll come, it'll come. But it does get anxious at times, where you're wondering if it'll ever come.

Hearing of this scholar's *need* for such moments of insight and feeling in scholarly learning and hearing about his persistence, I wanted to know more. "What's physics to you?" I asked, "What do you do in the name of the physics?" His initial response—"That's . . . a real tough question"—unfolded into a thoughtful answer:

Physics is part of such a large fabric to me. When I was deciding what field to choose . . . over twenty years ago, I had a dilemma between philosophy and mathematics and physics. Those are the things I was drawn to—those are the things which were important to me. And I never separate them in my mind . . . even though I've chosen to be a physicist.

And so the reasons I chose to study physics—[I realize that] this could apply to any academic discipline . . . [is that physics] is something that addresses what it means to be human. I think physics . . . like any truly analytical discipline . . . is a study of the human mind. It's the study of what it means to be who you are. It's a study of your own person. And so by looking *out there*, I'm looking *in here*. And physics, to me, is an unbelievably precise and efficient and beautiful—incredibly beautiful—way of studying myself. And of studying others, other humans . . . To me, that's what it's all about.

And it's similar with mathematics, and similar with philosophy. With philosophy, it's very explicit—you're asking questions about the human condition after all—and about the whole range of human emotions . . . With mathematics, you're studying conceptual structures . . . [and t]hough you're not studying the full range of human emotion, you're at least studying things which are in your head . . . But physics [is] about things *out [there]*. But after all, we're made of those same things . . . and [so] those things that we see *out there*, fundamentally replicate themselves *in here* [within oneself] . . . In studying the things out there, you're led to mathematical and philosophical ideas that, again, address the human condition. And truthfully, any focused thought [in any discipline] will address the human condition—any rigorous focused thought. And to me the one that speaks to me the most is this combination of physics, mathematics, and philosophy. [Italics added.]

Richard Marin explained that, to him, physics is a channel to insight, in part about the world out there and, somehow through that world, into his own self. For him the stuff of physics—what for others is the stuff of philosophy—is a gate that leads outward, toward knowing the world of which he, and we, are a part, but circuitously also a gate into himself. But how did he find that gate, again and again, in his life amid the boundless possibilities for study in physics? How did he settle on certain problems to solve?

"Sometimes I feel that I'm not even choosing them—they're chosen for me," he explained.

> I often feel that I'm naturally drawn to things . . . In the process of observing and . . . thinking—not with any eye to . . . research, [just] my brain latch[ing] onto something. And you know, I can't do anything [then] unless I study it. And so . . . I think physics is much more of an addiction than a choice of career. And sometimes problems are like that as well. I really think that problems choose me more than me choosing problems. And so from that point of view, it's very difficult to describe the process, but certainly, the problems that I like to work on have a certain smell and taste. They have a more philosophical side, and they have a more mathematical side. Unless I see those sides of them, they're rarely of interest to me.
>
> It's sort of one of those things . . . they come and get me more than me looking for them. And since I'm not really actively looking for them, it's hard to say what criterion I'm using. But . . . it's really . . . like taste. Why does broccoli taste good to you? It's really hard to say why broccoli tastes good to you, if you like broccoli, right? It tastes good. It's an immediate experience of tasting goodness. Right? I mean, it really is. And so it's really hard to analyze that further. It's like I've got an extra sense, and this sense could be touched in a good or a bad way, but . . . it's a sense. What is hotness? I don't know. It's just this thing I feel. What is a good project? This thing I feel . . . when something gets me.

As I listened to Richard Marin speak of the meaning, feeling, and power of his relationship with physics, I had to wonder where in his life more broadly he placed that relationship. How did his work with physics relate to other aspects of his existence? I asked him about the place of his scholarly work in his life.

"To me," he said, "one of the ways of fulfilling life is to do scholarly work."

> I . . . don't know how to say it really well. My first inkling, to answer [your] question, [is] that my life revolves around the scholarly work, but I don't think that gives the right flavor of what I'm saying. I really think that there's no separation between me and physics and mathematics and philosophy. They're just all one entity, and whether the work is scholarly or not . . . it's all part of the same thing. And you know . . . there are external things in my life which mean an awful lot, whether they be relationships or [athleticism] . . . It affects [them] . . . But my relationship with my work . . . philosophy, mathematics and physics . . . informs everything . . . those things as well. Those things don't fight my work. They [are] also connected . . . everything is very much connected, some [things] more than others obviously. And good or bad things in my work life can obviously feed into that. But that's true for everybody. I feel that the way I relate to athleticism or to friends or in relationships has a similar source to the way I relate to my work. Everything's very, very connected.

I asked Marin to clarify.

"Source," he said. "When I look at something . . . and I see something in it that I like, I really think about it. It has the exact same flavor to me [as] when I look at a problem [in physics] and see something. The source of me liking a person, or liking a sport, or liking a physics problem, or liking a philosophy question, is the same thing. And I don't separate them very much."

I asked Marin if there was any more he could say about that source. "It's a really tough one," he said. "In some sense I think all my work and all my studies have to do with finding out what that source is. And so I really think that I would love to know more about it."

What draws Marin to particular problems in physics shares its point of origin with what draws him to other experiences and relationships that also mean a great deal to him—to friends, his athletic activity, problems in philosophy. All are connected at a "source" of a related "flavor" or "taste" that he registers in experience, as emotional, physical, and intellectual feelings. Later in our talk, when Marin spoke more about the notion of a shared source, I asked him to elaborate on what it means to him to teach and mentor in physics. With hardly a pause, he answered: "It means doing high-level scholarly work and training the next generation of scholars. And providing for those people who you're teaching, who are not in your discipline, a clear idea of what your discipline is, and the reason why you're excited about it." I asked why that was important to him.

> I guess what I've come to realize over the years in . . . being a student myself and looking at . . . students who are around me, as well as being the professor and understanding how students react to things you say—I've come to see that inside of everybody, there's buttons. And certain buttons . . . —everybody has these buttons—and if you push them, it is no doubt almost 100 percent pleasureful . . . And some of the buttons we know from everyday life: there's the food pleasure button . . . the sex button, or whatever you want. There's [also] a mathematical button in everybody . . . and a lot of people don't know they've got it and the excitement [it can bring].
>
> Maybe I should generalize that. Maybe not call it a mathematical button but an analytical button. The excitement of analysis . . . it's partly selfish experience . . . just seeing that button pushed for the first time in somebody is such an exciting thing. Just to see somebody for the first time realize that this thing that either they didn't know about or thought was so dull could actually be unbelievably exciting—and sometimes life changing. Even if they never decide to do that work, it's an incredible experience. I think that there's a bunch of buttons like that, and at some point in my life, somebody pushed that—that history button in me . . . that religion button in me. And just to be able to return the favor, and to do that for somebody else with respect to my discipline. And there's an offshoot. I'm sure it's good for my discipline to have a general public that understands it, but that's truly not the primary reason that I find that interesting.

Marin said that what he feels in scholarly learning—its high points and insights revealed to him boldly in physics yet connected also to what he feels in philosophy and mathematics, in friendship and athleticism—is for himself. But in teaching, those feelings reflect, too, what he wants for his students. His experiences with the subject matters of physics drive his teaching—a process by which he eagerly seeks to engage his students, pushing "buttons" of potential insight. To engage others—to activate the unique excitement that physics can bring—requires that Marin know such excitement himself. And he does, in large part because others had once pushed those buttons in him. Marin teaches physics—he teaches *experiences in physics*. He teaches by activating experiences of physics in students that they might have sensed but did not know they could have.

NINA ALTMAN: "WHEN YOU'VE HIT A MAGIC TEXT . . ."

Newly tenured at Libra State University, Nina Altman creates a space of study and creative endeavor at the juncture of multiple literary fields. I found her office in a sprawling building, red brick and glass, gleaming hallways filled with students, graduate and undergraduate alike, talking and reading, staring in silence at text-filled screens, rushing to class, well filled packs on their backs.

I was struck in both interviews by the intertwining of Altman's learning in her scholarship and her life. The problems she worked on personally and autobiographically were mirrored in her scholarly strivings. Through our last interview she seemed keenly aware of that personal and intellectual blending, speaking about it at length, as when I asked her what literature was to her.

> It is a form of translation to me, first and foremost. Not only because I work with different languages, but even within English, any active interpretation [is] a form of translation. When you're trying to read a poem or lead a discussion about a poem in class, you're translating it for a particular context . . . you're drawing off certain things but leaving others. That negotiation and mediation I describe as translation—or [as] ways of allowing something to resonate and vibrate with different possible meanings. But I also think [that my] recurring preoccupation—what interests me—in literary study is a moment when you're suddenly aware of languages in a material form, whether it's written on the page

or it's sound. [In that form] it's unintelligible. Even though it's making meaning and you understand it in a certain context, you also confront it in this moment of strangeness. And that moment of encountering something in its radical foreignness is a recurring obsession in everything I . . . write about.

[My] book, this new project—what it means to encounter a letter in a foreign alphabet that you can't really voice. It's not spoken. It's a dead language. That encounter with letters is literature. It's kind of [a] primal scene . . . for me . . . because . . . I came to the [United] States when I was eight. I didn't speak any English, but I was conscious of language, sensitive to issues of language. So I really remember what it was like to be in this country where English was spoken, and [I] knew [that the English being spoken] had to signify something, but [I] couldn't make sense of it yet. And then all [I] could really see was this foreign language in written form, or [I could] hear it in spoken form—but it just didn't signify. And I think that's a very traumatic experience. But it's also an interesting one. And that . . . [is] what keeps drawing me into studying literature. You think about literature as expressive or communicative, but I'm very interested in the moments when there's resistance to communication—[when] you have this trace of something else. I don't want to make it too exotic or idealized. It's just that that, to me, is what I try to do in the classroom. And sometimes it frustrates students because they would like something to mean . . . and I keep pushing. I allow things to mean, but at the same time I keep pushing points of resistance to that.

I wanted to know more about the ephemeral thing she was invoking.

"So you said that we think of literature as expressive and communicative," I echoed what she had just said, "but then [that] there's this other something. Do you have any other ways of talking about what that other something [is]?"

"[It's the] materiality of language," she said, "I guess sensuous absorption into that, a loss of self into something that's other. And not necessarily a subjectivity or person. But just like this thing outside the self. I'm sure this sounds very romanticized. I don't know if I have other ways of describing . . . [it]—an affect of self-estrangement probably."

"So . . . is literature something that both has a meaning and has the no-meaning?"

"Yeah, yeah. Right. There are all these contexts for it to mean something, and there are ways in which it doesn't reduce the meaning. Not that it transcends meaning and becomes universal, but just [that] it can't reduce . . . to its meaning function."

For a cultural newcomer encounters with language that have no meaning, that stand as material constructions, opaque, can be startling—in Altman's terms, traumatic. They are moments when meaning is longed for or expected but unavailable, instances when materiality is all that can be seen, heard, and felt.

Nina Altman said that translation had been a way of life for her since childhood. Meanings rarely settled fully or firmly in place. They flowed between *being there* and *not*. In listening, I tried to understand how Altman's self-experience and scholarly impulses joined—how she called on her lived experiences in her writing, how she positioned autobiographical knowledge for her readers to understand as the source of her scholarly thought:

> "Translation . . . is pretty central to this book on [women a century or two ago and their struggles to learn the languages of ages long past]. I will be working more actively to theorize what that process [of translation through time and space] is and, in doing so, to communicate some of my own experience of it. Not that it will take a biographical or personal form in the book, like, 'This is what I feel when I translate' . . . I'm trying [rather] to communicate some aspect of my own translation experience, which has to do with this estrangement, or this hovering, and I will put that into my scholarship more. I feel like that's me—that's how I think. It's okay to write about that."

"So, whether you're actually actively doing translation or not, you could put some of that in there," I tried out.

"Yeah," she confirmed. "And one of the reservations I initially had about the book—oh, there's this weird specular identification or projection going [on], where I'm looking at [these] women [from a century or two ago] who were translating [ancient texts, languages no longer in use]—and [that] what I'm doing is [that] I'm projecting my own scene of reading into that. And maybe . . . I should separate the two. But . . . I've spoken to various people about this kind of specular, double reflection [and have realized] that that's the interest of the project. That somehow the way I'm involved in this scene of reading [and these women translating from the past] makes it interesting to write about . . . I am implicated in it, and I think I'm more comfortable in just acknowledging that. Without being confessional about it."

"You used the word *hovering* a while ago," I proffered, "how did you mean that?"

"You're in this space between languages, or at the moment, you're about to say something, but you can't—you don't have the words for it yet. That hovering—or what happens in the classroom when people are saying different things, and something's hovering in the air. And sometimes it precipitates into a comment, and sometimes it doesn't—but it's an experience that is valuable. And I think students see it as valuable, even if they can't walk away with something very tangible at the end of it. Do you know what I mean? . . . And translation is one way to get at that hovering. It's a certain kind of intersubjectivity . . . creating a space for mediation to happen. But not always having to do that decisively."

Altman's translational scholarship draws on herself, but without making that self an object of study; her texts in translation are object enough.

I asked Altman how she experiences her scholarly learning, albeit framed as translation. "Let's say you're reading something," I said, "and all of a sudden, you stop and say, 'My gosh, that's, that's a really nice idea.' [So for you,] what's the feel of a good idea?" Altman's answer was similar to Richard Marin's.

It's like a physical response, a sense of excitement . . . You know that you just hit a node. Or as a friend of mine says, you know when you've hit a magic text. You know, the text that brings all these things together . . . that's the magic text. Or Emily Dickinson . . . in response to [the question] "How do you know it's poetry?" Well . . . [it's] when the top of your head feels like it's been blown off. But I think for me . . . it makes me feel edgy, and sometimes it makes me panic . . . I feel like I'm getting too many good ideas all at once, and I don't quite know how to sort them out, or to organize a response to them. If they're coming too fast, then I panic.

Much like Marin, when Altman "hits a node"—or "a magic text"—she experiences being "edgy." She panics—"too many good ideas" and "how to sort them out, or . . . organize a response" when "they're coming too fast"—indeed, at times when "the top of your head feels like it's been blown off."

For Richard Marin and Nina Altman, scholars in different fields and in different universities, a moment of scholarly learning, at its height, is rife with physical sensation, movement, edginess, even agitation. The learner cannot sit still. That moment reaches inside to a "source," as Marin says, that touches the scholar's personal life—to friends and relationships for Marin, to a sense of self and personal history for Altman. In either case a scholar gains insight through sense and emotion that, as Marin explains, "gives you the results . . . while hiding the reasoning," which, he says, you "have to go back and reconstruct."

Both of these professors engage their scholarly learning. Both have clear-cut access to it. But what of professors whose work arrangements block their access to scholarly learning? I now turn to a scholar who struggles to get back to her "core" subject of study but who sees and feels it "thinning," year by year, as she pursues efforts quite separate from those that she once cared for deeply.

SANDRA COVINGTON: ADDING NEW PROJECTS ALONG WITH THE CORE

I found Sandra Covington in a historic campus building—ivied walls in sunlight, darkened halls and polished floors, piles of books and journals surrounding the corner of the desk at which she wrote.[6] A professor of public health, Covington was tenured at People's State University on the basis of her research on the epidemiology of staph infections in hospitals, schools, and other public spaces, a topic she had studied for years. Staph infections are common. They can be serious, yet many people have them— for example, on their skin—and do not become ill. Covington had long been fascinated by the social spread of a relatively benign strain of this organism, referring to it as her "core research" and "major interest . . . very self-initiated." At about the time that Covington was tenured, a virulently antibiotic-resistant strain of a different yet related bacterium had gripped the attention of medical and public health communities nationwide. A number of federal agencies suddenly announced the availability of large grants for research on "the bug" with a focus on prevention and treatment.

In response to strong university urgings to improve research funding in the biological sciences, Covington and some of her colleagues pursued these monies. They organized to write grants to support research on the virulent strain, many of which they "landed." Covington soon joined other grant-writing teams across the United States and later abroad. She was quickly absorbed by the new pursuit, which was quite different from the work she really cared about.

Realizing Covington's attachment to her long-term core subject of study, but her felt obligation to the university and to society broadly to join the worldwide network concerned with antimicrobial resistance, I wondered whether and how she balanced her attention between what she defined as two very different programs of work. As she described her newly emergent projects—on the antibiotic-resistant bacterium and later on other strains of growing public interest—I wondered what she did with her initial "major interest," whether it still mattered to her three years post-tenure. What might it mean for a scholar to leave behind a long-term quest that was her core interest and central to her identity, especially if she felt that she had not yet reached its end? In our first talk, during her first post-tenure year at People's State University, I asked Covington how she felt about her new line of research on antimicrobial resistance relative to her own long-term commitments to the study of the less virulent strains.

"My earlier work is still my major interest."

"But [this second and emerging line of work] is really different from the [first, isn't it]?" I asked.

"It's very, very different," she said.

Not yet satisfied, I returned a minute or two later to ask her again, "You mentioned that this [second study of antibiotic-resistant bacteria] is very different from your first set of interests . . . Have you been able to keep that earlier work up as well?"

"Yeah . . . I'm trying . . . Yeah, I have two [funded programs of research] going on at the same time, and it's the balance problem. And it's been quite—this year in particular has been really strained. But both [research programs, continuing and new] are going right now, not probably at the pace they should be, but they are going . . . I have funding for both."

Covington describes herself as having to juggle two demanding lines of inquiry in her field. But she had more to say through our talk about the kinds of things, campus wide, that were increasingly keeping her from her true research interests.

"I think the multitude of demands . . . I think with the current state of the university system—where we are now wanting to do community service, but we are . . . supposed to do [it] on top of institutional service, teaching, and research and not change, and get more extramural funding, but not reduce your teaching load . . . this extra layer of demands that we get every time we turn around. I think as you get more into the middle ranks, too, you get so many more service responsibilities . . . but nobody ever eases up on any of the responsibilities that you had before. So I think that's what I'm most, right now, concerned about, that each time we turn around [there's] another layer of responsibility without any recognition that you already have a lot of them.

I asked Covington what she worried about.

"I worry about getting my work done," she said, "and in some sort of a timely manner. So that's been a problem . . . Oh, and I should say, I worry about being burned-out. Ten years from now, am I going to be burned-out? And you see it here at People's State . . . burned-out fifty-year-old faculty members . . . I don't want to be one."

"What do you think makes that happen?" I asked her.

"Well, I think part of it is . . . just keeping up to level, keeping up to the hours per week . . . [that's] what I worry about . . . Part of it is just not enough pats on the back for a job well done. And I don't really even mean monetary rewards. I just mean recognition—where people start to lose perspective."

Covington was quick to point out that her feelings of overload arose not only from the greater number of campus-based requests made of her but also from increased requests from her field of study. "I think, too," she said, "that maybe . . . right now all the national-level [disciplinary] things you get asked to do are new, and you don't think you should turn [them] down because you don't want to lose that opportunity to connect [with colleagues] in that work . . . but it adds another layer on a very busy workday."

How does Covington make sense of the increasing complexity of her work—of the growing professional loads she has agreed to carry? How does she explain to herself the increased responsibilities that distance her from her favored research at a time when, with tenure in hand, she might conceivably pursue the core work—and scholarly learning—more ardently than ever before in her career?

"You're older," she explained. "You have to take on . . . some more responsibility for the department [and discipline] . . . that you don't have to take on and really shouldn't feel obliged to take on [during your early years until] you've been around for a while. And if you have [a] feeling of where you want your department to go, if you don't do anything, then you can't, you don't have the right, to complain." Covington took on the new work on antimicrobial resistance in response to a felt obligation more than out of desire anchored in personal interest.

As she had foreseen, by her third post-tenure year Sandra Covington was engaged in more work that she felt obligated to take on in support of her university and her field. By then she was conducting several research projects that were unrelated to her core interest yet was holding onto that core and "balancing" multiple other responsibilities in response to the external pressures she sensed:

"I still have that one thread of research going," she explained, referring to her core work on the benign bacterial strain, "but then you're picking up projects . . . And so, [there have been] no big shifts in my core work, but adding new projects along with the core work is, I guess, how I would describe [it]."

"How do you get new projects going?" I asked her. "I mean, [do] they, kind of, come to you? Or do you go out looking for them?"

"The other [research projects, beyond my core work] have come to me," she said, "they have come to me."

"Do you feel equally committed to all these projects?" I continued.

"Well, it's actually real hard to balance the time," she said.

After she described her approach to chunking up her time so she could work on her multiple research projects, her teaching, and her growing service obligations, she reiterated, "I find it really difficult to balance . . . yeah, it's really hard."

What can be gleaned from this three-year review of Sandra Covington's work and learning through her early post-tenure career? Covington is occupied with learning many things—certainly in her research and increasingly in her teaching, administration, outreach, and service. Over the years Covington's research portfolio and the new learning it requires grow, but *not* in her long-nurtured core area of interest. Her learning in research expands over multiple and diverse domains as she responds—indeed, responsibly—to her university's priorities, her field's current concerns, and society's needs. But Covington's interviews indicate that she never lets go of the scholarly learning, in research, that she refers to as her "major interest." That persists in the form of a personal pull on her intellectual desire. Yet by her third post tenure year, Covington described her scholarly learning as but a "thread." Once rich, full, and promising of growth, it has "thinned."

Competing contextual forces—colleagues and administrators seeking expertise and energy, opportunities and obligations that she sensed—succeeded in pulling Covington away from her central interest. In just three years that interest, her scholarly learning, went from being the core of her research to only a thread. By her third post-tenure year Sandra Covington's scholarly learning, though still there, had been squeezed by "multitudes of demands" on her to learn other subject matter content. Covington was clearly struggling to balance all her commitments, especially in research, while maintaining that thread.

Right after getting tenure, Sandra Covington worried about the "burned-out fifty-year-old faculty members" she saw at People's State University, claiming, "I don't want to be one." Another concern was that without a better balance—between work for others and work for herself—Covington's feelings of engagement and desire to learn would dissipate, as would her desires to build a job and career that could support such experiences in others.

I offer these three cases as "live examples" of scholarly learning that grows, or struggles to grow, in scholars' lives. Richard Marin and Nina Altman strive to extend their learning of subjects that have meant a great deal to them throughout their lives. As Marin reflects, "There's no separation between me and physics and mathematics and philosophy." And as Altman says of her writing, "I'm implicated in it." Covington, also has a subject she holds as central to her interests. Yet her words about it are more diffused, and as she admits, increasingly so are her efforts. She speaks of her "self initiated . . . major interest" but then, more strikingly, of that ever "thinning thread" that she fears her favored work has become. More and more, myriad demands separate Covington from work she loves. She fears that her fires of inspiration will burn out.

Two Studies of Recently Tenured University Professors' Scholarly Learning

To better understand the experiences of professors like Richard Marin, Nina Altman, and Sandra Covington, I designed and carried out two three-year studies of professors' experiences of the early post-tenure career with attention to their scholarly learning; I initiated the first study around 1993 and concluded the second around 2001. The first study, the *People's State University Project,* explored thirty-eight professors' passages through the third post-tenure year. These professors all worked at one university, People's State, and on the whole represented diverse disciplines and fields. Yet given the university's vivid and historic land-grant commitments, well reflected in its present-day tenuring patterns, most study participants claimed membership in professional and applied fields of study (e.g., nutrition, engineering, or business). The *People's State University Project* started out as an exploration of how recently tenured professors respond to the organizational and collegial realities of their "new," now more senior status; I wanted to understand whether and how professors' jobs changed once they acquired tenure, how they felt about such change, and how they managed it. That project concluded in part that behind the newly emergent organizational and collegial realities of the early post-tenure career lay a deeper, more personal and meaningful reality. Most of the professors I interviewed *loved* interacting with their subjects of study: exploring them, performing them, sharing them with others, coming to know them ever more deeply. The *People's State University Project* ended with my own desire to understand what that love—of a subject of study—was all about, why it mattered, and what, if anything, professors did to pursue it in changed or continuing ways post-tenure.[7]

I designed the second study expressly to address that question. I invited a fresh crop of professors, forty in total, tenured at one of four major research universities during the three years leading up to the first project interview. The twenty men and twenty women in this second study were distributed fairly evenly across the sciences, social sciences, arts and humanities, and professional/applied fields. Their home campuses, two public and two private universities, two urban and two suburban, were located across three states. The *Four Universities Project* offered a five-year look into university professors' scholarly learning. Although professors' scholarly learning had been visible at the margins of the *People's State University Project* (leading me to assert the need to study it), the *Four Universities Project* brought that learning into sharper view.[8]

I devoted the *Four Universities Project* to exploring professors' scholarly learning across a substantial range of disciplines and fields and from within individuals' unique experiences of such learning. The experiential perspective on scholarly learning is central to the story I tell: it allowed me to probe *what* scholarly learning is to those who engage in it. To foreshadow a key study finding, I learned that participating professors' scholarly learning mattered greatly to them, often in very personal ways. Something in the subject matter content of professors' learning connected deeply, and indeed personally, with questions, challenges, or desires in their lives—senses of knowing and feeling that they had sought to grasp, sometimes for many years, and that their subjects of study let them pursue more fully than other subjects could. Professors' subject matter content was a window that let them look deeply into matters of personal meaning. This looking, and thinking about what they saw, was their scholarly learning. Toward that end they mustered their well-honed professional skills, deep disciplinary knowledge, and significantly, personal understandings, energies, and interests.

Research on professors' scholarly learning is uncommon in extant writings about American higher education, which emphasizes topics such as professors' career trajectories, scholarly productivity, socialization and acculturation, job roles and responsibilities, reward structures, compensation and programmatic support, alignments of faculty jobs and institutional missions, power and politics in the faculty career, participation in governance, strivings for equity in the workplace, and faculty development that facilitates professors' adaptation to organizational imperatives that are not well related to substantive concerns. Although functionally supportive of the American higher education enterprise, research on these topics gives virtually no attention to changes in professors' subject matter interests and involvement over time.[9] That research overlooks the substantive enterprise of the "higher learning."

Because higher education research rarely examines professors' scholarly learning in relation to institutional priorities and practices, university policy rarely reflects it. Policy makers and the general public seldom hear about professors' scholarly learning except with regard to major—and rare—knowledge breakthroughs. The kind of slow, continuous, painstaking scholarly effort that conditions and precedes such breakthrough rarely enters the public discourse and, thus, the public mind. What enters instead is myth: images of university professors as failing to live up to their promises and capacities, as neglecting their teaching and scholarly responsibilities, all at public cost—in a word, professors with lifetime tenure in decline. Sandra Covington spoke to bits of this image as she described the "burned-out fifty-year-old faculty members" around her. She feared becoming one herself, given the new load of work she took on post-tenure and her self-distancing from the scholarly learning she loved. My study design did not allow me to explore whether a professor's self-distancing from work that she loves, possibly in combination with mounting demands on her time, does indeed lead to "burn-out" or to other forms of decline. Clearly, however, it was a concern to Covington.

In and of itself tenure cannot and should not be associated with professorial decline through the early post-tenure career; the vast majority of the recently tenured university professors I interviewed were fully and energetically engaged in their scholarly learning. I call attention to this insight from my study because it does not align with the all too common public view that once they earn tenure, professors become increasingly lax in their learning, teaching, and other responsibilities. Although I do not subscribe to that view—chapter 4 will show that it is fundamentally mistaken—its status as a public myth requires that I address it here.[10]

On Myth and Matter in the Early Post-Tenure Career: A University-Based View

Contemporary social myth portrays the tenured university professor in one of two ways. In one version tenured professors spend little time in their classrooms, labs, and offices. With tenure in hand, they become less accountable—and less connected—to their students, colleagues, fields of study, and occasionally profession. They relax, so the story goes, perhaps too much.

In a different but related version of the myth, the newly tenured university professor is free and unfettered to write and think and "lead a scholarly life"—to become a fully intellectual being. In this view the professor's intellectual horizon is unconstrained. Virtually anything is possible. Yet the myth also says that few professors take on the opportunity to learn freely that tenure offers. Therefore, the myth states that after getting tenure, few professors work—or learn—as diligently as they did before. Hence, the myth connects a professor's talents and work ethic to her success or failure. It states that capable and diligent scholars achieve academic success, sometimes academic stardom. Such scholars publish extensively, teach in informed and energetic ways, and exert leadership among their university- and field-based colleagues throughout their careers. They are productive through the full length of their tenures. They are high performers. In contrast, those less capable and less committed to their work are not. They tire out or burn out. They fail to keep up with their fields, which shows as they teach from notes yellowed by years of reuse. They stop publishing. Although some of them become leaders in university governance, they lose touch with their fields of study. They stop learning. Sadly, many decline into "deadwood." The handful of tenured professors who do "make it" intellectually possess both "natural smarts" and cultivated intelligence; they activate these resources through disciplined effort. The many who do not succeed "simply don't have it in them," or they squander the rich possibilities that tenure offers for their intellectual growth.[11]

The harm of this view of post-tenure decline lies in the policy treatments and academic environments that university leaders and public officials invoke to correct it: post-tenure assessments that focus on professors' productivity absent consideration of their scholarly learning and substantive contributions, instructional development programs that emphasize "customer satisfaction" and fail to anchor pedagogical improvement in the advancement of subject matter thought, faculty development schemes that focus more on professors' acquisition of tenure and promotion than on the crafting of jobs and careers anchored in scholarly learning, teaching improvement programs that go nowhere near the classroom and that unnecessarily reify distinctions between research and teaching. In relying on such measures—none of which address directly the health of professors' subject matter commitments—leaders and policy makers who may indeed want to enhance higher education's substantive contributions may inadvertently push professors away from this goal.[12]

Without attending directly to the *substantive learning* that drew many professors to their academic endeavors in the first place, and that continues to hold many to it by virtue of its emotional pull, policy shifts in higher education are unlikely to elicit substantive change from professors. In the end university leaders who bolster nonsubstantive features of the academic enterprise (e.g., assessments and professional development programs attuned to productivity, customer satisfaction, rewards acquisition, career progression) as means toward the end of scholarly learning, or as signs to track how professors move toward it, may find their faculties more enmeshed in those means and signs than in scholarly learning. My research indicates that the widespread myth of post-tenure decline is patently misguided. Because no one has looked behind this myth to consider how professors truly experience their scholarly learning through the early post-tenure years—thereby offering a replacement image—the myth becomes a self-fulfilling prophecy. By elevating myth-based talk and action about needs for "faculty development" that remediates or prevents decline, for example, the myth elevates assumptions about needs for remediation and prevention that have never been tested. Although some professors may well decline in their scholarly learning in the post-tenure years and could therefore benefit from programs and policies aimed at stemming such decline, those who continue to learn and grow in their subject matter work or who authentically struggle to do so, may not get comparable support.

My aim in attending to professors' scholarly learning is to advance understanding of what that learning means, what forms it may take in professors' work and lives, and how best to support it, given its core value to higher education. We can improve professors' scholarly learning—and create conditions to foster it—only if we know what it is from within the experiences of those positioned to enact it, professors such as Richard Marin, Nina Altman, and Sandra Covington.

University Professors' Learning, with Attention to Their Scholarly Learning

I define learning as the construction of knowledge and of coming to know. A person who learns does one or more of the following: she glimpses, realizes, or otherwise comes to know something altogether new to her; she expands her knowledge of something she knows partially; she questions, or doubts with reason, something she has known and believed; and she revises something she knows or how she knows it. Learning, viewed this way, requires a *learner*. It also requires *something* to be learned. It assumes the learner's mental engagement with that something, be it the politics of her academic department or the content, new to that professor, of a book she has chosen to teach to her freshman English class.[13] Although learning may occur without the learner's full awareness of it, my use of the term assumes enough awareness for a learner to bring it into the talk of a research interview. Learning may occur in the moments of an event, in action, or upon reflection.[14] The following five propositions, derived from literature from several areas concerned with human cognition and development, summarize the perspective on learning that framed my research:

> *Proposition 1. Professors' learning as part of professors' work:* Professors' work requires that they learn.

Proposition 2. Learning as someone learning something: To say that someone learns implies that someone is learning something. Thus, to understand a professor's learning also requires knowing who the professor-as-learner is and what she learns at a certain point in time.

Proposition 3. Professors' scholarly learning: To understand a professor's scholarly learning is to understand how she learns *what* she professes through her practices of research, teaching, and service: her subject matter knowledge and ways of knowing unique to it.

Proposition 4. Professors' scholarly learning as personal and emotional experience: For many professors scholarly learning holds personal meaning. It may be intensely emotional.

Proposition 5. Contexts as, in part, the contents of learning: Professors' learning happens in contexts that shape *what* they learn (content). Yet professors can also learn new ways to think about those contexts, thereby influencing what they learn in them.[15]

These propositions frame the stories, explanations, and images of virtually every professor I interviewed and whose words I quote in the following chapters. The propositions were also embedded in the voices of Richard Marin, Nina Altman, and Sandra Covington. These three professors envision themselves as working and learning at one and the same time (proposition 1), though what they learn, especially by way of subject matter, differs among them (propositions 2 and 3). Each of the three pursues the learning of a subject that means a great deal to her or him (propositions 4), whether with seeming ease (see Marin and Altman) or through struggle (see Covington). Finally, for all three, a context of one kind or another conditions the content of the scholar's learning (proposition 5). Altman and Marin attend to the question of where in their lives their scholarly learning comes from; their lives are contexts for their scholarly learning. Covington speaks to the power of her present-day institutional context over her choice of work and thereby learning. What remains unclear is the extent to which these scholars (Covington in particular) try to reshape features of their immediate contexts in ways that enhance individual freedoms to learn as they wish (pt. 2 of proposition 5).

Together, these propositions also helped me articulate the questions guiding the research:[16]

— Given professors' unique subject matter attachments, what are some useful ways to bring together one's doing and learning across the range of faculty work: teaching, research, service, and outreach? (Proposition 1)

— If professors are learning, what is the range of the topics, subjects, and actions (in the form of ideas, practices, and so on) that they learn, and how do these mesh (or not) in their experiences? (Propositions 2 and 3)

— What more may be said about the emotional side of learning—about desire and even love in learning? How does emotional meaning hold up in the context of a professorial career and academic life? (Proposition 4)

— In what contexts—of work and life—do professors in fact learn what they learn, and how helpful are these contexts to them? Where especially do they engage in scholarly learning and in what ways? (Proposition 5)

— What can professors do to position themselves for generative learning, scholarly and otherwise? To what extent can they turn the places in which they live and work toward advancing their scholarly learning in particular? (Proposition 5, pt. 2)

— How do universities mediate professors' learning, for better or for worse, and what might this imply for university policy and leadership? (Proposition 5)

In closing, I want to recap some of the distinctive features of my treatment of professors' learning. First, scholarly learning is often linked publicly with academic research, defined as objective inquiry that differs from everyday thought and feeling. I expand on this view by exploring the emotional content of professors' scholarly learning as well as its biographical positioning: what scholarly learning may contribute to a scholar's own life story and the personal colorings of professional endeavors.[17] That said, I recognize that professors sometimes engage in scholarship that, though substantive and well crafted, even socially important, holds little personal meaning for them. I strive to distinguish this kind of learning from that which is more personally meaningful. Second, in tracing professors' scholarly learning, I recognize that its content—and its personal meanings, too—may change over time because learning, in and of itself, implies change. Third, my view of learning addresses far more than the definitive acquisition or creation of particular knowledge in a certain field or discipline, job, or life situation. It considers all facets of the pursuit of knowledge—choosing what to learn (or being chosen by it, in Richard Marin's terms), awakening to an interest or a turn of mind on a long-term interest, raising questions or simply struggling to raise them, experimenting with thought or images, becoming aware of misconceptions and responding to them, watching and waiting for insights, speculating, among others. Learning, as I use the idea, refers to any or all of these facets of the experience. And fourth, though limiting my attention to scholarly learning in the early post-tenure career and within elite universities, I assume that it also grows in other stages of professors' careers, in other careers and jobs, and in other types of institutions—indeed, that it should be widely fostered. My aim here is to establish that scholarly learning exists and that it matters—to professors and university leaders alike and to people beyond the university who care about creating institutions for learning.

CHAPTER TWO

The Heart of the Matter

Passionate Thought and Scholarly Learning

Serious scholarly work is rarely discussed in terms of scholars' emotions. Yet scholarly learning implies the pursuit of thought, with feeling at its center. For some, that learning is nothing less than the pursuit of beauty. Drawing on the experiences of two participants in the *Four Universities Project*—an astronomer and a musician, a man and a woman, working at two very different research universities—I elaborate on the place of emotion in professors' scholarly learning. Then, stepping back, I contextualize the astronomer's and musician's voices in those of the other thirty eight professors participating in the same project. Melding the voices of scientists and applied/professional scholars, humanists and social scientists, I portray professors' scholarly learning as emotionally complex and as punctuated at its high points by an experience that I call "passionate thought," at times amid strivings for beauty.

Passionate thought, as I envision it here, applies to the *disciplinary, or subject matter, content* that infuses professors' careers, and not the career apart from what goes on in it. That distinction, between a professor's subject of study and her career, merits a closer look.

Choosing the Subject versus Choosing the Career

Much has been written about adults' occupational choices, including features of work and personality that explain why teachers become teachers, doctors become doctors, lawyers become lawyers, and so on. A fair amount has also been said about why some people hold to their initial occupational choices for life while others shift their commitments.[1] Regardless of what happens in the long run, the initial choice often entails additional decisions, among them, which specialization, or subspecialization, to pursue and, relatedly, which community or subcommunity of specialized practice to join.[2]

Consider the modern-day physician. Assuming admission to relevant communities of medical training practice (e.g., teaching hospitals and medical training programs), the twenty-first-century American physician-in-training may specialize in one (or more) of numerous medical subfields, each reflecting specialized medical knowledge and a community of practitioners of that knowledge—for example, she may specialize in gastrointestinal health, metabolic functioning, cardiac care, or mental and psychological well-being, among many others. Setting aside external considerations (e.g., financial, lifestyle), what is it, about the content of a particular specialization, that drives individuals who have already chosen to be doctors to specialize in particular areas of medicine, thereby declining attention to others? What is it—about personal desire—that draws some novice physicians to specialize in surgery, pulmonary care, ophthalmology, hematology, or psychiatry, each represented by one or more communities of practitioners with expert knowledge and certified membership in that medical subfield?

But another choice may loom on the horizon of some doctors' careers: given a set of well-trained physicians, committed to particular medical specialties, what might lead some to deepen their own and their field's medical subject matter knowledge through research as they continue to care for patients exhibiting ailments in their areas of medical expertise? That is, how do individuals with strong interests in gastroenterology, endocrinology, cardiology, hematology, or psychiatry choose to become contributors to the specialized knowledge of their specialized fields—that is, to become medical researchers in their fields in addition to being expert medical practitioners?

To probe still further: what might draw a physician-researcher specializing in, say, radiology—and beyond that in mammography and its uses in the detection of breast cancer—to devote long portions of her career to formulating criteria differentiating early-stage cancer from precancerous changes in breast tissue? This physician-researcher makes not one but multiple occupational and substantive choices: she decides to enter a field (medical practice); specialize in a particular subfield (radiology); specialize yet more intensely in a particular set of practices (mammography);

devote her career to knowledge production (conduct research to improve breast cancer diagnostics) alongside medical practice (practice radiology toward breast cancer detection); and focus her research and medical practice, for years to come, on a particular medical problem (differentiating early-stage breast cancer from precancerous conditions).[3]

A similar branching of choice—from global occupation, into occupational specialization, then subspecialization, and eventually into specific topics—may be applied to the career making of lawyers, schoolteachers, and college and university professors, among others. For individuals who do eventually become university professors, the initial choice may not be one of occupation as such (becoming a professor) but, rather, of subject matter (one's field of study), or the two may be intertwined. A professor of organizational psychology, for example, may have a complex career choice story to tell: there is the narrative of how the organizational psychologist came to be a professor, as opposed to a management consultant. But there is also the (usually prior) narrative of how she became a subject matter specialist in, say, organizational psychology instead of mathematics, history, or something else. I am concerned here only with the latter narrative: professors' decision making relative to the subject matter knowledge, and ways of subject matter thinking and inquiring, that they make it their life's work to learn and to inspire others to learn as well.

Considering the distinction between career and subject of study, and my concern with how professors experience scholarly learning, leads me to ask: What does it mean, and what is it like, from within professors' experiences, to engage in scholarly learning that is personally meaningful? What does such learning entail that is personal? What draws professors to particular areas of study or creative endeavor or to particular questions, topics, and themes within them? To address these questions, I turn first to the experiences of two professors who search for beauty in scientific research and creative endeavors.

The Pursuit of Beauty as the High Point of Scholarly Learning

How is beauty, and the emotional desire that it stirs, given voice in professors' scholarly learning? I turn to David Mora, an astronomer at Libra

State University, and then to Carmen Elias-Jones, a musician at Signal University, for responses that they draw from within their own experiences of the very different subjects that they pursue.

DAVID MORA: "I LIKE TO OBSERVE—I LOVE TO OBSERVE"

Sitting in a brightly lit office atop a towering modern building, all concrete and stone, steel and glass, I interviewed David Mora, an astronomer, in the first year of the *Four Universities Project*. In the window behind him the long arm of a huge mechanical crane hung soundlessly in midair, a diagonal slicing the blue-gray sky.

> AN: What is it about your work that you love?
>
> DM: I like to observe—I love to observe.
>
> AN: You love to observe?
>
> DM: Yes.
>
> AN: Can you say more about that?
>
> DM: Well, okay . . . on a ground-based observatory [as opposed to satellite based] . . . you . . . have to do a lot of planning . . . you go there, and [in contrast to satellite-based observation,] you actually carry it out . . . [In] ground-based observing on a typical night . . . you'll have a problem with the clouds. You'll have a problem with the winds and you'll have a problem with the humidity. The telescope will break, the detector won't know how to operate correctly. I kind of like that. This is nuts and bolts, really getting down . . . in the dirt here, and you're dealing with the real point of contact between the science and nature . . . [This] can be . . . exhilarating . . . also . . . extremely memorable.
>
> AN: It sounds like observing is really big for you . . . I'm trying to understand . . . what it is about observing that really gets to you.
>
> DM: Well, it's that dynamic aspect of it . . . The sun sets. It's not gonna wait. You've got to be ready. It's a challenge to use the telescope effectively all the time. It can be a challenge. We had a run in . . . June . . . where we wanted to know what we were getting instantaneously. So we had to reduce the data right there and see what we were getting. And that was extremely valuable . . . we were seeing the new information right in front of our eyes within minutes

of taking the data. So it's a very dynamic process. It could be very, immediately rewarding. It can be very frustrating. Let me just put it this way. Whatever it is, it's usually at the edges of your emotional response . . . You're rarely in a position where you're just sort of, la, la, la, you know. You have a strong impression of something going on . . . it can be very exhilarating, very frustrating, whatever. But it's always very something . . .

AN: Sometimes it's really hard to talk about what's going on inside of us when we have experiences, like observing, that you just talked about . . . I'm wondering if you could . . . try to put even more into words what's going on inside of you [when you observe].

DM: No, I know very well, I mean . . . when things are going well and you really feel intimate, you feel like you're just working very effectively, and you've got all cylinders going. And outside distractions are not entering into the process and disrupting this flow. It's nice. I mean, it's hard. And I think this is why there's a certain analogy here with people who do things that require very intense concentration. You can really sense that all of your efforts are working very effectively, in harmony, to do this one thing. So, yeah, occasionally I'll notice that as I'm observing and say, "Wow, we're clicking here. Things are going well. Everything is working to the same purpose, and we're getting good results." And you get feedback, too, from what you're doing. So you can see the whole cycle. You're working hard to get something to work well, and you can see that it's actually working well. The flip side of that [is that] it can feel terrible if you think you've made a mistake. I mean, really terrible.

And later in the interview:

AN: Looking back at your life, do you have a sense of where this fascination with observation may have come from, or when it started for you?

DM: Ah, well, I can remember a few things that happened. I remember once when I was twelve or . . . maybe ten, I went to Mount Rushmore with my parents . . . I don't know if you've been there at night . . . But they turn on the lights at night, and they have this show of . . . patriotic songs. And then they turn everything off, and everyone heads home. And it's out in the Black Hills. It's quite far away from any big cities. And, of course, once all the lights on the mountain are off, it's pretty dark. And we were there in July . . . And there was the Milky Way. And the Milky Way is really one of the most beautiful things you can see from Earth. People don't get a chance to see it very often, but when you do, and I remember—that made a very good, very strong impression . . . I did then, and I still do now, appreciate it. It's just a beautiful thing.

AN: What's a beautiful thing?

DM: What you can see through these telescopes. It's really spectacular . . . it's true, the visual, and nowadays the nonvisual, images that we get are the thing that really turn people on in astronomy. It is the thing that gives you primal feedback . . . and sometimes you'll really think about it. There will be nights [at the observational site] I can see the Milky Way. Or a night, for example, that I wasn't actually on the telescopes, so I could let my eyes get adapted to the night. I'd look up, and you really, suddenly feel that, "Wow, we're in this galaxy, big, big galaxy, and we're out here on the edge, and there's the galaxy. I see it." And . . . you can say, "Wow, it looks just like these other galaxies that I just took a picture of the other day in this system that's separate from all the others." Suddenly you can start to feel the whole picture of it.

And it's a combination of both what you see, an instinctive or primal thing, and also your knowledge of what you put together. That's encouraging, too. . . You really do get a feel that, "Wow, we're just here sitting, floating on the edge of this galaxy." I mean, you really should do it . . . It's spectacular, and you really see your location in the galaxy. So, yeah, that's one example. But there's other times where you just appreciate—this is a very beautiful thing to look at. Through a small telescope, even there, [there] are some objects that are just . . . they're different . . . they can be really pretty, very colorful, intricate in detail.

Through this interview the astronomer explains that his present-day research is, in part, a response to the aesthetic draw of his past experiences—from his childhood memories—of witnessed beauty. Asked about the sources of his fascination with the night sky, David Mora describes his first sighting, at age ten or twelve, of the Milky Way, a summer night in South Dakota on a family trip he never forgot. His words suggest that even his earliest memories of experiencing beauty still course through his life. These memories, still vivid, connect directly to his work today, lending it continuity, folding it into the narrative he knows as his life. Although they are ongoing, these memories evince a bounded immediacy; they speak to experiences that start and stop, caught in time. Whether as experience or memory, Mora's imagery portrays an aesthetic realization, an encounter with beauty that frames his research and, more broadly, his learning as a scholar and as a scientist.

To grasp the feeling of the work that Mora describes, I turn to the philosopher Elaine Scarry's book-length essay *On Beauty and Being Just* for insights—on the convergences of beauty and understanding, of desire, curiosity, and pursuit— about scientific inquiry as about art. [4] Mora's narrative suggests that research, even in a highly technical science, may grow from vivid images and sensations that a scholar experiences in bounded moments of time (for example, or in childhood) and then recalls, through memory, over subsequent years. In *On Beauty* Scarry asserts that pursuits of beauty, of immersion in it, may incite desire, intensely felt, to know that beauty in fullness, to understand it. A scholar may respond to such beckoning from an object of beauty through expressions of awe and curiosity: a desire to submerge oneself in the beauty at hand, a desire also to know and believe it, a passion, then, to inquire, to explore, to ponder, to come to know. In his interview Mora describes how he saw the brilliance of the galaxy—how he took it in—for the first time in the blackness of the night on Mount Rushmore. His first experience of the Milky Way was impressed in his memory, and it remains with him nearly thirty years later as he explores the sky, though now equipped with the tools and concepts of modern astronomy. Although technically skilled and conceptually trained, David Mora still returns to his childhood memories of beauty, connecting them narratively to his professional efforts as a practitioner of the scientific method, a constructor of the expert knowledge that constitutes his field. In memory he is pulled back to desires for knowing and feeling still more.

Scarry also says that beauty is an abstraction, requiring materials for its expression. Scholars, many of whom are spurred by visions of beauty that beckon them to strive for meaning, choose their subjects of study in light of images that they had once glimpsed in them. In a scholar's life choosing one's subjects of study and teaching, and identifying the "fields" within which those subjects can be found, may occur in moments of witnessed beauty. Such choice may occur long before college advisement sessions and orientations. It may well occur on a summer vacation or in a child's backyard—as she stares up at the sky, pores through a book, or looks deeply into a pond.

Mora's interview substantiates this line of thought. He says that he witnesses beauty through particular subjects in astronomy. These subjects seem to awaken in him a capacity to see and engage with beauty and its meanings in ways that other topics and subjects in other fields do not. He seems able to see something, within certain stuff in astronomy, that he cannot access as deeply or fully in other matter. The beauty he sees in the night's brilliance beckons him to strive for meanings expressed in the terms of astronomy as a scientific tradition of thought. Mora thereby pairs the search for beauty with a search for truth. He engages in this dual venture as an extension of the vision he encountered, fortuitously, on a summer night in his boyhood.

For Mora, a striving for beauty and meaning can be deeply emotional, touching a number of deep feelings. Mora expresses awe for the beauty that a telescope reveals; he describes the exhilaration of a good observation. His draw to beauty—to the stars of the night sky, in memory and more immediately—is one of desire, of passion expressed through disciplined thought within a long-cultivated subject of study.

Although much may be gleaned from the scientist-aesthete about how a scholar is "pulled" to his research subject, in passion and thought, more may yet be gained through a parallel analysis of the day-to-day experiences, and memories, of a scholar in a different field and university, one whose scholarship is better termed "creative endeavor." Carmen Elias-Jones is a professor of music, a teacher primarily of undergraduates at Signal University. Notwithstanding the contrast, I couple the words of Elias-Jones with those of Mora, such that each illuminates the other—paradoxically so, in that the complexity of modern-day academe does not at all facilitate these two scholars' cross-disciplinary, cross-institutional, and cross-career meeting. Despite the distances, their words converge in meaning and experience.

CARMEN ELIAS-JONES: "THIS THING THAT MOVES YOU SO"

I met with Carmen Elias-Jones, newly tenured at Signal University, in the oddly shaped room that served as her studio, which, though crowded with musical instruments, exuded brightness and light. She was exuberant as we talked, thrilled less with the tenure she had recently been granted than with the music that had long filled her life and which she wanted to pursue further.

AN: This internal experience that people sometimes have in different ways, when we are doing something creative—I'm wondering if there is any more that you can say to help us understand what it is?

CE-J: Oh, that's a really difficult question to answer. But it is really . . . listening to music, and really listening to it . . . as a musician in a different way than most people would. It is like you are inside it and living it, and it moves you across a gamut of emotions. Then, there's the actual act of playing . . . when there is naturalness about it, it is very hard to explain . . . It is a thrill, it is a huge thrill . . . it is like a complete focus of oneness with the instrument. And then you can hear yourself producing this thing that moves you so. It is a challenge and a reward all at the same time on so many different levels.

AN: So, you said . . . first you were in it, and then you are actually making it.

CE-J: Yeah. You are actually making it, yeah. And then, physically—you spend so much time, physically, actually with the instrument—being able to conquer it, and then [you] hear this—and it is a good sound. It actually doesn't happen that often. Because if you interview many musicians, you find that most of the time they hate their performances, can't stand to listen to them. But listening . . . [when] it is a good sound—I don't think there is anything that equals that feeling. And being able to do it . . . It is big physical thrill . . . feeling the instrument—and that when you change how you play, you get a different sound. And the different sound makes you feel a different way.

Describing the "big physical thrill" of music—how "when you change how you play, you get a different sound" and how then that "makes you feel a different way"—prompts Elias-Jones to talk about her role as a teacher. "I want to communicate this," she says.

> CE-J: Actually, I think it does make a difference to a student. When I say [to the students], "I don't think you get this—listen to this." And I speak to them with great earnestness, I say, "How can this not affect you? Listen to this." And they look at me, and there is almost a different—it is like all the ions in the air are completely different. And then [the student] sit[s] down, and there is a completely different sound, and it is a wonderful feeling. Because then I feel it, I hear it, and I help someone do it. And then I look at the face, and I say, "Did you feel something different?" They say, "Yes."
>
> AN: So, part of your teaching is also helping people be moved by their own [work]—
>
> CE-J: Oh, yeah, absolutely. And knowing the difference . . . between what is moving and what is not. Care . . . caring enough. But, to communicate that, you [yourself] have to care a lot about it.

The artist revealed how her pursuit of beauty in music connects with her work as a teacher, as a cultivator of musicians—that is, of aesthetic experience, musically expressed, in others' lives. As a teacher of music, she strives to help students find and open spaces within themselves of knowing and feeling and of "caring enough" to "know the difference between what is moving and what is not." To do this, Elias-Jones points out, she also must "care a lot" about the musical subjects and skills that she shares with her students.

Much like the astronomer David Mora, Elias-Jones reveals the sources of her passionate engagement with music in her childhood—in experiences unmediated by formal education, a musical imagery of sound that got converted into memory, illuminating and guiding her current professional work. Elias-Jones positions the musical memories of her childhood as guides to and inspirations for her creative effort in the present day—as pulls on her creative scholarship. She also positions these memories as resources for her teaching, working with students who themselves are just at the edge of discovering the fascinations of music that will, she hopes, draw them in.

CE-J: There was a lot of music in the house . . . My father had an expensive record collection . . . [The music] just made me dance around the house. I still remember the pieces, yeah, I actually have very clear—they are very defined moments. The [musical instrument] came in—yeah, the first time I heard [this instrument] . . . was in the church, and I thought to myself, I want to learn that.

AN: Uh-huh. How old were you . . . about that time?

CE-J: Five or six years old. Then the [instrument] came in. That was a big deal, you see. My sister learned [to play it], and I just sat on the floor and howled and had tantrums until they let me start. Because they thought I was too young. So then I was seven. And I tell you, the other defining moment . . . is an aunt of mine . . . at the age of fourteen . . . came to visit, and she played a piece [in our living room]. And I was just saying this to a student the other day who was playing the same piece. And I remember the exact moment, I remember exactly what she was playing—I remember how it sounded, and I remember exactly how it made me feel. It is very clearly defined.

AN· [What] was she playing?

CE-J: [Names the piece and composer] . . . it always stands out as being special. And I think it was more special because it happened right there in my living room on that [instrument].

Elias-Jones's passionate desire as a child to create music continues to animate her work today; a bridge of fascination—much like David Mora's of the stars—connects her present and past. Sometimes when she hears her students play, she also hears those earliest sounds ("I remember exactly what she [my aunt] was playing . . . how it sounded") and alongside them the emotions ("I remember exactly how it made me feel"). For Carmen Elias-Jones, accomplished creative endeavor enacted today, or taught today to others, is linked through memory to experiences of related endeavors in her past. The aesthetic thus infuses her teaching—her musical work with students—as much as it does her professional creative effort. It helps to join her creative and intellectual work with her teaching, anchoring and pulling at her attention, desires, and creative energies. It animates the daily work of her professorial career.

Some might argue that the beauty in Elias-Jones's art—which she creates in emotion, even as that beauty incites emotion in her—cannot be generalized to a science that seeks to distance the "self who studies" from an object of study.[5] To the contrary, researchers', scholars', and artists' attempts to know cannot be represented as strivings for selfless understanding. Rather, theirs are strivings for honest understanding: for thought that is emotive in its honesty, drawing its creator to it equally for what, in honesty, it is and also what, in substance, it represents.

Through a decade of listening to university professors describe their early post-tenure careers, I have come to understand that their construction of subject matter knowledge is hardly free of emotion and is intimately connected with themselves. Professors' scholarly learning—expressed primarily through research, as for David Mora, or more complexly through creative scholarship and teaching, as for Carmen Elias-Jones—is often rooted in what I call "experiences of passionate thought." Anchored in professors' memories and desires, professors' passionate thought pulls hard on the disciplined attention and professional energy that contemporary intellectual endeavor requires.

Professions of Passion

In interviews Carmen Elias-Jones, David Mora, and thirty-six other recently tenured professors participating in the *Four Universities Project* described their subject matter learning as being deeply emotional—as marked by what Mihaly Csikszentmihalyi, the eminent psychologist of human development, refers to as "the optimal experience" of "flow" in human consciousness: experiences of powerful "concentration," intense "absorption," "deep involvement" yielding a "sense of accomplishment" and "joy."[6] These are the high points of intellectual endeavor; they are markers of the professors' passionate thought.

Yet the passionate thought that these professors described involved far more than the bright spots of what Csikszentmihalyi refers to as the peak experiences of flow. Professors' high points of passionate thought were surrounded often by many other emotions, all bearing on it.

Responding to questions about what it is like to engage in work they love, professors participating in the *Four Universities Project* invoked images of *peak (positive) emotion, absorption, sensation,* and *intensified awareness,* all resonant with Csikszentmihalyi's imagery of the flow of optimal experience. Individual professors voiced these images selectively—some drawing on them all and others on a few; some speaking smoothly and with ease and others more haltingly; some saying they had already thought deeply about such experiences and others, less so. Acknowledging such variance, I nevertheless present these images summarily as expressions of passionate thought in professors' scholarly learning—in moments of discernment and creation amid their construction of subject matter knowledge—in research, creative effort, or teaching. In this view passionate thought is an expressed high point of professors' scholarly learning, one they both know and feel in their subjects of study and teaching.

Peak Emotion

Just as Carmen Elias-Jones describes the "huge thrill" of the musical beauty she creates ("I don't think there is anything that equals that feeling") or that she hears others create ("listening to music . . . really listening to it"), other study participants describe their own peak experiences: a gerontologist recollecting the "runner's high" in realizing "I've got a fix on what it is that I think"; an anthropologist recalling the "huge high" of "incredibly wonderful" experiences in the field; an environmental engineer explaining that her research "can be a high . . . this completeness you have" when "anxieties and tension melt away"; a professor of finance describing the "exhilaration" of seeing the "pieces" of his research come together; a chemist describing the "sense of fulfillment" he feels in watching "very talented people doing very beautiful things" in science.

Absorption

These peak experiences grip attention. Professors describe themselves as engrossed, in deep "concentration," even "obsessed": David Mora, the astronomer, notes that at these times "distractions are not entering into the process," nor are they "disrupting this flow," but, rather, "you can really sense that all of your efforts are working very effectively, in harmony, to do this one thing." And Carmen Elias-Jones explains that in these passionate moments she feels "a complete focus of oneness" with her music. Other participants echo this theme: a philosopher describing the "all-consuming" research at the center of his first book; a writing teacher equally "consumed" by the craft she teaches and practices; a gerontologist so "involved with the ideas . . . really, really wonderful" that in "looking at [her] watch" she wonders "how it got to be that time"; a psychologist who, at "times during the day," finds himself "lost in what I'm doing" and "not thinking about . . . anything other than the work itself . . . getting satisfaction in the whole process, seeing it all come together."

Sensation

Professors also speak of a palpable, even physical imagery of scholar and subject, or creation, in dynamic interaction. When an observation works, says David Mora, he finds himself at the "the real point of contact between the science and nature," a moment suffused with feelings of "intimacy." Carmen Elias-Jones's allusions to "feeling the instrument . . . spend[ing] so much time physically . . . with the instrument" and "being able to conquer it" also suggest reciprocal, physical forces—images of an instrument being as alive as the musician, its sound "moving her" as she creates it. A professor of writing who "create[s] a scene that suddenly is . . . alive" as she hears it "sing on the page" also calls up an image of interaction; as a writer, she both creates and experiences the creation.

Other professors also describe sensations (and sometimes feelings of adventure) that their work, in its high moments, can evoke. Asked what it is like to be in the "different place" (as he calls it) of passionate thought, Richard Marin, the theoretical physicist at Hope State University, portrays his subject of study, first, as physical terrain that, soaring birdlike, he scans (though "nonvisually" and "nonverbally"), then as bathwater that he passively soaks in or as turbulent waters in which he "swims aggressively . . . really trying to get somewhere":

The picture I've come up with, maybe a romanticized version of what is actually going on . . . [is that] there are different modes that you can attack problems in. There [is] certainly a passive mode, and then an aggressive mode, and . . . all shades in-be-tween. And so when you are in passive mode, the work is very nonvisual. It is not that you are visualizing things inside of you—at least this is not the way I work . . . it is a completely nonvisual and a nonverbal experience. It's connecting to symbolic forms in a way that's direct but yet not verbal or visual. It is hard to de-scribe from that point of view. I often give visual analogies—like sometimes you feel like you are soaring through mathematical landscapes and you are just seeing what the landscape looks like. But the seeing there shouldn't really be taken literally as visual. Be-cause what you are doing is you are looking at mathematical land-scapes with a different eye. Sometimes I describe the passive mode as . . . like you are sitting in a mathematical bathtub, and you are letting the mathematical waters wash over you. And you [are] just letting it soak in . . . immersing yourself in this world, and you are not really trying to go anywhere within it. You are letting it take you where it may. There [are] other times where you are swim-ming aggressively in those waters, and you are really trying to get somewhere . . . but it is in a very strange symbolic sense.

Although Marin qualifies his sensory metaphor (indicating that he means nonvisual and nonverbal imagery), he nonetheless invokes images of his interactions with his subject of study that are as palpable as those of Elias-Jones and Mora.

Intensified Awareness

In describing work they love, the professors often refer to intensified awareness—expanded, deepened, or refined understanding—of the sub-jects they study or create and sometimes of the processes of study and creation. Carmen Elias-Jones speaks to deepened awareness, both of the music she creates and her process of creation, when she says, "It is like you are inside it and living it." As she apprehends the changing music ("when you change how you play, you get a different sound"), she re-fines her (emotional) understanding of what she is creating ("the different sound makes you feel a different way"). David Mora similarly invokes expanding awareness of the research process in astronomy, for example, when he says, "You can see the whole cycle." Mora points out that one gets feedback from the process, leading one to see, under the best of circumstances, "that it's actually working well."

Other professors portray intensified awareness in other terms. "It is the only possible experience where you . . . can surprise yourself . . . where suddenly you come across a thought that you didn't know you had," says a scholar of comparative literature, "and . . . that's a really startling experience, because you always . . . anticipate that other people have [thoughts] that you don't have, and you always anticipate that you have thoughts that . . . you have, but you never anticipated that you have thoughts you don't have, you didn't know you had." For this scholar a broadened awareness of subject arrives by surprise. A scientist also describes a surprising insight: "A light goes off," he says, "or something clicks, or something happens that you go to the next level of understanding. And that's where it becomes exciting is that you start to go 'Uh-huh, now I've got [it], I see now where this is going,' or 'I see something that I didn't see before, which tells me where to go next.'"

WHAT PASSION SIGNIFIES

In expressions of peak experience, absorption, sensation, and intensified awareness, one may hear passion. Yet what evidence exists of that passion's substantive worth—its connection to professors' scholarly learning? How can I know that, within the passionate thought that a professor describes, something of substance is happening—the making or remaking of a substantive thought? Although I approach this question as fully as the data allow in the next chapter, I broach it here by reentering professors' experiences to ask what that passionate thought may signal. As I will show, the interviews suggest that for some professors passionate thought signals an instance of discernment and for others, of creation, yet for both it always occurs relative to a particular subject matter thought (a subject, question, idea, or image in disciplinary or cross-disciplinary knowledge in astronomy, music, literature, social work, and so on) or experience of subject matter knowing (e.g., in an instance of telescopic observation, musical creation, writing, or ethnographic reflection). In the professors' narratives a scholar's passion is for, and her thought is about, a particular subject of study. It is in this sense that professors' passionate thought—its discernment and/or creation—may be viewed as a self-realized instance of scholarly learning.

Discernment

Based on these data, *to discern* is to apprehend a pattern, order, or meaning amid an assumed absence of order and meaning. The scholar usually does not view herself as crafting the order but as sensing or inducing it. She identifies, describes, and analyzes preexisting patterns, orders, and meanings that others have overlooked or left unexplained. A social scientist, recently tenured at Signal University, describes what he derives personally from his research:

> I used to do crossword puzzles a lot, and at times it would be immensely frustrating when it was a puzzle written by a particular person who had a particular mind-set when setting the clues to the puzzle. I have no idea how to actually answer. I'm talking here about a puzzle like the *Times* puzzle where there's a larger theme to it, and you're completely screwed if you don't figure out what the larger theme is. What I think of productive research as feeling like is those all too rare occasions when I was successfully able to see what the structure of the puzzle was . . . and at the same time not just the structure but to see how all the little pieces fit into it. That satisfaction of filling in the last square. And my father used to do crossword puzzles with me when I was a kid . . . He used to write *QED* at the very end when he was finally done. He used to routinely be able to finish the puzzle. What I like to think of in my research is finally being able to get to that point where you can write *QED* and set it aside and feel that it's something that you've done and can look back on with some satisfaction at some point in the future, that you successfully have shown something. You've successfully illuminated something that had been obscure before.

Through the metaphor of the crossword puzzle this social scientist represents an affinity for discernment: he describes a distant puzzle creator who, given his "particular mind-set," creates a puzzle that reflects a "larger theme." Identifying with the puzzle solver, the social scientist says that "you're completely screwed if you don't figure out what the larger theme is." On the other hand, a puzzle solver who discerns "the structure of the puzzle" is more likely to solve it—or translated into scholarly terms, to yield "productive research" that "successfully illuminate[s] something that had been obscure before."

Another social scientist at Signal University similarly equates scholarly discernment with puzzle solving: "I love being able to make sense out of these little remaining . . . traces of the past . . . It's very comparable to the satisfaction of solving a puzzle. It's like . . . detective work, except you get to pick the murder cases and then investigate them, and it's a very, enormously satisfying thing to all of a sudden recognize that there's a pattern out there, and then figure out what that pattern means." This social scientist relishes the scholarly "detective work" of "investigation," pattern recognition, and pattern definition that his work affords. A professor of policy studies echoes this view. "My strength as a scholar is that I see things other people don't," he says. "People don't understand why you would write about [this subject], and yet when you give papers about it, they go, 'Well, my God, this is great.'" For this professor, and for the social scientists, research requires a discerning eye cast on particular aspects of the social world.

Professors who cast their scholarship as acts of discernment strive to unearth and explain patterns and meanings in the phenomena they study. For some of them discernment may emerge with great force. The scholar of comparative literature who views inquiry as "the only possible experience where you . . . can surprise yourself" captures this well as he adds, "In that sense it is really in a way . . . a revelation." This literary scholar echoes the words of another study participant in a different field and at a different university, Richard Marin, the theoretical physicist at Hope State, who portrayed the high points of his scholarly learning as instances of "revelation."

Creation

Based on these data, *to create* is to make and/or assemble meaning, through a particular medium or subject, in a time and place that does not (yet) reflect such meaning. "You are actually making it [i.e., music]," says Carmen Elias-Jones, "and then, and then physically, I mean, you spend so much time physically actually with the instrument, and being able to conquer it and then hear this, and it is a good sound." Elias-Jones portrays herself as creating—as bringing, through her performance, a new musical sound into a space that held no such sound before she began to play.

Similarly, a scientist speaks of passion for creating "new ways of doing things," which, prior to her creative action, are nonexistent within her research group's protocol. Asked to describe what she is doing in moments of "fascinating" work, the scientist, recently tenured at Signal University, says: "It's normally figuring out a clever way of doing something, and I . . . would say if I were evaluating myself as a scientist . . . [that] I am probably more interested by the process than the results . . . I must say . . . when I'm thinking about new ways of doing things, I'm not normally talking about new science or discoveries. I'm thinking about new ways of building a piece of equipment . . . So it's not fundamentally a new idea. It's a new way of doing something to get you to [where you might want to go]." This scientist says she is intrigued by the challenge of creation—inventing the particular instruments or methods whereby she and others engage in science.

Participating professors' expressions of passion in acts of discernment and creation include allusions to peak emotion, personal absorption in the work, physical sensation of and interrelation with a subject of study, and intensified awareness of the subject studied and the process of study. These images suggest that passionate thought may materialize among scholars in diverse fields pursuing diverse aims in diverse ways but always through a particular subject, discerned or created and thereby learned.

Viewed from within itself, and in its multiple manifestations, passionate thought appears complex (internally diverse) and dynamic (active and changing, responding). But from afar that passionate thought seems static and disconnected. How is passionate thought, as a high point of scholarship, situated among other experiences in professors' scholarly learning? How diffuse or contained, continuous or evanescent, predictable or erratic, are the high points themselves? I have so far examined passionate thought in isolation from the rest of professors' experiences of their work, and of scholarly learning specifically. Next I will explore the optimal experience that passionate thought represents in relation to other experiences of scholarly learning. In this expanded view scholarly learning encompasses and exceeds the high points of passionate thought, thereby contextualizing them and possibly even contributing to their coming into being.

Beyond Passionate Thought: Scholarly Learning as Its Source and Surround

Study participants typically portrayed passionate thought as pockets of deep insight or creation, and of intense "fulfillment," "excitement," "exhilaration," and "gratification," instances of beauty frozen in time and space. But do such experiences hold up over time? And what about the frequency of professors' experiences of passionate thought or about what happens in the spaces in between them? What does it take, on professors' parts, to call such high points into being, if that is even possible? Although instances of passionate thought matter deeply to professors, scholarly learning is a broader experience encompassing passionate highs and lows and gradations of feeling in between. That broader experience of scholarly learning, including its sparks of passionate insight, is itself embedded in still larger and more complex experiences of human existence.

EXPLORING THE SCHOLARLY LEARNING SURROUNDING PASSIONATE THOUGHT

A professor of business at Signal University describes a good workday. It's afternoon, and he and his colleague have, through the day, uncovered patterns of real interest in their data. As the patterns crystallize, he edges toward the exhilaration of significant insight. He then describes what he encounters in the cold light of the next morning:

> P: A really good day is a sunny day with the radio on and I'm programming a statistical package and running a regression 'cause I'm learning stuff, and at five o'clock I've got two new factors that I know that I didn't know when I walked in at eight. That's a great day. That's a really great day. The bad day is I walk in the next morning and discover I've got a programming error, and they're wrong. That's a disastrous day. We had one regression on one of

our earlier papers—we ran this regression—and do you know what an *r*-squared is?

AN: Yes.

P: Okay. We're getting *r*-squares of 20, 21, percent, we ran this one regression and got *r*-squared of 70 percent. This is fabulous! And I said, "Tom, something's got to be wrong." He says, "Listen. We're in a good mood. We have a good result. It's six o'clock at night. Let's go home, have dinner, talk to our wives, we'll come in tomorrow. If we spend fifteen more minutes and find out it's wrong, it will ruin the rest of the day." So we went home and had a great night. Came in the next morning and found out it was programming error.

Sometimes passionate moments abort, like they did for this business professor. Sometimes they represent false starts and false hopes. Some professors say that false starts absorb most of their time, with only a few initiatives yielding the passion for which, as one put it, "they bust their butts." "Ninety five percent of the time I get nowhere," says a chemist, "but that 5 percent pays off for the rest." And a historian notes that for her a passionate flash of insight "happens like every three years." The music professor also says that "the good sound" of truly good music "doesn't happen that often" and that "most of the time they [musicians] hate their performances." The theoretical physicist says that although "you are spending your life for those experiences," one might have them only "once every couple of years." The scholar of comparative literature sums it up: passion in scholarly thinking "is a very rare experience . . . to be sure."

For most professors the passion of high thought is rare and fleeting. As the chemist says: "It is a brief sense of fulfillment—like the following morning it is already old, and 'Why didn't I think of it before? How come no one thought about it?' But for five minutes it is, it is nice." Passionate thought is also erratic; it cannot be guaranteed. Though immersed in music, Carmen Elias-Jones glimpses the unpredictability of passionate musical experience—the lack of any assurance that it will recur—when she says she is "glad that it [her music] does that to me still." The professor of comparative literature also acknowledges the finite quality of knowing in passionate thought as he describes scholars who, in reaching for passionate intellectual expression, "suddenly find that maybe there isn't anything in particular that I want to say." Reaching for passionate thought does not guarantee its accession; it comes, as this scholar also has noted, quite "by surprise" and sometimes not at all.

For most of the professors I interviewed, experiences of passionate thought were brief, rare, illusory, and sometimes flawed; they also were unpredictable and at times deeply disappointing. Despite these draw-backs, professors devoted abundant time and energy to pursuing them. In between the high points, in the larger expanses of scholarly learn-ing around and between them, professors struggled for their realization. Within those larger expanses of struggle, of effort to learn in scholarly ways and in honest deliberation, such moments—of passionate thought recalled—were goals and beacons, objects of desire, though at times inac-cessible ones.

EXPLORING PASSIONATE THOUGHT THROUGH TIME

At Libra State University a professor of philosophy describes how he typi-cally paves the way for experiencing passionate thought.

> P: Ah, in the kind of work that I did in the book especially, what tends to happen is you are thinking about some problem, and usually it takes a while to get clear about what the problem is. But then you come to a point where you appreciate that if I'm going to be mak-ing any headway here, there is a certain problem I have to solve. Sometimes it's a mathematical problem. Other times it's a concep-tual problem. Then what . . . happens to me usually . . . is I end up going through a period where I'm experimenting, and I try a bunch of things, and they don't work. So I keep in my drawer over there—and I have a drawer at home [too]—I keep old sheets of paper with one side [that] have been typed on. And what I do during this period is I take a . . . pen, and I just write on these pieces of paper, and I literally go through stacks of paper—like this—in a week. I just try something out, and it doesn't work . . . I throw them away.
>
> AN: And you throw them away?
>
> P: Yeah, yeah, I throw them away because they didn't go anywhere, and usually . . . during that period what is happening is I'm working

on this problem, a few minutes here, a few minutes there . . . and it's very, very frustrating frankly because I'm not getting anywhere. But then in a few cases what will happen is you'll get an idea . . . which turns out to be promising, that you think you can make some headway on. And then what happens to me is I get—there isn't any other word for it—completely obsessed for a while, maybe a few days, maybe a week or two.

AN: Obsessed?

P: Obsessed with this problem, and I'm obsessed because I really like it because I'm making progress now on this problem that has been bothering me for a long time. And . . . during these periods, which are reasonably rare—if they weren't rare I couldn't even live my life—but, I don't do anything else really. I just think about this problem, and you have the feeling, all the way along, that now I'm getting somewhere. And then, in some cases, you actually do get some place, and that's great. And [in] some cases you don't, and that's not so bad. Then it's back to the drawing board. But that's the part of the research that I most like.

This passage exemplifies the larger processes of thought (narrowing down and clarifying a problem, experimenting, making mistakes, and finally happening on a promising result) and emotion (e.g., connection or occasional frustration) within which one scholar's passionate thought is set. But these dual processes of thought and emotion continue after the defined moments of "obsession," for example, if the scholar finds that his initial hunch was wrong.

AN: So let me take the alternative route here, and say, you got into this feeling of being almost there . . . and really went into it deeply, and all of a sudden you realize that there was a mistake, or [it] didn't work out—What happens then? What does that feel like?

P: Well, I typically get upset and depressed, but I guess I've always thought that my greatest intellectual strength is that I'm very dogged . . . I really never let go of a problem once I get my teeth into it. So . . . one of the main results in my books, there's this one important . . . result—I worked on that for two years—and it happened all the time that I thought I had it and I didn't, thought I had it and I didn't. There's another problem which I would have liked to have been able to tackle in the book which I worked on, I don't know for how many years, and it's happened over and over that I've thought that I almost had it, and it just turns out I don't. It's a hard problem. It's a problem that's been unsolved for years and years and years . . . but when these things happen, I feel upset and I feel depressed, but I don't ever— . . . I always try to think of what's the next thing to do. I never . . . get so upset that I think that I don't want to work on this anymore. Because once I've committed to a problem, it's sort of—

AN: You're committed.

P: Yeah, it's there.

This scholar says he persists "in dogged ways over and over" when his first effort fails. In the aftermath of an "obsession" that yields nothing, "upset" and "depression" displace excitement.

This professor explains that his peak moments, signaled by obsession, follow from an extended period of mucking around in various avenues of thought. During this time he engages in both planned and unplanned activity. He encounters accidents, makes mistakes, and revises. He expends significant effort with little payoff. He senses little or none of the clarity of direction, energy, accomplishment, and joy associated with passionate thought. Instead, in these off-peak times he stands at an emotional balance point that often shifts toward frustration, upset, or depression. At other times ("reasonably rare," he says), he shifts toward "promising" moments of hope in which he feels, "I'm getting somewhere." And sometimes he indeed does "get somewhere," and as he says, "that's great," but at other times "it's back to the drawing board." This scholar's words suggest that the flash of peak emotion and absorption punctuates a larger experience that, if not negative, may be simply less than optimal.

The comments of other professors I interviewed resonate with those of the philosopher. A professor in the sciences says that his passionate thought is part of a longer process: "It's not like there's a moment when there's nothing, and then all of a sudden there's something. It's more like a long sequence of small steps." Emphasizing the ups and downs of research, he adds: "It's challenging. It's a good thing when things work out. But things don't always work out. There are frustrations." And a social scientist, considering the larger process of his fieldwork, echoes that in contrast to the moments of intense "clarity of thought," "there were many days when the research just didn't go well . . . I didn't find the animals. I couldn't follow the animals; they went up a cliff." Like the philosopher, the scientist and social scientist portray moments of passionate thought surrounded by long stretches of less pleasurable though persistent effort.

Scholars express the range of emotion that marks their work in various ways. At times the highs and lows are side by side, as in the case of the scientist who speaks of being both "excited" and "frustrated," and two writers who describe their compulsions to create but then switch to portrayals of writing as "frustrating, overly consuming, solitary" or as infused with a "sense of loss or sadness or mourning." An engineer similarly describes research as "fascinating" and "pleasant" but also as riddled by "whatever pain it's gonna take to get there." And Carmen Elias-Jones's experiences of music are anything but a steady high thrill. Rather, the musician experiences a "gamut of emotions" as she performs. The astronomer David Mora also evinces an emotional complexity when he says that his moments of intense thought are less about a particular feeling than about the extremes of multiple feelings, from "immediately rewarding" to "very frustrating," but "whatever it is, it's usually at the edges of your emotional response." "You're rarely in a position where you're just, sort of, la, la, la," he says. "It can be very exhilarating, very frustrating, whatever—but it's always very something." For many study participants passionate thought represents momentary exhilaration, often accompanied by other feelings, such as frustration or depression. The "passion" of passionate thought is thus far more complex than its initial representation—the high point—conveys.

Passionate thought is variegated, spanning multiple emotions, but for some professors, so is each of its component emotions. Although some professors portray these emotions as being consistently extreme ("always very something," Mora says), others describe them as varying in intensity. The theoretical physicist says that "there are all levels" for a particular emotion and that "it is not like . . . it is all zero or one." Some scholars value the muted moments. Referring to his high moments of thought, the philosopher says, "If they weren't rare, I couldn't even live my life." Some even take willful action to still passionate engagement for a period of time. Elias-Jones says, "It is very important that I get away from it [music]"; she builds into her life occasional "music-free days." Scholars striving for passionate thought in their scholarly and creative work may aim for moments of emotional quiet alongside the exhilarating and depressing times.

Interestingly, not all participating professors view the larger process of scholarly learning—the times in between realization or insight—as secondary experiences. Some relish the times of struggle or "negotiation" in between, for the culmination of such struggle in peak insight broaches loss even as it offers gratification. A professor in literary studies says that what drives her is the protracted process of research into a question or idea important to her, less so than its resolution: "Being [in]side the process . . . in dialogue with it . . . is what I love about it . . . When you are . . . negotiating your relationship to different ideas." She adds, "By the time it's become a product, I usually fall into despair." Passion is at the heart of the process of this scholar's efforts to learn and know. As one of her long-term struggles to learn something important to her culminates in insight, as a "product," she grieves its departure from her life.

In these professors' experiences, passionate thought appears momentarily within the larger process of its pursuit as an experience of scholarly learning. The process, for some, reflects exploration and accident, mucking around and mistake, waiting and persistence, as well as extremes of fluctuating emotion—from exhilaration to despair. Although most professors described the larger process of their scholarly learning as less productive and exhilarating, or as emotionally quieter, than the peak insights of passionate thought that punctuate it, some said that they relish the entire process. Thus, the high points of realization—of coming to know in passionate thought—are but sparks of experience within more complex streams of diverse thought and emotion in professors' scholarly learning.

Varieties of Passionate Thought

Rather than associating passionate thought with the pursuit of beauty, some of the professors I interviewed associated it with a search for expressive space. Rather than positioning it consistently within a single subject of study, some presented it as cross-cutting multiple areas of study.

Rather than casting it as an individual experience, some professors portrayed their passionate thought as shared.

The Search for Expressive Space

Asked to describe the work they love and its origins in their lives, some interviewees, notably women, describe modes of thought that they invented in childhood or adolescence as spaces, protected from the public view, in which they might express ideas, insights, questions, and sensations disallowed in their daily lives. Some portray these modes of thought as, originally, spaces of retreat—escapes from other forms of more public thought (which they paint as uncomfortable or hurtful) within their families, schools, and communities. These scholars also say that the ways in which they learned to think years ago, in these alternative childhood spaces, have in part, framed their scholarly thought in adulthood.

Asked about the biographical sources of the special "focus" that lets her "shut out everything else" as she engages in scholarship, a professor of landscape architecture at Libra State says:

> I was just thinking about that this last [long holiday] weekend
> . . . I had quite a bit of time to just read and write a little and do
> what I wanted . . . And for some reason . . . some time during one
> of those days I happened to think, "Why is this so gratifying?"
> And [I] thought about the past . . . One of the things I thought
> about . . . was the sense that . . . this satisfaction does go back a
> long way for me, goes back to childhood and . . . that internal
> feeling of focus going back a long way . . . it's an escape in some
> ways. It was a way to not think about and not deal with other
> things going on in your life but to be able to just kind of bury
> yourself in something and get satisfaction out of learning that
> came with that . . . I do think it goes back a long way.

Asked if the feeling of focus was just about "escape" or if it indeed included "learning" and its "satisfaction," she adds: "I think it [was] both because if it had been just the former, an escape, I could [have] watch[ed] TV all the time or read comic books or smoked on the corner with my friends or whatever. I didn't do those things because . . . there was . . . some inherent satisfaction, in addition to being able to block out real life—the rest of the world . . . be[ing] able to leave that, there was the inherent satisfaction of—boy, learning." For this scholar escape from the thought that dominated her childhood entailed more than departure; it also entailed an entry into learning, which she achieved through "focus." Focusing was for her a different way to think, constructed in childhood amid "real life." The experience continues in this scholar's life today, situating the thought of her research.[7]

Moving Beyond a Single Subject

Many professors participating in the study said they stumbled, early in life, onto particular subjects that have served as the primary sites of their passionate thought throughout their lifetimes. Such was the case of David Mora, who found astronomy as a ten- or twelve-year-old on summer vacation in the Black Hills of South Dakota. The same is true of Carmen Elias-Jones, the musician who at age five or six first encountered her instrument in the church that she and her family attended. For these scholars the link between childhood passion and adult commitment is clear.

For other scholars that connection is less direct and more thematic, spanning multiple subjects in which the professor has learned over the years. A professor of business at Horizon University says that her present-day fascination with organizational studies that exhibit "simplicity . . . [are] aesthetically pleasing . . . elegant . . . very intuitively appealing" are related to her childhood love of "books and novels and stories" reflecting "nice, clear-cut theme[s] . . . simple . . . short . . . evok[ing] a very strong emotional reaction." Noting that her childhood literary interests and her interests today in organizational studies (both locations of her passionate thought) are indeed "very different," she says that for her they connect in her fascination with aesthetic form.

In a sense this aesthetic form, materializing over time in different subject matters, is this scholar's subject of study, perhaps as much as is the organizational subject matter of her current intellectual endeavor. As an adult, she has adopted the knowledge and questions of organizational studies as the "new" media of her ongoing aesthetic pursuits. Professors may then commit early in their lives to a particular subject, yet where and how they go about realizing it can change in surprising ways from childhood through adulthood. Despite the change, their subjects stay with them, as do their memories of coming to know them.

Passionate Thought as Shared

Although most scholars portray their passionate thought in relation to their own activity, others present it as a person-with-person experience. A professor of gerontology, newly tenured at Horizon University, describes passionate thought as materializing in the subject-anchored conversations of a research group of professors and graduate students who, in building ideas together, also build "intense" excitement about their scholarly pursuits: "We had one experience this year where we locked the door with everybody in here and had laptops . . . computers. It was strenuous and not the right way to do it. But the product turned out to be pretty good. And I think everybody had that sense of getting [excited] about it as the intensity about it built up." This scholar describes an emotional and intellectual "intensity" that, she says, arose within the group as each member became excited about the "product" that collectively they were creating.

But conversations such as these are not restricted to research settings. A professor of romance languages, working at Hope State University, describes a classroom teaching experience that is just as intellectually intense:

> Sometimes it [creative insight] happens when I'm talking about something with a reasonably . . . receptive class, which, in fact, happened this afternoon. I mean, we discovered a whole bunch of things that I really hadn't ever—it was pretty cool . . . we were reading [this] novel . . . this was the second week of discussion. And nothing we said is going to make Western intellectual history . . . but there were a lot of connections. There were a lot of things that hooked up and made sense and that we could circle back to, and a lot of things you could come back to from the week before that had been left dangling. And there was the occasional remark from a slightly obstreperous, productively obstreperous student . . . and I was able to funnel [his remarks] back into the discussion and show how [it] looks at first like a smart-alecky response. It was, in fact, rather profound if you looked at it long enough and from enough different angles. It was very enjoyable. It was fairly intense. Everyone was really quite focused.

This scholar emphasizes the "rather profound . . . connections" of knowledge that she experienced and that she witnessed in her students: "Everyone was really quite focused" on the "fairly intense" learning. From her standpoint these learners created, through dialogue, a passionate thought that no one person could create alone.

Both the gerontologist and the scholar of romance languages describe instances of high thought and emotion created in their interactions with others. They describe themselves as feeling their own passionate thought and as sensing it in others around them: as thought grew interactively, so did emotion—in both cases, relative to specific knowledge that the people involved created together. A scholar of literary studies, on the faculty of Libra State University, summed up her experiences of such instances: "It has to do with establishing connections. And what's satisfying about it is when you've reached the point in a dialogue with someone where that kind of energy—this sounds very New Agey—. . . gets exchanged. And . . . it's not located in one's self or the other self, but it just . . . emerges. That's really very satisfying. So in a way it's a giving up of something but also getting something back, but it's not about ownership." This scholar describes the insides of her passionate thought as an experience of "connection" and "exchange" of "energy" with others, as an experience of the "giving up of something, but also getting something back," though not about "ownership." It is thereby shared.[8]

Passionate thought appears in diverse forms and may thus be viewed as being contingent on the resources in and constraints on professors' learning in any portion of their lives (e.g., community conditions prompting needs for adolescent "escape" from them); the particular intellectual resources available to individuals for thought at any point in their lives (consider the shifting substantive media of professors' subjects from childhood through adulthood); and not least, the conditions of professors' work (such as the availability of collaboration as a work mode).

Between Self and Other

Most professors participating in the *Four Universities Project* experienced their scholarly learning as being powered by a search for passionate thought: sporadic, often unpredictable instances of discernment into or creation of substantive ideas or images, appearing as flashes of insight within still larger experiences of subject matter study (in scholarship or research) or, more broadly, as subject matter representation (teaching). The idea or insight so discerned, or the image so created, may in the long run be a gift to others—to students and colleagues, to practitioners and citizens beyond the university. But in the moment of its coming into being—its "revelation" (as the scholar of comparative literature called it) or its "making" (as the musician Elias-Jones portrayed it)—it is a gift of deepened and surprising realization, in passion and thought, to the scholar who feels and knows it. In such moments it comes in flares of peak emotion, as experiences of absorption and intense sensation, of heightened awareness, for some a crystallized beauty.

Passionate thought, as an instance of beauty, is surrounded by the emotions that mark its pursuit through broader experiences of scholarly learning. Yet passionate thought is itself an instance of insight that professors experience in different ways: as ideas and images to protect or relish in moments of escape from daily life; as insights that move through diverse subject matters as a person's learning opportunities re-form throughout her life; and not least, as experiences of oneself or among oneself and others. In all its forms this passionate thought, however brief and rare, draws scholars, through desire, repeatedly back to it. It draws them to scholarly learning in depth, potentially through the extended expanse of their careers.

David Mora, Carmen Elias-Jones, and their colleagues offer an inside view of intellectual desire: scholars' strivings for passionate thought, occurring in flashes of discernment and creation, within larger and more complex processes of scholarly learning. Yet even with this view, questions remain: about the kinds of thinking that professors muster toward their scholarly learning; about where and when scholarly learning materializes; about other kinds of learning that may occur alongside the scholarly, and how these interact with the scholarly. I turn next to these questions, again from the standpoint of professors' experiences—and understandings—of them.

CHAPTER THREE

Mindwork

What and How Professors Strive to Learn

Professors' peak experiences of passionate thought are infrequent, brief, and unpredictable; a person cannot simply call them into being. What professors can more realistically strive to bring into being is the far broader and more complex experience of scholarly learning that situates those high points, making them possible. Scholarly learning, as the "mindwork" that situates passionate thought, may be viewed as part of the soil in which that thought grows. Passionate thought does not appear from out of the blue but grows amid the vicissitudes of scholarly learning.

Professors' Conceptions of What Their Scholarly Learning Entails

When one encounters an intellectual problem, she cannot simply summon up the knowledge that passionate thought would provide. If what one faces is indeed a problem of scholarly thought, she has to work at it mentally. To do that, she can call up, consciously and willfully, the armamentarium of thought and of ways of thinking and inquiring that she has developed through her career and life to explore other such problems: ways of garnering ideas and information related to those problems, approaches to viewing and interpreting the problems, approaches to their interrogation and exploration, practices of experimentation and analysis, habits of trust and belief in what counts as knowledge about them. As she selects and activates certain portions of that armamentarium of thought to address her problem, she positions herself to engage in scholarly learning about it.

Professors participating in the *Four Universities Project* referred to this armamentaria of thought openly as they described their scholarly learning. The question "What activities of mind did participating professors see themselves as undertaking in the spirit of scholarly learning as I have defined it?" helped spark the discussion.

I identified four such activities of mind, including professors' efforts to extend their subject matter knowledge; re-form that knowledge; re-contextualize it; and represent, or project, that knowledge in terms and through images that others can grasp, thereby exploring meanings that acts of projection may bring to light.[1] These activities of mind, viewed as approaches to scholarly learning, are summarized in table 3.1.

EXTENDING SUBJECT MATTER KNOWLEDGE

Study participants frequently portrayed their scholarly learning as *subject matter knowledge extension.* To extend one's knowledge of a subject is to grow it out, thereby increasing its volume or scope. Participating professors typically portrayed extension as acts of addition to an established knowledge base or as acts of filling in gaps in that base.

Asked if her students influenced her thinking as a teacher and scholar, a literature professor at Horizon University exclaimed, "Graduate students, yes, absolutely," then added: "The things they work on . . . the things they know and learn about . . . it's real important . . . to keep up with what . . . the graduate students are reading." "You know," she observed, "they're more au courant than I am in that respect." The professor of literature says that her graduate students bring to her what they have gained from their readings beyond their class assignments. Thus, they point out to her, and to peers in class, subject matter developments that the professor herself may not yet have accessed. They serve as scouts to new knowledge, helping to extend the teacher's grasp of the knowledge she teaches.

Such comments were by no means restricted to professors who taught graduate students. An anthropologist at Libra State University said that in both her graduate and undergraduate classes she purposefully assigns readings that bring her into contact with disciplinary knowledge that, in her words, is "new and interesting to me" and that this results in her

TABLE 3.1 Scholarly Learning: Professors' Views of Their Own Activities of Mind

Form of Subject Matter Change	Definition	Enactment
Extend	Expand or fill in knowledge of a subject that one has developed to date	• Adding in newly emerging knowledge about the field • Reviewing the field's classics for new insight • Improving grasp of field's foundational ideas
Reform	Bring together distinct ideas, rethink the meaning of one or more ideas	• Bringing together ideas within accumulated knowledge • Rethinking established ideas or perspectives
Recontextualize	Position an idea developed in one knowledge environment within another so as to view it against a changed background; analyze comparative views	Moving substantive ideas to: — fields of study other than one's own (cross-disciplinarity) — new or unusual social and cultural settings — practice — one's personal life
Represent	Project one's knowledge of a subject of study for others' best-possible understanding, explore emergent meanings in so doing	• Teaching • Writing • Presenting • Other modes of expression

Source: Derived from the Four Universities Project, year-3 interviews, n = 39.

"learn[ing] about areas or new topics or read[ing] new literature that I wouldn't otherwise read." Professors who, while teaching, learn in this way—at the edges of knowledge they previously mastered—promise to bring new thought, and possibly a spirited interestedness, to their work with students. As their students learn, so do they.

The theme of additive scholarly learning within teaching pervaded the majority of interviews, suggesting that for university professors, certainly at the graduate level, to teach is to maximize possibilities for learning for students and teacher alike. Carla Duran, a professor of biological sciences at Hope State University, exemplifies the approach:

I teach graduate seminars, and I usually pick a topic that I know I need to learn more about. I took that to an extreme this semester.

Usually I pick topics that I know quite a bit about but need to learn more about. But I picked a topic that I really knew very little about, and that was plant breeding systems. And I knew that most of my students don't work on [that] . . . but I've gotten a couple NSF grants to work on [it] . . . [but] I don't have a good background in botany, so I thought, "Well, I'll just teach . . . this graduate seminar in plant mating systems, and we're gonna work our way through this really dense and difficult book because . . . [otherwise] if you held a gun to my head, I wouldn't sit down to read [it]." [I wouldn't] be able to read through this book.

I found four students . . . [who] signed up and . . . seemed to be very agreeable. And so we've just taken it a chapter a week and we've read this book, and we've all learned a lot . . . Some things we've learned more about than we've wanted to know, but it's worked . . . It's achieved our objectives. And so now that we've worked through this book, we're reading . . . some primary literature, and it seemed like the students were fine with [that], too. But they needed something, two credit hours or one credit hour, to force them to learn a subject that is a little bit impenetrable . . . so I certainly have learned a lot, and it seemed to work.

As Duran's statement indicates, her teaching about a topic she did not understand well—in this case, plant mating systems—made her students' learning, and her own learning alongside theirs, possible.

As these scholars note, to extend their knowledge is to add to it, to enlarge it, or to fill in gaps in light of developments in the field. Knowledge extension also may involve a professor's going back to her field's "primary literature"—its classics—to plow for deepened understanding. Although she acknowledged in one portion of our interview that she was "not at all sure what value [teaching] has to me as a researcher," a physicist at Libra State University exclaimed later in our talk that her teaching made her think through deeply some of the foundational ideas in her field: "It's not like I don't know the basic facts about introductory physics . . . I definitely do. But . . . there's always a nuance . . . a potential question . . . You . . . have to actually . . . think about it . . . I have to definitely work through a lot of the stuff. Some of it [is likely to] be things that I should have learned in graduate school . . . but didn't. And there

[will] be other things that I probably did learn at one time that I've totally forgotten." Although she feels well versed in the "basic facts" in her field, this physics professor realizes that in teaching, she may "work through" ideas for "thinking about" such facts in detail, gleaning "nuances" she had not previously considered.

It is worth noting that some of professors' scholarly learning, through extension, involves more than gaining mastery of subject matter knowledge, basic or advanced. It also involves gaining research skills. A professor of engineering at Horizon University said that even though most of his scholarly learning is situated in research that "there are always things in the textbooks [I use in my undergraduate class] that . . . are a little bit outside of what I learned before, or . . . things that I do in my research, [and] so there are various [research] methods I've learned about [in teaching]." He described a computer software package that he used initially in his research then brought to his undergraduate class, where, in order to teach it, he had to learn it still more deeply; this then helped him as he returned to his research. "I started using it [software] in the research," he said, "and then I introduced it into the class. And I kind of go back and forth between them, on the software . . . I've acquired a lot of skill in using [it]." This professor uses his teaching as a site in which to hone his research skills and his research as a site for sharpening a practice he teaches.

As these examples suggest, participating professors said they extended their subject matter understandings by adding new (advanced) knowledge to what they knew already and also by collecting or recollecting ideas and perspectives foundational to their subjects of study, though not bearing directly on their own research. As the examples indicate, professors in different fields and on different campuses, teaching graduate students and occasionally undergraduates, described their scholarly learning as occurring by way of extension, typically within their teaching or research.

RE-FORMING SUBJECT MATTER KNOWLEDGE

To extend one's knowledge is to enlarge or fill in its already established base. To *re-form* it, a scholar may act more boldly: She may join seemingly distinct, even disparate, understandings. Or she may rethink the meaning of a familiar idea, possibly in surprising ways.

Bringing Together Seemingly Distinct Ideas

Some professors portray their scholarly learning as a creative act: they may glimpse resonances between two ideas, or groupings of ideas, typically held apart and bring them closer together to view them against each other or in combination. Jennifer Oldak, a mathematician at Libra State University, referred to connection as a primary mode of her scholarly learning: "And so we've seen that there are some very interesting, strong connections between [one mathematical field] which is really what I've been working in, and [another mathematical field], . . . which I knew very little about before, and now, I know a little bit more about, and I can see the connections. And so I'm . . . more interested in going down that avenue. I'm more interested in connections between [mathematical] fields than [in] particular fields themselves. That's a new connection that seems to be there—I'm heading off in that direction, trying to pick up some knowledge from [mathematical field newer to her]." Oldak portrayed herself as learning in two locations: within one or more mathematical subfields and, even more important to her, across them ("I'm more interested in connections between [mathematical] fields than [in] particular fields themselves"). As her last sentence suggests, the mathematician's connective, cross-field effort is what drives much of her within-field work; she defines her central interest, then, as one of connection. Echoing this mathematician, a professor of comparative literature at Signal University also explained his own field's valuing of "connections," in contrast to searches for the "big, great, good idea," which, he said, "doesn't exist" in his field. "You don't have suddenly the idea that then leads to . . . the discovery of a new element," he said, but rather, "you see connections, and you see interesting questions that you want to formulate."

Why might connective work matter so much to scholars? Serena Mandell, a professor of history at Libra State, offered her own experience as a partial response: as "things come together," she said, she begins to feel "the sense of significance" that her efforts in studying contemporary European history represent. And she added, "I feel it in teaching, I feel it in reading, and I feel it in writing." And struggling to put into words the meaning of connection, as opposed to work with single ideas, one at a time, she proffered, "I can get kind of obsessed about details of things . . . but what's more a site of pleasure and excitement is . . . bringing things together rather than . . . looking at the structure of [a single idea]."

Emily Lifton, a professor of environmental engineering at Signal University, also drew on her deep involvement with subject matters of her field to describe the significance of connection in her scholarly learning: "I work at the interface [of multiple scientific and applied fields,]" she said, "but I think all good researchers do that. I mean, you tend to do your research in a way that hasn't been done before, and you try to come up with new connections or different connections, and that's why it's research, right?" For Lifton connection is what defines research as a primary mode of her scholarly learning.

Rethinking Established Ideas or Perspectives
Through their scholarly learning professors may also rethink—or strive to rethink—their own and others' established ideas or perspectives, thereby positioning themselves to re-form meaning, newly acquired or long-held. A chemist at Hope State referred to such effort as "stirring the pot of knowledge" in his head, and Serena Mandell, the historian at Libra State, spoke of it as "shifting my frame on a particular issue." Such change in a scholar's thoughts about a subject central to her expertise can yield a sense of movement, even awakening (knowledge "stirring"), or of focusing (frame shifting). But it can yield feelings of substantive movement as well, sometimes heaving a scholar from one side of established understanding to another. A social scientist at Signal University said that her recent conversations with friends—and in parallel with undergraduate students—had led her to see and understand that "the other side" of a position she had long held, on a controversial social policy issue at the center of her research, could have "every bit as much integrity as I have." At the point that I last saw this scholar, she was considering the implications of this insight, from the other side, for her well-developed research stance.

Professors participating in the *Four Universities Project* varied in how they experienced such rethinking of established ideas: it felt bold and exciting to some, unremarkable to others. Emily Lifton, the engineer at Signal University, said that her work with students, undergraduates and graduates, could lead her to glimpse new ways to think about features of her field that, until such moments, she had not fully appreciated. "I love teaching a course the first couple of times, particularly if it's really engaging my learning," she said. "Now, any time you teach something, you always learn . . . through the students . . . The students always bring new questions, and . . . I'll say, 'God, I've taught that for ten years, and no one's ever asked me that question before. That's really interesting. I'd never thought of that.'" In contrast, Esther Sharan, a literature professor at Hope State, referred to such rethinking, and the insight it yields, as part of a more commonplace "working out" of ideas, blending as quickly as they appear to her into the background of her knowledge. "Every now and then I'll have the sense of elaborating an idea and working it out a little more thoroughly in response to a question from a student . . . It's not a particularly dramatic thing," she said. "Often I don't have time to note it down . . . it sort of happens, and then it's gone. I can't always remember exactly . . . I don't really have time to stop and figure out exactly what it is that I'm working out on my feet, as it were."

As these examples suggest, to re-form knowledge a scholar usually reflects on the knowledge at hand, then going in search of more insight, she moves that knowledge around, feeling its movement in her mind, occasionally being moved by it herself. Alternatively, she may bring its parts together in unusual ways or explore it in a new or different light, at times one suggested by students. A scholar may experience her knowledge re-forming efforts as dramatic or subtle, as happening slowly or rapidly. These efforts may appear in the context of her teaching and research, in work done alone or with others.

RECONTEXTUALIZING SUBJECT MATTER KNOWLEDGE

Professors may engage in scholarly learning by recontextualizing their long-held subject matter ideas—in other words, by thinking about their ideas in new and different settings that bring out unexamined features. This means more than engaging in a thought experiment; it means actively moving an idea from one location to another and working with it in the new place.

Before pursuing the recontextualizing of subject matter knowledge as a form of scholarly learning, it will help to define what I mean by the phrase *contextualizing knowledge*. To contextualize knowledge is to locate an idea in a larger, encompassing knowledge environment that by virtue of its unique meanings, slants the idea in particular ways or brings out certain of its meanings while making less of others (though those remain latent). I can envision the idea of thirst, for example, a physical experience that on a stifling summer afternoon in most twenty-first-century middle-class American homes means something distinctive: discomfort, the desire to reach for a cool drink, a sense of physical annoyance that one knows can be soothed and is only a temporary state. This, I trust, is a thirst that many people in twenty-first-century America can relate to. I have so far *contextualized* the idea of thirst in a certain time and place that lend it a certain meaning.

I turn now to the *recontextualizing of subject matter knowledge,* which I define as moving an idea from one knowledge context that brings out certain of its meanings to another context that brings out other latent meanings, possibly covering up those that were more obvious in the first setting. Extending the previous example, I recontextualize thirst now in the life of another person who is presently recalling the horrors of constant thirst, bodily deprivation in wartime, when thirst and war have no end, when to have thirst means to be or not be. This person's knowledge of thirst, drawn from that other time and place, is clearly not the same thirst that someone who has never been there, physically and psychically, knows.[2] Thirst in these two settings means very different things. For a learner to shift a thought, like thirst, from its long-term positioning in one environment (a twenty-first-century middle-class American home) to quite another (wartime imprisonment or present-day memories of such) for a hard comparative view involves recontextualization.

This view echoes the oft-heard comment in schools that a word can mean different things in different contexts—in effect, that words hold special meanings, given different usages and different surroundings. Ideas, including those with which scholars work, behave this way as well: moved from subject to subject, or from usage to usage, aspects of their meaning can change, however subtly. This view of contextualization— and of recontextualization—resonates with proposition 5 given in chapter 1: that professors' learning occurs in contexts of knowledge that shape it uniquely. To recontextualize a piece of knowledge—an idea—involves moving it from one knowledge context to another. Doing so may bring out facets of meaning in the idea that were unseen in the earlier environment, though muting others that were previously visible. I view insights gained through recontextualization of a substantive idea as scholarly learning, especially when that recontextualization is intentional. I also count a learner's searching out and entering into new contexts with this aim in mind as scholarly learning.

How might a professor go about purposefully recontextualizing an idea? She might do so, first, by moving an idea that is associated with one discipline or subdiscipline to another, as often occurs in cross-disciplinary study, a topic I take up in the next chapter. She might also do so by moving an idea that in the past she explored exclusively within traditional academic settings (in a lab, fieldwork site, or classroom) to other settings beyond academe, among them: new or unusual social or cultural settings; professional and/or occupational practices other than the academic; and scholars' own personal lives and autobiographical knowing apart from their professional endeavors. Each of these alternative settings reflect certain kinds of knowledge that may contextualize scholars' ideas in ways that are new or different to them, thereby shaping their meanings.

Moving Substantive Ideas into New Settings

Professors may move the problems they have studied previously in academic settings (e.g., among their disciplinary colleagues) into the lives of individuals and communities where those problems may "come to life" in new and substantial ways: in the terms of people's social, cultural, and personal realities. In her final interview Emily Lifton, the professor of environmental engineering at Signal University, spoke at length about differences in meaning between a scientific idea expressed as a chemical formula and its "live form" in a natural environment that physically touches the lives of people in a nearby residential community.

Lifton describes herself as belonging to a field that "seeks to protect human health and hopefully to protect ecological health as well . . . [by promoting] better understanding of chemical interactions, biological interactions, physical interactions." Among her chief interests is the effort to "understand chemical interactions of pollutants . . . either as way[s] to remove those pollutants from various environmental phases . . . from water . . . But then if . . . released into the environment . . . figure out where [they] go" with the aim, ultimately, of "mediat[ing] the impact of pollutants on the environment . . . to protect both environmental health and human health." Lifton, who has contributed substantially to chemical understandings of water, its treatment and safety, was recently reminded that scientific interpretations of "live problems" in her area of study are incomplete if divided from knowledge of people's very real life struggles with those problems—physically and biologically (thus medically), psychologically, socially, and culturally. To get closer to the "lived" versions of the environmental problems she studies, Emily Lifton moved her chemistry problems, long situated in the discourses of her scientific community, to an alternative site: the discourses of policy formulation and city residents' everyday lives.

Lifton learned to engage her continuing subject of research between two sites in ways that respond and contribute to both, a shift she talked about briefly through her year 1 interview. Describing her past and current work as analytically lab based ("trying to figure out what happens to the organics as [water] goes through this treatment [process]"), she added, "I'm now looking at natural process, natural systems like a wetland," in light of related problems with our water supply. Elaborating on part of the "why" of her locational shift—from the lab-like water treatment station to a wetland—Lifton explained: "When I first started my academic job I was trying to understand what happened to organics in a [water] treatment process. That was all well and good," she said. "It's just . . . not interesting. Now I'm trying to use the technique to understand what happens to different water bodies." Before I could ask Lifton what had led her to this view, she said, "After a while, you ask the question . . . what is the value? . . . what has the greater value?" She raises this question in light of an interest that, by her year 3 interview, has "become more acute": whether to continue in her long-term "focus . . . in a more fundamental hard science area" (the water treatment process) or "to move into an area that's a newer interest which is a little bit more—policy related" and attentive to "the consequences to society for the legacy of pollution" (the wetland perspective).

Throughout our interview Lifton spoke at length about her growing desires to understand the science of water pollution as existing, in her words, "within the story" of a larger ecological-community interaction within which problems of water safety play a significant role. For Lifton this meant learning "how to do the algebra of partitioning chemistry" (her core intellectual interest) by way of a broader but equally rigorous social-ecological analysis that pointedly asks: "What's the harm? What do we need to do? What's the decision?" Rather than viewing her lab-based research as distinct from studies of society and culture, Lifton describes how social-cultural perspectives on scientific problems can heighten scientists', policy makers', and citizens' appreciation of the complexity of the science at issue—and of the "real life" that it touches. Lifton has, in effect, moved her knowledge pursuits from one context, namely a community of scholars of the topic, to another, a broader community of citizens, policy makers, and water treatment workers in a "live community." That new community context brings out facets of her topic that were less visible, and perhaps less graspable, than they were in the purely academic setting. Thus, Lifton engages her scholarly learning in two worlds at once: in her lab and in that part of the natural world where the problems of learning exist.

Moving Substantive Ideas into Practice

Professors, especially in professional fields—education, business management, social work, engineering, and so on—may benefit from thinking through professional practitioners' understandings of the ideas that those academics typically pursue by way of research. A real-world perspective can on occasion helpfully direct the academic view. Professors of education, for example, who want to identify teaching practices that lead to students' improved understandings of school subjects, of students' own identities, of society or culture, or of humanity broadly may benefit from watching and talking to expert schoolteachers, culling bits of their wisdom of practice. Professors of management who study the meaning of leadership may likewise benefit from watching and talking to management practitioners who have had to learn, on the job, how to think about organizational strategy. Professors of social work and engineering may reap insights for their research by exploring subject matter ideas as they "come to life" in the practices of skilled social workers and competent engineers. A number of the study's professors, all in applied/professional fields, did in fact move their research-based problems and theories into sites of practice, exploring how knowledgeable practitioners use them, or enact them, on the job. As a professor of engineering at Horizon University remarked, one can learn for research and teaching from "observations of real things" in a field of professional practice—for example, through "site visits [or] talking to people working in industry" or in other work settings.

In this spirit participating professors' conversations with practicing professionals—some of whom were their own students—sometimes served as sites of those professors' scholarly learning. Les Thompson, a professor of business at Signal University, said that his practitioner students, many in corporate jobs, have taught him a great deal about some of the topics that he has sought to teach them:

> It's very nice to know the people that generate the data. We wrote one paper—we were trying to explain the rate small businesses pay on their loans. When you're a small business corporation, you go to the bank, and say, "I'd like to borrow ten thousand dollars." And they say, "Okay, you have to pay us back." And as part of that loan contract, they [bank officials] say, "If you don't pay us back, we get the truck that your corporation owns as collateral." That makes the loan less risky. Except if you don't pay them back, they can come get all the assets of the corporation. But corporations are limited liability organizations, so they can't go through the corporation back to your house and your personal car. Unless when you sign the contract you say, "Yes, you can." So in about a third of these contracts you say, "Not only can you come get my corporate assets, but you can come get my personal assets." Well, if they do that, that makes them [loans] a little less risky [for the bank]. And if it's less risky, they [the bank] should give you a lower loan rate. [So, I] run the regression, and . . . find it has no effect on the loan rate. So, what I'm doing is, I'm letting you come get my car if things go [bad], but you're not giving me a cheaper loan.
>
> And so [my colleague and I] wrote this paper. "You know," [we said, as we reviewed the analysis] "this fact makes no sense." And [so, later] we were teaching this [research finding] to students because this is something they'll go do [on the job]. And I had a student come up after class and say, "Makes complete sense to me." "It makes no sense," [I argued back]. He says: "No, think about it. The small businesses that do this, when they went into business to get it started, they liquidated the college fund, they sold off the second car, they took a second mortgage. They don't have any personal assets, so they say, 'You can have all my personal assets.'

But there aren't any assets there." It's a kind of thing, [I realized,] that if you talk to the people that generate the data [like this student as a practitioner,] sometimes you'll understand it much better. [But] not always. Sometimes the perception of what's going on is very inconsistent with the data. But even those cases—it's kind of interesting because here's what they say they're doing when you talk to them . . . Here's what . . . really they're doing when you look at the data. Now, why is it that they think they're doing something that is not what they're doing? And again, that raises a potentially interesting question . . .

If you asked me ten years ago when I started, "How much are the students gonna help you on your research?" "Zero—I'm here to teach them finance." But these people—you teach them how financial markets work. In return, they come back and tell you how they really work, consistent with theory or not consistent with theory.

Les Thompson was stumped with regard to the question of why banks might insist on offering high-interest loans to some seemingly low-risk borrowers. Their doing that, Thompson said, defied prevailing financial logic, namely that a lender should assign high interest to high-risk loans; she should lower the interest rate as risk lessens. A student whose day-to-day work involves handling such loans explains to Thompson the pragmatics of the "illogic" at hand: upping the collateral on a loan does little to lower the interest rate if the value of the collateral is negligible. In this scenario Thompson, a highly regarded and accomplished scholar, gains substantially for his research from his student, who also happens to be a practitioner. That student drew Thompson's attention to a salient discrepancy between the assumptional logic of the field and the pragmatics of professional practice. He helped Thompson to resituate his intellectual problem from a purely academic setting to one of "live practice." In doing so, he broadened Thompson's view.

Moving Substantive Ideas into One's Personal Life and One's Personal Questions into Scholarship
The substantive insights that scholars gain from their scholarly learning may respond to questions in their personal lives. Scholars' personal

questions may also ignite some of their scholarly pursuits. According to this view scholars conceptualize their subjects of study and their lives in relation to one another. One may be regarded as constituting a context for understanding something in the other: a subject of study may then mirror some feature of the life of its creator or analyst, and her life may, alternatively, mirror features of the subject. I have already represented this kind of self-reflexive dialogue between a scholar's personal life and her professional work in the case of Nina Altman, the scholar of literary studies at Libra State University discussed in chapter 1: Altman studies the incompleteness of translation, drawing insights for her research in part from her life as an immigrant to the United States—but also for her life from her research. In this double view a scholar's life contextualizes her research while her research contextualizes features of her life.

Like Altman, William Alana, a professor of education recently tenured at Hope State University, offers a compelling narrative of what the study of teacher-student relationships has meant to him—what such relationships have brought into his own life as a teacher and how his learning in life, among significant relationships (with a parent and grandparent), has informed his pedagogy as well as his studies of pedagogy. Throughout both our interviews Alana offered vivid stories of family relationships that taught him what it means and feels like to learn, engage with a text, and subsequently, help another person learn something hard yet rich with meaning and emotion. Alana knows that how and what he learned about teaching and learning through his family relationships shape the educational relationships he creates today with the students in his classes. That early learning also shapes his research in education. With the recent loss of a parent who was central to his own experiences of learning in childhood, Alana finds himself looking ever more intently to his teaching relationships with students, a constant reminder of what he gained from his parent:

> I find in my teaching this fall, I'm with students in a way I don't feel like I've been before . . . Just existentially. I feel older. Losing a parent really makes you feel that way . . . But that's also made me feel like . . . I can give something in a way I've not quite felt before. And I'm not sure if I have words for that, but I feel like

I've been a guide . . . in both [my] classes in a way I've not felt before as a teacher. There just seems to be a bit more depth to it, or the stakes seem a little higher. The importance is stronger . . . One thing I never have done as much as this fall, for example, is . . . We have these three-hour classes . . . once a week . . . intense . . . and when students [get] kind of upset or confused about an idea, or troubled by an author . . . or by an idea, I tend to go right to them at the break or after class. I don't wait for them to come to me . . . But more than I remember doing [before], I go right to them. It's interesting. So . . . there is some difference . . . I feel [in] the teaching . . . I feel like these ideas matter more in a way.

William Alana's personal life—and especially his own teaching and learning relationships with a parent and grandparent—provides a backdrop for what he strives to do now professionally in his classroom teaching and what he strives to understand intellectually about what teaching can mean. In mirror image what he does in his teaching and in his research on teaching illuminates a central point of meaning in his personal life.

These various views of knowledge recontextualization suggest that scholars can learn, in-depth, even in subjects they know well already, by moving core ideas, topics, or questions into different but intellectually promising knowledge environments—for example, into fields of study other than their own but ripe with fresh insights or, alternatively, into new social and cultural sites, settings of practice, and reflectively their personal lives. Moving familiar knowledge into a new context may highlight features of the subject that were previously unseen. As the preceding examples indicate, this form of learning has strong potential to grow in the work of scholars in applied and professional fields (e.g., as they move academic thought into professional endeavors or engage in public service that is academically grounded), though it may also be visible in the work of scholars of the humanities (e.g., as they draw from personal experience for intellectual insight). I did, indeed, find numerous examples of such learning among scholars working in applied/professional fields and in the humanities; I also found them among scholars working in universities with strong missions of public service.

To represent one's subject matter knowledge—that is, to verbalize or otherwise project one's knowledge of a subject of study for others' best-possible understanding—also is an act of scholarly learning. This is especially so when the person representing the knowledge (e.g., a teacher) gains insight into it *as* she shapes images of it for others' (e.g., students') benefit. Teaching a subject matter idea, writing a research report, and publicly sharing research findings are all acts of representation. They involve a person (here a professor) projecting her mindwork into a public space—or into a space where at least one other person strives to grasp the ideas the professor projects into it. To project, in this case, means to make public, to articulate, to designate, to express, ideally in ways that grant a listener access to the subject projected. Within this act of projection the professor can learn: as she sees her ideas outside herself; as others respond to the ideas, possibly reconfiguring them as they project them back to her; and not least, as she herself reshapes those ideas in novel ways for others' understanding. Cast this way, acts of subject matter representation are themselves environments, or contexts, for professors' creation (or re-creation) of subject matter. I will say a great deal more about this topic in the next chapter. For now two points are worth making about what professors learn through acts of knowledge representation.

First, as she engages in acts of knowledge representation, a scholar may, quite simply, come to appreciate the representational qualities of the subject matter knowledge that she and others produce. In representing an idea, the scholar may cast it in different ways. In doing so, repeatedly, she realizes that she *can* cast it in different ways: that knowledge can bend, though within limits of what defines it as knowledge of a certain kind. "I have found different ways of conveying concepts," said Carmen Elias-Jones, the professor of music at Signal University. We may infer that in finding those "different ways" to "convey concepts," Elias-Jones comes to think of those concepts as conveyable—as representable to others. The same may be true of a professor in the sciences, also at Signal University, who described her recent efforts to "convey all this [subject matter] information with absolutely, essentially . . . no equations . . . relying a lot [instead] on graphics . . . don't replace equations with text . . . replace equations with pictures, because then students can understand it." This scientist's active involvement in acts of alternative representation may drive home to her the depth to which such representation is possible. A philosopher at Libra State University similarly described the power of example in knowledge representation. "My experience has been that . . . a really good example to illustrate what you're talking about is usually worth . . . half an hour spent trying to explain a theory," the philosopher said. "So I now spend a lot more time than I ever did . . . constructing really good examples of things to bring into class to illustrate." This scholar has also learned that he can represent his knowledge not merely by way of explanation (defined as one way to project knowledge) but also by way of example (another such way). In responding to their interlocutors' needs for alternative representations, professors make use of the representational qualities of their knowledge. In doing so, they position themselves to appreciate that quality of their subject matter knowledge—and of their abilities to use it to advance their own learning, even as they advance the learning of others.

Second, and relatedly, a scholar may come to realize that due to its representational qualities, subject matter knowledge may be shared in different ways with different audiences, depending on what audience members are primed to learn. Ron Vendelin, a newly tenured professor in Hope State University's school of business, says that this insight has led him to construct different knowledge representations for different students to whom he has taught the same idea. He describes how he casts the concept of research sampling, first to undergraduates and then to graduate students as audiences for his teaching:

> One of the things that I have learned is they [students] need to relate the principles [I teach them] to their everyday lives . . . MBA students will be okay if you relate [what you are teaching] to the[ir] work lives because many of them are working. But undergraduate students—some of them are working, but they may like [to see] more [of a] relationship with life situations. For example, [when] I talk about sampling . . . if you're a production manager [as many of his MBA students are], I can talk about sampling, in . . . production: "You are making one million bridges, you take . . . *y* bridges and see what it is." But from undergraduates' [perspectives, you talk about sampling as follows:] "You are go-

ing for a job interview. You are there . . . one day, depending on what the company is. But the company . . . based on the one day, they are experiencing you for one day and they are assuming how you will do for the rest of your working career. So that is sampling" . . . I realize that it is important for them to understand it from a life experience perspective.

Vendelin explains that he represents research sampling to his master's students in the terms of the work that, as he has discerned, most of them do as production managers in corporate America. In teaching the same concept to undergraduates, Vendelin relies on different imagery. He knows that at the point that business undergraduates get to his class, they are preparing for job interviews. To teach research sampling, this professor draws on this fact of their lives: he represents a job interview as a sample that corporate officers construct to assess a candidate's fit with a job they seek to fill.

To share his own well-developed knowledge of sampling, this professor reconstructs that knowledge in at least two different ways to present it to student audiences primed to learn it in different ways. Doing so assumes that the professor knows his subject, sampling, "inside out" and that he can translate it, with minimal loss, into the terms of his students' distinct interests, which he also must understand quite well. What has the professor gained? I conjecture that, in addition to adding to his repertoire two new images of a concept that is core to students' understandings (sampling), he hones the subject matter knowledge that diverse images of that concept provide. He also hones his skill at producing such images, an act that is as substantive as it is communicative. As such, he conceptualizes his subject matter further in the context of an act of its representation.

In addition to learning their subjects of study by extending, re-forming, or recontextualizing them, professors may thus learn them by creating and exploring multiple images (representations) of them. They learn a great deal about expert knowledge as they create and reflect on those diverse images. This requires an awareness on the part of the scholars that this is possible: they have to know, first, that knowledge can bend and also that they themselves can bend or otherwise shape it, clearly within the limits of its meanings. And second, they have to know who their learners are as well as how to use that "knowledge of the people" to shape the subject matter knowledge they will offer to them (by way of representation), in ways that those people can grasp. Although the targeted learners stand to gain from such effort, if done well, so may the scholars themselves—because pursuing an alternative knowledge representation may involve an alternative conceptualization. Participating professors portrayed this kind of representational learning as occurring heavily within their teaching and also in their research. This form of scholarly learning was in no way limited by field of study, level (graduate or undergraduate), or university, though it was especially prominent in programs and departments in which professors valued their pedagogical roles.

WHAT SCHOLARLY LEARNING ENTAILS, FROM THE STANDPOINT OF PROFESSORS' EXPERIENCES

Scholarly learning, including the passionate thought it encourages, can materialize in different ways for professors. As such, they may experience their scholarly learning, and themselves as its learners, in different ways: they may view themselves as extending their subject matter knowledge, re-forming it, recontextualizing it, and representing it. Such experiences appear in a variety of academic work locations: in professors' research, in their teaching, and in their public service, among others that I will discuss in the next chapter. Yet as most academics will attest, professors do not live by their scholarly learning alone. They live in good part by creating, maintaining, and developing the sites of work that sustain it, that give it places to be. That other work, often institutional and instrumental in nature, also needs to be learned—and as I will show later, it also needs to be intertwined with scholarly learning in supportive ways

What Else Do Professors Learn?

As noted in chapter 1, once they cross the tenure line, university professors take on new senior-level work while continuing in established programs of scholarly learning or revising them. Some of that new work—and the learning that it requires—is unrelated to their scholarly learning; it requires knowledge fully unrelated to professors' favored substantive learning. I refer to such activity as "instrumental." Professors may view their instrumental work and learning as important nonetheless and gladly take it on, for example, out of a sense of obligation or a desire to "give back." Some professors try to minimize their involvement in instrumental efforts, or to avoid them altogether, preferring to attend to their own scholarly learning agendas.[3] Drawing on the study data, and on my own experiences as a tenured professor in two major research universities, I submit that it is impossible, or at least unwise, to avoid instrumental work and learning, given the academic community's valuing of intellectual autonomy. To maintain that autonomy, professors must exercise it, instrumentally, in those parts of the academic enterprise that touch their scholarly work and learning.

But instrumental learning need not always be problematic. At times an opportunity for instrumental learning coincides helpfully with a professor's scholarly learning. Consider a professor of finance whose current research examines budgeting in major research universities and who is appointed to a faculty committee charged with rethinking the structure of budgeting in that professor's own university. Or consider a professor of chemistry who joins a college committee to evaluate the utilization of space on the university's sciences campus. The business professor gains an additional "work space" for thinking through her favored topic, budgeting in research universities. The chemist gains the opportunity to equalize the distribution of space relative to colleagues' true needs.

At times, however, scholarly and instrumental learning do clash, as for example they would for a newly tenured historian who struggles to complete his decade-long analysis of voting patterns in major American urban centers while serving as associate department chair, an intense service role in his university. For some professors instrumental work distracts; sometimes it annoys. Managed unwisely, it can derail a professor's scholarly learning. This is something that some professors may anticipate and fear, as did Sandra Covington, the professor of public health at People's State University, who worried about the growing distance between the work she loved and the work she felt compelled to do. As her professional obligations increased, drawing her further and further from the work she cared about, she worried about "burning out." To avoid such anticipatory anxiety and "to get on with scholarly learning"—but without shirking instrumental responsibility—professors must orchestrate their jobs and careers with care. They must try to blend and balance the scholarly and instrumental features of their work and their learning. In chapters 4 and 5 I take up the question of how professors participating in the *Four Universities Project* approached this task. For now I address a more basic question: if learning increases post-tenure, what is the full range of what professors strive to learn? And especially, what besides the scholarly are they learning?

Table 3.2 summarizes the range of what professors participating in the *Four Universities Project*, all of whom were three to five years post-tenure at the time of the final interview, indicated they were learning (col. 1), definitions and examples of what that learning constituted, (col. 2), and the prevalence of each kind of learning in the study sample (col. 3).[4] Row 1 shows that virtually all participating professors (90% or more) portrayed themselves as being engaged in scholarly learning. Professors indicated, however, that they were learning other things as well, most of which had little positive bearing on their scholarly learning at the time of the interviews. Rows 2 through 7 highlight participating professors' more instrumental learning.

Table 3.2 shows that more than half of the participating professors were involved in learning subject matters that they characterized as being unrelated or distracting to their core scholarly learning. Some saw this additional subject matter learning as competing for the scarce time and energy they would have preferred to devote to learning the subjects to which they were deeply committed. People's State University professor Sandra Covington talks about the challenges of pursuing her favored research on the epidemiology of a benign staph infection in the face of a strong university- and field-based pull on her to pursue research on newer antibiotic-resistant bacterial strains. She sought to carry out research on both these fronts but felt pressured toward the more salient and better-funded antibiotic resistance effort. As she saw her "core" interests thin over years of neglect, while working continuously to meet her rapidly mounting instrumental responsibilities, she worried about "burning out."

Table 3.2 also makes the point that subject matter learning—reflective of one's committed subjects or not—does not come into being all on its own. It arrives at professors' doors by way of the practices in which professors engage at work day by day: through research and other scholarly study (reading, conversing, and listening), teaching and preparing to teach, outreach and consulting, and service and administration. Thus,

TABLE 3.2 What Recently Tenured Professors Learned ($n = 39$)

What Professors Learned[a]	Definitions and Examples	Prevalence in Sample[b]
1. Subject matters related to scholarly learning	Construct subject matter knowledge for scholarly learning (via extension, reformation, recontextualization, representation).	* * * * *
2. Subject matters unrelated/distracting to scholarly learning	Construct subject matter knowledge unrelated to scholarly learning.	* * *
3. Professorial practices: research/creative endeavor, teaching, mentoring, outreach, administration, service	Conduct research, inquiry, artistic craft. Teach, mentor. Engage in faculty service (to institution, field, community).	* * * * *
4. Key academic contexts (academe, discipline/field, campus)—how to identify, use, manage resources and constraints	Understand/navigate academe, field, campus. Manage, orchestrate professorial work. Work with people.	* * * *
5. Bounded qualities of academic communities and practices, potential for their reform	(Re)create workplace and worklife. (Re)create academic work and community, tolerate dissipating community and changes in familiar patterns of work. Know when to push against established boundaries, and not. Understand one's power and options; understand limitations. Understand one's own (personal) limitations.	* * * *
6. One's own identity as person, scholar, professor	Balance personal and professional concerns/values. Appreciate/value oneself (strengths, weaknesses). Navigate/reconstruct career. Create one's social identity.	* * * *
7. Containment and inaction	Refrain from immediate response; learn to withhold.	* *
8. Disengagement from scholarly learning, research, and/or teaching	Withdraw from professional activity or scholarly commitment.	*

[a] (1) Categories are not mutually exclusive. (2) Rows 1 and 3 present data collected in study years 1 and 3 of the *Four Universities Project*; other rows present year 3 data only. (3) Data reflect professors' responses to questions about learning and relevant comments made while responding to other questions.

[b] Proportion of year-3 study participants indicating the particular learning:

at least 90% * * * * *
at least 75% * * * *
at least 50% * * *
at least 25% * *
15% or less *

professors' subject matter learning becomes recognizable within the *academic work practices* of a recognized social role: that of the university professor. From within these professional practices of teaching, research, service, and outreach, professors may indeed learn diverse forms of subject matter—or they may gain other knowledge or skills that, though valuable to the academic enterprise and to their own jobs and careers, have little substantive bearing on their scholarly interests (e.g., managing large-scale grading, reading and monitoring budgets, understanding curriculum approval processes). Although learning of this sort matters to professors' careers, and although some professors do enjoy it, it can become substantively problematic if it displaces professors' scholarly learning for extended periods of time, distancing them from sources of their intellectual excitement. Row 3 indicates that virtually all participating professors were learning the key practices of the professoriate. Some experienced this learning of practice as supportive of their scholarly learning, although others did not. A case in point is a professor of philosophy at Libra State University who, post-tenure, took on extensive undergraduate teaching, doctoral dissertation mentoring, administration, and service responsibilities, none of which aligned well with his core interests: the study of gain in decision theory and of causal inference in statistics. To carry out his increasing instrumental responsibilities, he had to learn the practices and knowledge that the new responsibilities entailed as he carried them out. The load of new work and its simultaneous learning distanced him from his desired learning for an extended period of time. He struggled for time to devote to his new work.

Table 3.2 shows that a substantial majority of participating professors (at least 75%) also were learning about the varied environments in which they carried out such practices, among them: the *academic,* including how colleagues work together, relate to administration, and manage their research, teaching, and service; the *disciplinary,* including the standards and expectations, cultures, norms, and values of a particular field; and the *institutional,* including the cultures, priorities, and expectations of professors' employing university and more localized work spaces (e.g., the academic program, department, or network of scholars). Participating professors were also learning how to use these environments' unique resources (who to call on for advice about how to manage large-class teaching, how best to access information about research funders) as well as how to manage environmental constraints (how to craft careers in the absence of clear-cut "rules of engagement and professional advancement," how to train students in research methods not represented in a curriculum). And because so many of their tasks were social and interactional, professors also learned "how to work with people." In light of all they were taking in, professors also learned how to juggle and balance their tasks. Such learning is evident in Sandra Covington's experiences as, post-tenure, she gained insight on the university's priorities for its faculty: although she believed that she would continue to pursue her favored area of study after earning tenure, perhaps among other topics of growing importance, Covington learned that People's State University had its own agenda for her own and her colleagues' research, and with which she would have to contend, given that her own interests did not line up neatly with those of the university.

Professors learned, too, how far they could stretch their subjects of study, work practices, and work environments without distorting their integrity. They learned what was "in and out of bounds" among the members of the communities to which they belonged, how far they could go in reforming those communities, and when they had overstepped community norms. Table 3.2 shows that most professors in the study claimed to learn the boundedness of their professional practices and of participation in the communities within which they enacted their professorial work. This also entailed learning the limits of reform in community life, including the boundaries that, to preserve a community's identity, they should not cross. Sandra Covington at People's State came to understand that she could not bypass her campus's priorities, which emphasized highly salient research, in order to devote more time to her favored scholarly learning.

While they were learning in and about their professions, the participating professors were also learning about themselves: realizing strengths they did not know they had, and also weaknesses that they had previously not had to acknowledge. In taking on new university-based service responsibilities, for example, some professors were surprised to realize how effectively they could organize, lead, encourage, motivate, and support others. Conversely, other professors brought their self-conceptions down to size upon realizing that some of their colleagues could outdo their best efforts. A number explored ways to balance their personal and professional lives. In brief they were learning self-identity: personal, professional, and intellectual. Table 3.2 shows that most participating professors deepened their efforts to explore or define their identities in these ways. A social scientist at Hope State University exemplifies such learning a year into the program coordination duties that he assumed post-tenure. Although initially fearful of the role and of what he could do with it ("I hate roles like this . . . don't think I'm good at them"), a year into it he felt otherwise. "It has been good for me," he said, "[to] confront my fears and my limitations . . . and learn more about myself."

Through the early post-tenure career some professors may also rethink their views of effective professional action, especially its pacing. Rather than always striving to be immediately responsive, direct, and outcome driven (e.g., taking clear and positive steps to pursue a grant on the horizon or solve the latest administrative problem), they saw themselves as benefitting occasionally from delayed action or inaction. They may learn the value of timing in action and response. Table 3.2 shows that at least a quarter of the study participants referred to such learning. A bold example is a scientist at People's State University who learned to invoke a containment strategy in his research. Due to growing responsibilities in teaching and service, he sharply limited his research involvement through the school year but returned to it fully each summer.

Unfortunately, at times professors go still further: they learn disengagement. Some disengage from learning or from one or another practice in which they were previously involved. Table 3.2 shows that this was the case for a small number of professors participating in this study. One struggled to distance herself from a university whose "sexism," as she called it, devalued her presence. Another who had previously been very active in faculty governance withdrew from service as she awoke to the limitations on faculty power in the university. A third began to disinvest in teaching because she saw very little opportunity to teach courses that mattered to her. Two more withdrew from research due to felt needs to address family, service, and teaching obligations that they took very seriously. Yet these professors, notably all women, did not take the decision to disinvest lightly. They described, in detail, the emotional strain that had led up to and accompanied their decisions to let go of an activity they valued. And in fact, though retracting portions of their committed professional efforts, four of these five women found ways to reinvest their energies elsewhere: for example, from withdrawing involvement in sexist university dynamics to writing about the positions of women in such situations; from the inabilities of one to exercise governance powers effectively, and the inabilities of another to teach in favored areas, to the reconstruction, by both scholars, of research agendas that positioned them powerfully in their respective universities; from a scholar's overinvestment in financially productive research, lucrative to the university but of declining interest to the scholar, to her recommitment to teaching and academic administration as alternative routes for expressing her subject matter interests. The fifth professor, among the youngest in the sample, and feeling torn between home and work, withdrew consciously from all university activities other than the basic requirements of her job.

In chapter 1 I suggested that to appreciate professors' learning requires understanding what they learn. What, then, *do* they learn? Professors participating in the *Four Universities Project* portrayed themselves as learning the subject matters to which they were deeply committed, even as some also learned subjects of lesser personal interest. They also were learning their key professional practices. The majority of participating professors also were learning "the lay of the land" of their work environments, including normative boundaries, as well as their own personal and professional identities. Smaller numbers were learning practices of reflective response, including, at times, studied inaction. A fraction of the study professors were learning to disengage from their scholarly learning or from one or more practices to which they had committed portions of their careers and lives.

University professors in the early post-tenure career—and up to five years post-tenure—can learn a great deal both in their committed subjects of study and beyond. Interestingly, only a few of those I studied indicated the kind of disengagement from learning or practice that the prevailing post-tenure myth would predict: none of these professors, including the few who openly talked about disengagement, showed any signs at all of slides into "taking it easy" once they had earned tenure. In fact, the five who reported disengagement in one portion of their work lives or another did so with deep regret and under emotional stress, in fact, out of hopelessness rather than selfishness, and after expending great effort "to make things right," rather than simply avoiding hard work (see table 3.2, row 8). Further, four of these five found productive and thoughtful ways to reinvest the energies that they had initially withdrawn from diverse forms of academic involvement.

From Desire to Duty, from Learning to Labor

It is noteworthy that the vast majority of professors participating in the *Four Universities Project* remained engaged in scholarly learning through the final interview, for some up to five years post-tenure. Further, they were all learning other forms of work critical to their jobs or careers (see table 3.2). I conclude that the post-tenure myth of professorial decline simply does not hold up in this sample of early midcareer professors drawn from diverse fields and working in four major research universities across the United States: tenure in no way extinguished these professors' desires to engage in scholarly learning, the central resource they bring to American higher education. They certainly did not "hang it up" after acquiring tenure. They did not distance themselves from their committed subjects of study (although, as one would expect, those subjects sometimes changed through their learning). And as their other learning—instrumental and largely institutional—shows, they did not distance themselves from their professional responsibilities either.

Professors participating in the *Four Universities Project* positioned themselves to pursue multiple forms of scholarly learning: as a group, they sought to extend their subject matters, re-form them, recontextualize them for comparative views, and represent them in order to leverage insight. Only five (less than 15%) showed signs of withdrawing from their intellectual or professional commitments; further, four of these five ultimately reinvested their energy in other parts of the academic enterprise. Looking outward up to five years post-tenure, the post-tenure myth of professorial decline is flatly wrong as a representation of what happens to university professors, as learners and professionals, after acquiring tenure. They clearly strive to learn, many of them working hard to hold onto their scholarly learning and also to learn other new responsibilities that come their way at this career stage.

Yet some significant issues remain unexplored. Some of the examples I have presented so far suggest that professors' scholarly learning goes on in academic work other than research. Teaching, in particular, appears as a prime location for professors' scholarly learning; interestingly, so does service. Given this insight, and given the broad range of possible learning that appears to go on through the early post-tenure career, it is worth asking several other questions. First, where else, besides in research, may newly tenured university professors engage their scholarly learning? That is, in what contexts, work-wise, are they learning their favored subjects of study after tenure? Second, how can teaching and service, both viewed traditionally as antitheses to professors' scholarly learning, become sites for such learning? What would that look like, and how might this imagery—of learning in teaching and learning in service—be explained? Third, given the range of learning in which newly tenured university professors engage, one can view them as being pulled in different directions: between work they feel they must learn and do in the name of duty and work that grows from their authentic interests and desires. But what might it take, on the part of a newly tenured professor, to manage all this learning and doing without being pulled apart? In other words, how might a professor manage her workload and learning load while remaining responsible, equally and synergistically, to herself and to communities and persons beyond herself? How can that professor position herself to carry it all out? Fourth, what can a tenure-granting university do to facilitate its recently tenured professors' learning along its multiple dimensions, though with attention to its scholarly components? What, in particular, can university leaders, as people who set the tone and shape the contexts of professors' work, do to facilitate that learning?

CHAPTER FOUR

Location

Where Professors Pursue Their Scholarly Learning

I argued in chapter 3 that the post-tenure myth is flawed: it is not true that with tenure in hand, university professors withdraw from their scholarly learning. Nor is it true that their teaching and institutional service decline. Data provided through the *Four Universities Project* indicate that through the early post-tenure career, professors can—and that those in the study do—continue to learn those subjects that inspire their deepest intellectual passions and curiosities. But this is not the only learning in which they engage. The study shows that through the early post-tenure career professors learn to teach, advise, mentor, be a colleague, carry out service, and administer programs and activities, among other things. Of course, they do more than just learn this work. They do it. Clearly, being a tenured professor entails more than learning, and it entails more than scholarship. Given the load of new effort that newly tenured professors assume, where and when do they find the space and time to engage in scholarly learning? This chapter identifies the locations and, in some cases, the moments of scholarly learning: *the contexts of work and life* within which professors find time to construct their core subject matter knowledge.

But why does context matter? I argue that context matters because some of its features have the power to shape or at least influence the subject matter content of professors' scholarly learning: something about where and when a person learns (location and time as context), including who a person learns with and from (interaction as a certain kind of context), get into the *what* of her scholarly learning (subject matter). Drawing on research on learning in educational settings, I view subject matter as absorbing selected features of the setting in which it exists (parts of that setting become part of what a learner learns) and also as impressing itself on selected features of that setting. Thus, to understand scholarly learning, one must understand the larger settings—of professors' work and lives within which that scholarly learning occurs.[1]

I turn now to a discussion of the contexts that situate, and thereby help to constitute, professors' scholarly learning. I attend first to the obvious contexts: the disciplines and fields within which professors were trained as graduate students and within which they continue to create themselves as scholars. I then turn to the less obvious and sometimes taken-for-granted contexts of professors' subject matter learning: their day-to-day campus work and, beyond that, their lives more broadly.

Scholarly Learning in Disciplines and Fields and across Them

Where professors engage their scholarly learning can bear on what they learn; the context and content of their scholarly learning intermix. The academic concept of "discipline" reflects this intermixing of the content of professors' scholarly learning (disciplinary knowledge) and the context within which it occurs (disciplinary community). The same may be said of a disciplinary specialism or a multidisciplinary field, both of which can indicate a community of knowledge practitioners and the substance of its members' shared practices.[2]

SCHOLARLY LEARNING IN ONE'S HOME FIELD

In order to pursue their scholarly learning, professors participating in the *Four Universities Project* positioned themselves to engage in distinctive activities of mind: most said they were extending, re-forming, recontextualizing, or representing their subject matter knowledge. They pursued their scholarly learning in different ways through the early post-tenure years. I found this pattern among professors who remained squarely in their own disciplines and fields, though moving around within them.

At Horizon University a professor of organizational studies, describing her exploration of business organizational strategy as broadening out after tenure, serves as a primary example of within-field scholarly learning. Originally a specialist in United States–based corporate strategy, post-tenure she joined with other scholars from throughout her field who were exploring it in an international perspective. Although remaining in her field (organizational studies), this scholar broadened the purview of her learning within it and thereby her colleagueship as well. "Most of my pre-tenure and even immediate post-tenure research tended to . . . focus on U.S. firms," she explained, "but over the last couple of years, I'm getting more interested in . . . international strategy." Asked why she had broadened her within-field view, she said: "You want to rejuvenate yourself, you want to find more—interesting [work to do]—not that the work I was doing wasn't interesting. But it was kind of narrow. So [I've done this] to . . . rejuvenate myself and identify topics which I can see myself working on several more years." Although remaining committed to the agenda on corporate strategy for which she was tenured, this scholar took her scholarly learning, post-tenure, to other corners of her field, where she found ways to extend it. Her interests did not shift as much as did the intellectual and community resources she brought to bear on them as she moved about her field.

Professors may enlarge their within-field subject matter knowledge through their research, as did the scholar of organizational studies at Horizon. Yet they may do so also through teaching, as did a biologist at Hope State University. "Certainly, anything I teach at the graduate level contributes to my career," the biologist said, "because even if I know . . . quite a bit about a field, we're reading things that I haven't read." The biologist indicated no need to look beyond her own field for new and relevant material that would advance her scholarly agenda. A historian at Libra State University, heavily involved in undergraduate teaching, echoed this view: "There are lots of possible detail[ed] . . . things that I didn't know until I needed to teach them." And she added: "There are also times when students have asked things that I didn't know the answer to, so I went and found out. And sometimes it's . . . individual little bits of information . . . [or it's] 'Oh, wow! That makes sense!' . . . it helps me understand things that I thought I already understood but didn't." The historian, like the biologist, expands her field-based knowledge in the context of her teaching.

Although much is made of out-of-field learning, some scholars relish opportunities to look deeply within their own fields, whether through research, teaching, or thoughtful scholarly conversation. Having recently participated in a prestigious field-based seminar, a social scientist at Signal University described what it was like for him to be "sitting down for a week . . . in real isolation . . . talking with people who worked [in my field] and had different perceptions [of topic of interest to the field]. It was a huge education for me," he exclaimed. "What it means is all of a sudden over the last two years, I've been exposed to a much broader range of [field-based] research than I would have been before. It's like getting a tutorial in [my field]," he added. "I'm still trying to sort out what that means, but I think it makes me a better scholar . . . for being able to see the range of what's out there." Yet not all the participating professors' experiences were so positive. Although most spoke excitedly in interviews about what they gained from their post-tenure explorations of their fields, at least one, a humanist at Hope State University, said she was "put off" by field-based ideas she had recently encountered and that, in her words, resembled "animal[s] . . . coming off a different planet other than the one I would like to live on."

Whether enjoying the knowledge they encountered or not, professors who pursued their scholarly learning within their own "home fields" claimed to improve in their understandings of their fields' offerings. To stay in their home fields did not mean that these professors stopped learning. Working within those fields, professors unearthed new knowledge, and often they established relationships with new colleagues whose thoughts were unfamiliar to them. Although I did not follow participating professors beyond their early post-tenure years, I surmise that their expanded views availed them of knowledge—and of community—that in future years they could call on as needed for insight.

SCHOLARLY LEARNING OUTSIDE ONE'S FIELD

Some professors position themselves to learn outside their disciplinary or field-based communities of practice. This need not mean leaving one's home field "for good." Usually, professors who cross into disciplines and fields that are new to them pursue the new knowledge while remaining anchored in their own. Thus, their "trips out" serve as opportunities to "recontextualize" their learning agendas—to view their continuing topics of study in different ways and in different settings—thereby enlarging their understanding of them (see chap. 3 on recontextualization as a form of scholarly learning). Such trips out of one's field of study are usually temporary, intentional, and focused. By immersing themselves in the knowledge of other fields, professors expect to learn something relevant to their favored topics of study and then return their learning to their own field. Typically, these professors have no interest in separating themselves for good from their home fields or their favored subjects of study. Instead, they may take temporary leave to learn what they need, then bring it home for their own and their field's learning. Although ventures such as these, focused specifically on the learning of meaningful subjects of study, are often referred to as "interdisciplinary" or "multidisciplinary," for the sake of precision I refer to them here as "cross-disciplinary" or "cross-field."[3]

Some professors do, indeed, move themselves and their work into new fields for the long run—to new communities whose members create and teach subjects differing from those which the professor learned in the past. Some of them make such moves when they take new professorial jobs that are not well matched to their substantive interests. These scholars carry an unusual learning load. As one would expect, they have to learn the routines and work cultures of their new jobs. Yet they also have to resituate their favored topics of study in knowledge environments (a new field or discipline) whose members may not, at least initially, appreciate those topics. Scholars wishing to hold on to their scholarly learning may need to learn to express and work with the subjects they care for deeply in new ways; others may even go so far as to change their subjects.

Both of these approaches to learning outside one's own field of study—the temporary and the long term—require still other kinds of learning: a scholar who moves her topic outside her own field must have some sense of that topic's potential to re-form in response to the unique offerings and constraints of the new setting. That scholar also must understand the depth and range of her commitment to that topic of study and also to her original field of study.

Temporary and Focused Leaves

A professor who strives to identify new or different ways to conceptualize her topic of study may seek out learning opportunities in fields beyond her own. Although the topic that this professor pursues may be rooted in her field, she strives to identify knowledge in other fields to deepen understanding of it. She engages then in cross-disciplinary or cross-field endeavor.

The *Four Universities* study included a number of professors who crossed over briefly to new disciplines and fields to seek out knowledge in support of their long-term interests in topics that were already well situated in their own fields. Some of these professors explored new fields independently, and others collaborated with out-of-field colleagues. Richard Marin, the theoretical physicist at Hope State University introduced in chapter 1, has done both. In his third post-tenure year (the time of the year 1 interview) Marin said that the independent reading that informs his favored area of study, in physics, "has always been broad—in biology, in religion, in history, in literature, in criticism." By his fifth post-tenure year (the year 3 interview) Marin had deepened his cross-disciplinary efforts through joint work with a philosopher, also on the Hope State campus: "We . . . have developed a point of view which is . . . half-physics and half-philosophy," Marin said. "It's fed back into how I think about my mathematical physics." Although working out of field, Marin has clearly remained a physicist; as a researcher, he has continued to contribute intellectually to the field of physics. He enhances those contributions through short-term, focused visits to philosophy and other fields, through independent reading, and also through collaboration.

Other scholars spoke in related ways: a gerontologist at Horizon University who "retooled" her learning within the field of management, given its potential to illuminate pressing problems within her own; a mathematician at Libra State University who purposefully explored physics for concepts that might intersect with newly emerging ideas in mathematics; a social scientist at Signal University whose coteaching with a scholar in a different social sciences field yielded "huge learning" for him and, by extension, for his field. Professors wishing to boost their scholarly learning may step out of their fields in temporary but focused ways to gain ideas and skills that they then bring home to their own.

Longer-Term Leaves

Professors sometimes move into new fields—new scholarly communities—in more long-term and open-ended ways, without a clear promise of returning to the fields in which they trained and in which many had planned to spend their careers. Most do this purposefully but not willingly, easily, or with assurance of success.

A SUCCESSFUL MOVE. Marissa Velez, a newly tenured psychologist deeply committed to the study of women's transitions into and through midlife, described her decision, post-Ph.D., to accept a beginning assistant professorship on the tenure track at Hope State University. She had very much wanted a tenure-track position in a department of psychology. But to make it possible for her and her partner to live in the same city, Velez broadened her job search to include psychology-based positions in schools of business, virtually all at major research universities. She took a tenure-track job in Hope State University's School of Business, where she taught master's and doctoral students in a human resources management program. Through her years on the tenure track at Hope State, Velez was able to bring her expertise in psychology to her teaching and other work, though largely restricting it to business applications.

In her year 1 interview Velez said that her life outside work had developed comfortably and well—she and her partner were happily settled in a city they liked—but her job at Hope State University posed real challenges: pre-tenure, Velez had struggled to develop her understanding of human resources management as a field to which she could bring her well-honed expertise in human development and within which also she could continue her work on midlife women's development. To do this, Velez had to merge her well-developed psychological interests and expertise with new knowledge about human resources management; she had to join, or at least learn how to spend time productively in, national and international communities of scholars interested in the study and teaching of human resources management. At Hope State she had to establish a colleague base, learn the culture of a business school, develop her courses, learn how to advise, and think through how to craft her work in public outreach and institutional service. Velez worked diligently at joining her new business school; she also labored assiduously to learn the field of human resources management, also new to her. But Velez also sought to retain her disciplinary affiliation in psychology and to further her research on women's psychological development through midlife. How would she do this? This question—of how to carry out good and meaningful work simultaneously in her field of study and field of employment—framed the full length of Velez's career from initial entry through early post-tenure.

While working toward tenure and even beyond, for example, Velez tried to introduce her areas of psychological expertise—on human development broadly and on women's development especially—into her graduate students' programs of study, albeit in the context of their interests in human resources management. But she had a hard time "getting at" those students in the first place. Departmental dynamics around "who taught what" barred her from courses and advising assignments through which she might have connected, on her own intellectual turf, with graduate students whose scholarly interests resonated with her own. Although gaining tenure at Hope State University, Velez was at a low point when I first met her. As time passed, Velez's sense of being blocked from the learning she loved—in human development, in women's development at midlife—shifted into feelings of distance from that learning. That feeling of distance, real and emotional, bothered her. Echoing Sandra Covington, the scientist at People's State University who feared becoming a "burned-out fifty-year-old faculty member," Velez agonized, "I can imagine by the time I would be done with this career, I would probably not have a heck of a lot creativity left in me . . . I don't know how much room there is."

Despite this early post-tenure slump, Marissa Velez persisted, moving slowly, a step at a time, without a clear view of how things would turn out, and guided mostly by will. She was intent on pursuing the psychology-based research on women that, she said, she loved: "I really have to fight off the narrowness and the pressure and just—resistance . . . so that's how I see what I'll do." Yet Velez did more than simply "fight off" opposing forces. She kept her eyes open for opportunities that might allow her to merge her learning in her new field of human resources management with her long-term favored learning about midlife women's psychological development.

Shortly after our first interview, Velez connected with a new university institute situated at some distance from the School of Business and attuned to urban research and outreach. The institute crystallized a central university agenda: to connect, by way of applied research, to the surrounding city. In her application to spend a year in the institute Velez proposed conducting an ethnographic study of female corporate officers' personal and career challenges in midlife, with attention to how these women responded to incursions of work and workplace pressures into their personal and home lives and the spillover, too, of their personal needs and interests into their workplaces. Thus, Velez conceptualized a research project bearing closely on her favored scholarly learning but also reflective of the interests of the School of Business and the human resources management program with which she was affiliated and to which she would have to return after her year's appointment to the new institute.

Two years later in our final interview, Velez exclaimed that with her new project on female corporate officers' personal and career challenges at midlife now well under way, she had finally "found her feet" at Hope State University. She described how her growing work in the field of human resources management, tied now to her institute effort, let her pursue ideas in psychology in ways that mattered greatly—to her, to the School of Business, and to Hope State University.

A TROUBLED MOVE. Esther Sharan, a scholar of Russian language and literature, also at Hope State University, told another story of leaving a subject area and a related community of scholars to which she had long devoted herself, moving then into a new subject associated with a different colleague community and representing a different field of literary study. Yet Sharan's narrative differed from that of Velez in a few ways. First, unlike Velez, Sharan's cross-field move did not entail a change in the disciplinary sector (arts and humanities) with which she was aligned: Sharan moved from one corner of the humanities (and within that sector, one corner of literary study) to another. Velez switched sectors in addition to switching fields (from a pure social science to an applied/professional field). Second, though Sharan hoped that the move would strengthen ties between her teaching and research (previously the two were quite separate), Velez was much more intent on creating such connection than was Sharan.[4]

Sharan opened her first interview with sparkling images of the Russian literature and language that she had long studied and taught—the "beauty" of the literary content, its importance to her sense of self, personally and professionally, her fascinations especially with *Anna Karenina, War and Peace,* and other of Tolstoy's writings: "It is to a large degree . . . who I am," she said, "and I think if I grow at all, that's how it happens." And she added, "I don't want to discount teaching, but I think something more visceral, more fundamental . . . happens when I am researching." In the middle of her second post-tenure year, during our first interview, Sharan looked happily and calmly at her career. Through it she expected to continue to engage with the subject and community of scholars she admired greatly.

Yet I learned during Sharan's final interview, scheduled in her fourth post-tenure year, that her career desires had fallen short of her experienced reality. She and her partner, also an academic, had indeed found suitable jobs in the area; nonetheless, Sharan continued to commute great distances to work. During her early post-tenure career she had found herself struggling to respond to new institutional leadership responsibilities (coordinating a busy program), caring for a young child (a daughter struggling with personal and social developmental tasks), and addressing the needs of elderly parents (increasingly infirm and living nearby), as her partner did much the same, all in the context of the lost time of a commuting work life. To respond, Sharan created a new scholarly portfolio that prized substantive efficiency. Although she was in the middle of a rich vein of scholarship on the literary and historic sources of *Anna Karenina*, a book writing project that meant a great deal to her, Sharan set it aside in favor of a new line of work on the social-political sources of the contemporary European short story. The new agenda promised far more rapid payoff than did the Tolstoy work: clear publication routes (publishers interested in literary developments mirroring contemporary political change) and well-organized teaching opportunities (students seeking out literature courses that treat contemporary political change globally). Or so it seemed. The shift, heavily driven by Sharan's desires for scholarly efficiency in a personal and professional life that seemed to be bursting at the seams, entailed significant substantive change for her. In setting aside her work on *Anna Karenina*, Sharan set aside the scholarly learning she loved.

The changes that Sharan made in her plan of study failed. She missed her study of *Anna Karenina*. She found herself struggling to lay the groundwork for new writing projects on the contemporary European short story that, despite the reduced substantive complexity, were hard to get off the ground. She found herself straining to engage—much less to master—the new literary genre she had elected to pursue, possibly because its contents meant so much less to her than did the Tolstoy study over which she had long labored. The strivings for beauty that resounded in Sharan's year 1 interview were altogether absent in the year 3 interview. Instead, I heard a narrative of arduous labor; by year 3 Sharan had little to say about beauty. "I have a feeling that I ought to figure . . . out [the new work on the modern-day European short story, its core ideas]," she said, "but I don't know that I am."

The Tolstoy work that Sharan had loved for so long, and to which she had hoped to return after tenure, remained, as she said, largely untouched. Her new research, on the contemporary European short story, also made little progress. "If I could finish [the *Anna Karenina* study] and . . . move on, just so I don't feel as if I've got so much shabby luggage from the past to carry around with me . . . That would help . . . if I were just a little bit more professionally involved in research. If that . . . wasn't always where the change came out, I think I would feel better about things. I would just take a little more pride in my work."

In their attempts to change within their fields of study, Marissa Velez, a psychologist, and Esther Sharan, a scholar of Russian language and literature, illustrate the power of context in professors' pursuits of the content of their scholarly learning. To pursue the content of her scholarly learning (women's midlife development) but in the context of a new field (human resources management within a school of business), Velez strived to blend it into her departmental work. She struggled to do so. After several years at Hope State she identified an alternative context within which to position her favored learning and began to pursue it there in ways that would better match her department's mission. She used her year in the institute to start up research that better joined her interests to those of her department; at the end of her institute year she brought that work back to her department. Thus, Velez sought to change fields (moving from psychology to business, and to human resources management specifically) without compromising her core desires to understand women's midlife experiences. She worked very hard to reshape her topic in response to the interests of the new contexts that she entered, but without changing its core meanings—namely, the core substance that drew her to it. Doing that allowed her to move her favored theme (midlife women's development) from one field of study to another, albeit with modification. Her year in the institute made that move possible.

In contrast, Sharan fully redefined the content of her scholarly learning, originally on Tolstoy but now on the contemporary European short story, to better match the contexts of her post-tenure work life, namely, its calls for greater efficiency. While remaining within literary study, this change in literary subjects entailed a change in fields. Sharan did not construe her day-to-day work contexts as movable or changeable (as did

Velez, in moving to the institute for a year). What did Sharan's reshaping of her scholarly learning entail? To reshape her scholarly learning, Sharan set out to learn a brand-new area of study and to join a new community. She took little with her, and it is unclear whether she kept up her ties to her core community of study (of Tolstoy scholars). Sharan's interviews revealed little of the substantive thematic transfer evident in Velez's experience; in moving to a new field, she seemed to start her scholarship anew. She had to learn her new subjects deeply and in ways that would ignite in her the kind of emotional connection that her scholarly learning, in a different literary field (Tolstoy studies), had held for her in the past. In our last interview Sharan was struggling to do this. She missed the substantive meanings that her scholarly study of Tolstoy, now lapsed, had previously represented. The new project she created at Hope State University failed to connect to her core interests, and she felt adrift.

Disciplinary and Cross-Disciplinary Knowledge as Context and Content

Newly tenured university professors may remain well attached to their subjects of study through the early post-tenure career. Although continued attachment to a long-term subject may, at first glance, seem to be a sign of intellectual slowdown—or of risk avoidance—professors' comments suggest that that need not be the case. Newly tenured university professors who stay close to their subjects may well be "on the move" in their learning in two ways. First, as professors explore the subjects that continue to matter deeply to them, they may stretch out into substantive topics and communities beyond their own, though nonetheless relevant to their own, in other parts of their own field. Thus, their within-field substantive interests and knowledge may expand but in relation to their core interests. Second, professors also may explore other fields, gaining substantially from such ventures. In doing so, they engage in scholarly learning that is cross-disciplinary or cross-field. Such ventures are usually purposeful and brief: professors exploring new fields for particular insights and skills that they can take home to their own work and core communities. Professors who leave their home fields more fully, however, without a clear substantive reason or plan to return, would appear to face critical career reconstruction challenges: how to hold onto the personal meanings that their scholarly learning represents, how to align their new contexts with such meaning, how to reframe their subjects of study so that their scholarly learning retains its integrity yet in ways that draw on the strengths of a new workplace while sidestepping its constraints.[5]

Scholarly Learning on Campus and in Lives

Clearly, professors' disciplines and fields matter a great deal in their scholarly learning. What matters even more is whether and how professors position themselves within, across, and beyond their disciplines and fields to pursue their scholarly learning in their university workplaces (on campus) and elsewhere (even beyond academe). Drawing on study interviews, I contend that professors' scholarly learning can be associated with university professors' campus-based work—especially their teaching, service, and outreach—but only if that learning remains connected to their disciplines and fields and sometimes to other significant sources, as well, including professors' personal lives. What this means is that disciplinary or field-based expertise and affiliation with a community of disciplinary or field-based specialists do matter for scholarly learning, but so does daily campus work. It is their blending, within professors' work lives, that makes professors' scholarly learning possible.[6] But where—between campus and discipline—does scholarly learning happen?

Professors participating in the *Four Universities Project* portrayed their scholarly learning as located in one or more of three contexts: academic activity, academic collectivity, or personal existence. In the context of *academic activity* scholarly learning occurs within the traditional work roles of the professorate: research, teaching, and service (institutional, professional, and outreach). In the context of *academic collectivity* scholarly learning occurs within social groupings and social organization, on campus or beyond it, in disciplinary or professional communities and networks, including colleagueship (much of it campus-based) as a form of faculty relationship and interaction. In the context of *personal existence* scholarly learning occurs at the borders of career and personal life, for example, in instances of autobiographical reflection and meaning making, alone and with others. Each of these three contexts reflects a further array of places and times within which professors carried out their learning. It is important to point out that none of these contexts refers solely to professors' disciplines and fields. But neither do they refer solely to the campus. Rather, they amalgamate key strands of professors' disciplines/ fields, campuses, and biographies.

Table 4.1 indicates the prevalence of the three contexts in study participants' thinking for study year 3 (n = 39). Of the three contexts noted, academic activity was most prominent in study participants' discussions of the *what* and *where* of their scholarly learning: they thought of their scholarly learning in relation to their research, teaching, and service (internal/external)—that is, in the context of their specific work activities (indicated by over 90% of the sample), in contrast to the more amorphous context of the academic collectivity (66%), or to the still broader context of personal existence (33%). This comes as no surprise: professors, like most people, focus on those activities that are concretely on their minds— that they think about and carry out actively day by day—rather than on more abstract and distant "collectivities" and/or relational networks in which they and their work are embedded. Fewer still set aside time for thought and talk about their personal lives as sources of their research. Both the collective settings and the personal can count as contexts for professors' scholarly learning,[7] yet in professors' experiences day-to-day activity stands out as the prominent site of scholarly learning.

What is surprising, and noteworthy, about these data are the specific locations—and in this case, the particular academic activities—that participating professors associate with their scholarly learning. Drawing on prevailing images of professorial work, one would be tempted to associate professors' scholarly learning with their research activity more so than with their teaching and service activities, the latter typically cast as antithetical to scholarship. Table 4.1 shows that, indeed, over two-thirds of participating professors associated their scholarly learning with their research activity. Yet a larger number of them related their scholarly learning to their teaching (90% or more), graduate and undergraduate, and a substantial number (upward of a third of the sample) related it to their service activity, including institutional service.

Further, table 4.1 underlines the important point that the contexts of recently tenured university professors' scholarly learning cannot and should not be talked about simply as campus-based—or, alternatively, as discipline- or field-based—activity, as researchers and university leaders often refer to them. As table 4.1 shows, a more authentic representation of the contexts of professors' scholarly learning requires viewing them

TABLE 4.1   Contexts of Recently Tenured Professors' Scholarly Learning
($n = 39$)

Contexts of Professors' Scholarly Learning[a]	Prevalence in Sample[b]
Academic Activity	
Faculty work within traditional academic roles	
Research	**
Teaching	***
Service	*
Total: Academic Activity	***
Academic Collectivity	
Social grouping and organization in the campus and region, disciplinary or professional group	
Community	*
Colleague relations	**
Total: Academic Collectivity	**
Personal Existence	
Meshing of career and personal life in construction of the academic life: autobiographical reflection, meanings and worldviews, personal relationships	
Total: Personal Existence	*

[a] (1) Categories are not mutually exclusive. (2) Data were drawn from all portions of interview transcripts referring to contexts of professors' scholarly learning. (3) *Research* indicates all forms of intellectual/artistic endeavor; also informal study such as reading in one's field; attending lectures, talks, conferences, and so on to keep up with one's subject or gain new knowledge; interaction with practitioners for insight. *Teaching* includes graduate and undergraduate; in classroom, lab, and other sites, mentoring. *Service* includes internal institutional, public outreach, and disciplinary. *Community* refers to assemblage of individuals and groups with shared ethos, history, and meanings continuing through time and unique to a campus, discipline, or field, often shaped by surrounding social/cultural environments. *Colleagueship* refers to member relationships, interactions, communication within community, formal and informal; includes peer relations, mentorship, and collaboration.
[b] Derived from year 3 interviews of the *Four Universities Project*. Proportion indicating particular contexts:

    at least 90% ***
    at least 66% **
    at least 33% *

simultaneously as of the discipline/field, of the institution, and of the scholar's personal life: as streaming through professors' academic activities and collectivities as well as their personal existence. Attention only to campus or only to field, or reifying the separateness of campus and field, can distort researchers' and policy makers' understandings of professors' work by hiding from view the fullness of professors' learning that materializes simultaneously in the intertwining of these settings. To glimpse the fullness of professors' scholarly learning requires viewing it at once as of a scholarly field or disciplinary community well beyond campus and as of the campus as a local work site. A better view also incorporates perspectives from scholars' personal lives.[8] All these sites together, along with the resources that each provides, help to frame professors' scholarly learning.

Finally, table 4.1 suggests that within the array of spaces within which scholarly learning grows, two specific sites—teaching and service—deserve closer looks: a number of the professors participating in the study said they engaged in scholarly learning as they taught, prepared to teach, or reflected back on the teaching in which they engaged. The table also suggests that professors' teaching—of graduate and undergraduate students—may be a richer location for their scholarly learning than is their research. Table 4.1 also indicates that service can be a site of professors' scholarly learning. Stated differently, and contrary to extant policy assumptions and prevailing professional thought, teaching and service, as campus-anchored activities, need not be viewed as getting in the way of newly tenured university professors' scholarly learning; thoughtfully conceived, they may even promote that learning.

Further, professors' engagement in scholarly learning need not be cast as interfering with their teaching and service. When scholarly learning is thoughtfully—indeed, responsibly—embedded in professors' teaching and service, it need not be viewed as obstructing those important professional endeavors.[9] Yet professors and academic leaders do not often use phrases such as "learning in teaching" and "learning in service." What does scholarly learning in teaching and in service look like? I draw on the experiences of the professors participating in the *Four Universities Project* for insight.

A CLOSER LOOK: SCHOLARLY LEARNING IN THE CONTEXT OF PROFESSORS' TEACHING

What does it mean to say that professors can learn in their teaching? What might such learning in teaching look or sound like? I addressed this question by considering: the full scope of professors' teaching (preparing to teach, teaching in action, reflecting back on teaching instances); its learners (graduate/undergraduate); and its diverse modalities (class/

lab group, lecture/seminar, classroom/practicum, and so on). Drawing on year 1 interview data, I identified four general images of what professors' learning in teaching looks like:

— Uncovering subject matter knowledge: striving for mastery and breadth

— Discovering/constructing subject matter knowledge: teaching that doubles as research

— Representing subject matter knowledge: exploring within and between one's own and others' represented understandings of a subject of study

— Revising subject matter knowledge: critiquing, reframing, and opening flows of thought.

Uncovering Subject Matter Knowledge

Study participants sometimes described their teaching as an opportunity to uncover previously accumulated subject matter knowledge bearing on their scholarly interests. This might involve strivings for subject matter mastery or breadth, sometimes both.

STRIVING FOR SUBJECT MATTER MASTERY. A number of participating professors, teachers of undergraduates, indicated that they sought subject matter mastery, a continuous deepening and refinement of their subject matter understanding. A scientist explained: "If you have to teach something, you have to understand it pretty well . . . You do have [to] spend the time to really get at the root of understanding." A second scientist in a different field added that doing well in class requires being "prepared to death." "A thousand German scientists, no problem," this professor said. "One hundred fifty undergraduates, *that* you have to prepare for." And a third scientist affirmed: "You really have to know your stuff . . . You can't teach it to them until you understand it yourself." These scientists were not alone in their views. "The challenge is . . . to have a certain line or mastery on certain issues," said a professor of literature, and a social scientist asserted: "You have to know something cold in order to be able to teach it . . . You have to be on your toes. You have to know the stuff and you're constantly learning." But more than keeping him "on his toes," this learning, he said, has made him into "a much better [scholar] . . . than five or six years ago."

Collectively, these and other scholars portrayed themselves as seeking to comprehend, in ever refined ways, the subject matter content knowledge of their fields. Comprehension assumes a subject created, shared, and preserved within a community of which the scholar is a part.

STRIVING FOR SUBJECT MATTER BREADTH. In addition to striving for depth through mastery, professors sought breadth: expanded coverage of their subjects of study. A literature professor explained that her learning through teaching makes her broadly "a more knowledgeable person . . . let[ting] me play with some things that interest me"—as did a research scientist, who noted that "having taught [the science to undergraduates] . . . I think I understand . . . [it] better." Professors involved in graduate teaching echoed the point. "We have very, very good graduate students here," said an anthropologist, "and I certainly learn a lot from reading their work and talking to them about their work." "Often [these] students have time to read more widely than professors do," she added, "so I get keyed into interesting new articles that people say, 'Oh, you should look at that.'" A historian also claimed that her views of research have broadened from "working with graduate students and seeing the range . . . of work that they do." As a result, she said, "I'm reading more different things and writing about more different things."

Several professors in diverse fields portrayed their scholarly learning as a broadening out of their already developed core of subject matter knowledge. They used their teaching, undergraduate and graduate, to reach into topics that otherwise they might not engage. Their teaching taught *them* by bringing to their attention knowledge bearing on their scholarly learning.

Discovering/Constructing Subject Matter Knowledge

Professors committed to researcher training sometimes use apprenticeships and communities of practice to bring learners authentically into the research practices they seek to teach. In this view professors simultaneously teach and carry out research, thereby positioning themselves to learn with their students about a shared subject. In apprenticeship the teaching and learning are heavily one to one; communities of practice lift this approach to a more complex communal level of peer and expert interactive learning.[10]

A social scientist described her desires to use her teaching of research methods to elevate research in her work life: "I think research . . . has moved up [in my interests] and teaching has moved down, which means they are probably closer together now, than . . . in the beginning [of my career]. And [they are] also . . . becoming very linked. For example, I'm teaching qualitative methods . . . and [my] students are going into [the field]. So I'm . . . doing my research with the students, and I would actually like to get to the point where I can figure out how to teach them . . . to do qualitative methods stuff at the same time as run a research project that they are a part of." She describes efforts to infuse research, as a distinctive activity, into an equally distinctive activity, teaching—a sensible aim, given how well a course on research methods incorporates both.

A biologist similarly described efforts to entwine teaching and research, a normative practice in her field: "I have had several graduate students that were really good at fieldwork . . . I have one graduate student now that's just . . . great [in a specialization unfamiliar to me], and because of that talent, we've been able to do projects that I would never be able to do. I don't have time to do a lot of fieldwork, and I don't know that I'm all that good at it . . . It wouldn't even be an option to do really [without this particular student]." This professor's transformation of a teaching task (the research preparation of a graduate student) into a research opportunity (putting the student's technical skills to use in her research) opens doors to her own, the student's, and their field's learning of subjects that matter to them all.

In this image of "learning in teaching," professors engage in scholarly learning at the intersection of their teaching and research. The subject matter knowledge they gain in so doing may then be cast in two ways: as the learning outcomes of teaching (for students) and of research (for the field, including the professor as one of its established members). This approach was most common among scientists and social scientists teaching graduate students.

Representing Subject Matter Knowledge
In representational approaches to scholarly learning, professors in all fields, teaching at graduate and undergraduate levels, strive to understand subject matter as learners understand it; they compare learners' subject matter understandings to their own, and they position learners to negotiate subject matter meanings with peers, with texts, and so on. To capture such interaction, one might ask, what kinds of things does a teacher

need to understand in order to teach in this way? Ideally, the teacher will understand: that subject matter knowledge is representational; how to elicit and work with students' knowledge representations; and how to recognize and appreciate students' novel knowledge representations. Professors participating in the study referred frequently to their efforts to achieve such understandings.[11]

LEARNING ABOUT THE REPRESENTATIONAL QUALITIES OF SUBJECT MATTER KNOWLEDGE. Academic learning, including scholarly learning, is sometimes described as the construction and reconstruction of subject matter knowledge. To engage in such learning (and relearning), professors must understand and appreciate the social nature of knowledge construction (it is shared), the fluidity of the knowledge at issue (it flows), its multiple forms and meanings (it changes), and its malleability (it may be revised), though within limits.[12] A history professor who teaches large undergraduate classes spoke of how she came to understand the representational qualities of historical knowledge as they appeared in her teaching:

> I do enjoy . . . putting together a lecture in a way that works and has a structure and elegance to it . . . I play around with materials . . . Now what's really changed over time, especially as I've been able to teach some courses several times, is that I use different materials a lot more . . . I do a lot with film and video clips and music. And it's an immense amount of work putting this together in the first place . . . structur[ing] a lecture that has six video clips in it . . . twenty seconds each . . . It's always . . . work to run around and get the videos and queue them up, and have everything ready to go . . . And the same with using music. There are some lectures in which I play music . . . helps [my students]— helps highlight something more vividly or make something more memorable . . . [So] I do a lot more with . . . multimedia than I used to. I don't use the computer at all. I don't have a Web page. I don't do PowerPoint. My technology is pretty low-tech video- tapes, CD player, boom box . . . I've been doing a lot with trans- parencies . . . just . . . give them some images, help them to store ideas and information in more than one way.

Asked why she has become engaged with representational features of her teaching, the historian said, "Probably because it's fun and because I know it works." She then explained:

> It's intellectually fun . . . to create a . . . complexity and density for [students]. I can't stand . . . the basic three-point lecture . . . [you] just say them over and over again. I really want students to learn layers in relationships . . . ambiguity, especially. Because . . . history teaching in high schools is still very often . . . names and dates . . . very linear, a very simple version of the past. And by using images, or by reading—sometimes [texts] I put . . . in a course pack. Sometimes I just read them bits of literature, including poetry . . . I do think . . . [that] a vivid image may stay in their mind[s] in a way that a statement of fact won't. But I also want them to develop a sense of the past [that] is complicated and ambiguous . . . layer[ed] . . . [History is not] like this hard little set of facts . . . that you can clutch in your hand like a stone, and . . . I want them to have a more complicated idea of knowledge

This professor understands that she can represent historical knowledge in different ways, and she wants students to understand this as well, as part of their learning of history. She suggests, further, that working in a representational mode helps her share history with her students as she herself understands it. She explains that teaching in this way, in full awareness of the representational qualities of historical knowledge, cycles back into her own learning—for example, as she reflects on how she portrays historical knowledge. "One thing that they've [my students] done," she said, "is make me want to write better."

A number of participating professors, teachers of graduate and undergraduate students and across diverse fields, said that they had learned about the representational quality of their subject matter knowledge pretenure. Yet post-tenure, they continued to deepen their appreciation of this quality.

LEARNING TO ELICIT AND WORK WITH STUDENTS' KNOWLEDGE REPRESENTATIONS. In advancing their scholarly learning within their teaching, professors also learned to see, hear, and respond to their students' knowledge representations. A social scientist described how over the years he struggled to represent his subject matter knowledge meaningfully and to respond helpfully to students' in-class representations: "When I first got here [as an assistant professor,] I wasn't confident enough in my ability to convey the basic information, to . . . get the students involved in the discussion [of social science], even in relatively small student settings. I tended to spend much more of the class hour with recitation than in actual interchange with the students. Now, I find that much easier . . . to integrate students' comments into what material I'm actually discussing, all of which I found extremely difficult my first year or two." This professor, who, years earlier, taught through nonconversational "recitation," said he now teaches in between his own subject matter knowledge ("the material I'm actually discussing") and the knowing his undergraduate students offer through "comments" in class. He described himself as "integrating" students' thoughts into the thoughts that, as teacher and scholar, he "discussed."

A philosopher described yet another image of how professors can work with students' knowledge representations, this time in the context of graduate-level student research:

> When I . . . arrived here first and began to teach graduate students . . . I had a tendency to micromanage . . . They would hand me a paper and I would give them back . . . extensive comments on it . . . looking at every line and paragraph . . . I don't do that anymore . . . I . . . think that I was really hemming people in way too much. They weren't able to do creative work . . . I would . . . try to put in terms for them what they ought to think about. And so . . . now [I] try much more consciously, particularly in the early parts of a project, to confine my attention to broad [issues] . . . where the project as a whole is gonna be going, than with the . . . details of the thing. Now as it gets closer to the end . . . I become more and more a micromanager as . . . it becomes clear how the project is gonna look.

This scholar describes his students' knowledge representations, through writing, as evolving—requiring his support for their expression as well as careful pacing of his response. He has come to view his teaching less as the promotion of his own knowledge representations than as the elicitation and support of his students' representations. Rather than marking up students' early knowledge representations, roping them into his own—action that might stunt students' own thoughts—he lets the students "grow" their own. Later in the process, however, he does provide his students with more explicit feedback. At that point he can direct his comments toward students' more fully formed ideas, as opposed to struggling, earlier on, to bring their nascent ideas toward his own.

The social scientist and philosopher portray their knowledge representational activity as blended dialogue between teacher and students, rather than as a teacher's monologue. In this view teaching entails elicitation and support, in the words of a professor of literary studies, "allowing a process to start or to continue or to facilitate something in a student . . . not to profess but to . . . mediate." Together, these professors make the point that their teaching involves attending to their students' knowledge representations and in due time shaping their own in response. Professors of both graduate and undergraduate students, and in all fields, said they struggled to acquire this understanding.

LEARNING TO RECOGNIZE AND APPRECIATE STUDENTS' NOVEL KNOWLEDGE REPRESENTATIONS. In teaching professors may learn to open themselves up to their students' knowledge representations, usually to correct or redirect them. At times, however, such opening up leads the student to redirect the teacher's thinking: the teacher, frequently of undergraduates, may see in a student's idea a novel view on a subject that the teacher presumes to know quite well.

A mathematician explained that even in teaching foundational classes, one "can learn new mathematics sometimes." She then described the work of "a very well-known mathematician . . . [who] very much enjoyed teaching beginning calculus students . . . really claimed he learned something from it every time." Thus, she added, "It's not impossible to learn something from these courses." A physicist echoed the mathematician's views: "I think definitely . . . I've learned . . . especially in teaching the big survey courses . . . what different things people could bring to . . . class . . . They often are able to make very creative analogies to help them understand physical concepts," he added, "[some] I would never have thought of." A professor of English literature also said, in reference to her undergraduate and graduate teaching, that in class "there is almost always . . . one epiphany . . . Every semester somebody . . . does something that you didn't necessarily expect . . . [there's] a moment in the classroom when I see something in a different light." A professor of music also said she learned, for her own craft, from her intensive studio-based work with students: "In showing them something," she said, "and in seeing their reactions, it makes me think about my own playing in a different way." These cases suggest that, through teaching, professors may gain surprising insights into subjects they have long studied. Talking with students about their subjects and attending to students' developing subject matter thoughts can inspire new thought among professors. They also may learn, even in foundational classes.

Professors learn about the representational qualities of their subjects. They learn, too, what it means to extend those subjects outwardly toward other learners so that they may grasp them while opening themselves then to these others' extensions of that knowledge back to them. In this view professors in all fields and at both graduate and undergraduate levels can learn from knowledge that, by virtue of its representational qualities, is fluid, formative, pliable, revealing of multiple meanings that can be shared.

Revising Subject Matter Knowledge
Teaching is often assumed to involve ideas that move from knowers to learners and occasionally from learners back to knowers, in both cases with the expectation that knowers will redirect learners' misguided thoughts. Yet occasionally, teaching is part of a conversation between two or more individuals wishing to understand and explore each other's minds as peers—for example, through critique, trial reframings, or experimental juxtapositions. These peers can be colleagues, but they also can be students.

LEARNING FROM STUDENTS' CRITIQUES OF PROFESSORS' DEVELOPING IDEAS. Occasionally, professors represent their evolving scholarly thoughts to students who, as developing colleagues, respond with their own thoughts for improving these professors' work. In this view students openly facilitate the learning of their teachers who have purposefully dissolved traditional role-based distinctions, merging their own and their students' learning and teaching.

A philosopher explained the power of student critique, constructively directed, on his work and learning. On occasion, he said, advanced graduate students "read my stuff when it's in draft form and come into my office and tell me what they think is wrong with it . . . and . . . sometimes they're exactly right." "I think that this is a good thing for them," he explained, "and I think it's good thing for me." "There's no doubt, no question that . . . there were a number of places in my book . . . where I would have made a mistake if it weren't for . . . [graduate students] coming in and telling me that it was a mistake." The philosopher thus learned from his students' "corrections" of the substantive thoughts central to his evolving work.

LEARNING FROM STUDENTS' REFRAMINGS OF PROFESSORS' ESTAB- LISHED THOUGHT. Students can contribute far more than invited critique to professors' work in progress. In exploratory seminars, for example, students may reframe their teachers' understandings of ideas that, the professors believe, they know well and deeply. Asked what kinds of situations help him to learn best, a political scientist responded that this can happen "when I am . . . among peers or graduate students, and we have a chance to . . . talk about new work, and that new work gives us a chance to sort of get at it . . . in a way that is not simply a reproduction of the mantras that we've developed about all the old problems." "Sometimes," he said, "it happens in a graduate seminar where simply the presence of someone who has a very different background and habit of thinking is . . . illuminating . . . [leads you to] try to weave the unfamiliar into your existing beliefs . . . Almost inevitably that requires gestalt switches." This kind of thought, he noted, "is not really something that can be done in isolation . . . it's a matter of putting yourself in a position where you have to think out loud with other people from [and] about [your] work."

This professor stands to learn as he brings students into his scholarly thought, freeing those students to explore and recast his thoughts in light of their sometimes "very different background[s] and habit[s] of thinking." In doing so, the students may "weave the unfamiliar into [the professor's] existing beliefs," repositioning how the professor knows her subject.

LEARNING WITHIN OPENED FLOWS OF SUBJECT MATTER TALK AND THOUGHT. In the exploratory conversations of seminars and labs, teaching can involve opening up flows of thought across students' and professors' minds, enabling new or unusual formations—thoughts in negotiation and connection—that a more formal treatment (such as a lecture or write-up) could freeze and stop, or convert, as one professor said, into "fossilized" form. "It's hard for me to say what I love about the final product because I'm usually pretty alienated from it when it's done," said a professor of literary studies, "[but] being [in]side the process, and being in dialogue with it, is what I love about it." Such dialogues, this scholar said, infuse her teaching and other scholarly work as well as meaningful relationships extending well beyond work, each affording her with "moment[s] when you are kind of negotiating your relationship to different ideas, and [being] inside of them, and they're shifting around, and . . . they're not completely definite yet . . . just shifting around." At times, she said, this "shifting around" brings thoughts together in surprising "connections" so that "a certain energy gets exchanged . . . it's not located in oneself or the other self, but it just kind of emerges." This professor, a teacher of literature to graduate and undergraduate students, portrayed herself as being immersed in processes of thought and as striving to keep such processes alive—as "despairing" of the congealing of thought that highly published professorial careers typically require.

Other scholars in other fields make related observations of what happens in their classroom teaching or in their mentoring of groups, or "teams," of students. A chemist explains that learning happens for him amid a research team of doctoral students that perform, and thereby create, their science much as does a string quartet. "Each person has a very unique voice, a distinctive voice," he said, "yet what they're able to do together is more than what you could do as a solo instrumentalist . . . It's still individual but still part of a community." In this chemist's view the multiple, individually conducted inquiries of a small research team can yield learning in the form of collectively created thought—ideas that, though building on the work of unique minds, no one alone could create.

Teaching for these and other professors involves creating spaces in which diverse thoughts and thinkers "shift" and "connect" in unexpected forms, "crystallizing" meanings, as another scholar called it, previously unthought, unrealized, or untried. Whether through critique, reframing, or the opening of flows of thought, professors in all fields—teachers of graduate and undergraduate students—often explored each others' thinking, striving thereby to improve their own and their colleagues' thoughts. To do this, they usually positioned themselves as peers in interaction, striving for re-vision.

Scholarly Learning in Teaching

Teaching can be a rich context for professors' scholarly learning along-side that of their students. As a chemist said, teaching can "stir the pot" of professors' subject matter knowledge, thereby creating opportunities for hidden thoughts or unusual juxtapositions to surface. It is noteworthy that the four images of scholarly learning in teaching presented here resonate with professors' portrayals of the "activities of mind" that they undertook in pursuit of their scholarly learning. For example, both the first and second views of professors' scholarly learning in their teaching—their strivings for mastery and breadth, their making teaching double as research—parallel the view, in chapter 3, of scholarly learning as professors' extending their subject matter knowledge, namely, their further growing out, or filling in, of the base of subject matter knowledge that they have developed to date. The third view of professors' scholarly learning in their teaching—learning through knowledge representation—is virtually identical to the same-named view of scholarly learning discussed in chapter 3. The fourth view of professors' scholarly learning in their teaching—knowledge revision—resembles the view of scholarly learning defined, in chapter 3, as professors' re-forming their subject matter knowledge, namely, bringing together ideas previously deemed separate or rethinking of long-held ideas and perspectives. What this analysis suggests is that newly tenured university professors' scholarly learning can grow in their teaching inasmuch as in their research or scholarship broadly. Teaching appears to be as rich a site for professors' scholarly learning, as it is—one would hope and assume—for their students, graduate and undergraduate, and across diverse fields and disciplines.

A CLOSER LOOK: SCHOLARLY LEARNING IN THE CONTEXT OF PROFESSORS' SERVICE

Professors' teaching can be a site of their scholarly learning. Faculty service can be a site for such learning as well. I define university professors' service as their contributions to "the governance, management, and operation of their employing institution, in whole or in part, internally and externally . . . the work of their professional/disciplinary associations . . . [and] the maintenance of their disciplines and fields at large."[13] But what does scholarly learning look and sound like within individual professors' practices of service, whether internal (e.g., institutional operations and upkeep) or external (e.g., public service or outreach)? What more may be said about the kinds of scholarly learning that professors may gain through faculty service? With Aimee LaPointe Terosky I found that, in their service, professors can gain in-the-moment learning of the subject matters that bear directly or indirectly on their scholarly learning. They also may gain access to community resources—for example, intellectual expertise available through on-campus colleagues—that they can mobilize toward their substantive learning at a future time.[14]

Service that Provides in-the-Moment Substantive Learning

Recently tenured university professors can use their service responsibilities to gain subject matter knowledge that is valuable to their research and teaching, or simply to their own broad-based understanding of their subjects of study.[15] In the views of many professors—especially scholars in professional and applied fields—university outreach, or university-sponsored public service, is an ideal vehicle for such learning.

I have already presented an example of learning in public service through the case of Emily Lifton, the professor of environmental engineering at Signal University who developed and tested the chemistry of water treatments aimed at eliminating pollutants. Lifton's early work included several significant laboratory-based chemistry projects whose findings, reported in key scholarly journals, advanced understanding of the chemistries of water pollution and treatment options; this body of work helped shape research in her field. By her third post-tenure year Lifton had moved her research, still focused on the chemistry of water pollution, toward considerations of its use by—and usefulness to—others. Rather than limiting her analyses to the lab, she moved her analytic efforts into the world, where problems of water pollution, treatment practice, and environmental policy exist as part of people's everyday lives.

Post-tenure, Lifton continued to study the chemistries of water, but now in the context of "live" practices and policies bearing on the quality of water for human consumption. In effect, she moved her research problem from the lab into the natural and social world where it originated and where, in fact, people defined it as a problem. In doing so, she revised her own—and no doubt her field's—understanding of that problem's substantive complexity: water pollution, viewed chemically, looks and acts different in the natural and social world where it grows, and where it wreaks its effects, than it does in the more distanced lab. It looks different, Lifton said, in the context of the larger environmental "story" of which it is a part:

EL: I think I gave [you] this anecdote before. Right now I feel . . . more compelled and intrigued by . . . the ways in which society has harmed the environment . . . in a slightly larger picture than [just] to say, "Okay, class, today we're going to talk about the partitioning chemistry of PCBs." What's different? One is [that in the class discussion focused only on the chemistry of pollutants] we're taking the chemical, and we're just thinking about it *outside a story*. The other is to talk about the chemical's behavior *within the story*—I like that [within-story perspective]; that's more [meaningful] to me [italics added].

AN: When you say within or outside the story, what's the difference there again?

EL: Well . . . so what's the story? Let's talk about PCBs within the context of General Electric and the Hudson River . . . I can tell you the same chemistry [of PCBs from both contexts.] But in the traditional context [of lab and disciplinary discourses that exclude environmental/human concerns, hence *outside the story*], you're getting an answer as to how much . . . [of] PCBs are in a particular environmental sector—[the] concentration [of PCBs in an] environmental compartment. In the other [environmental/human perspective, hence *within the story*] you can do the *same* calculation—but you go a step farther. You say: "So now, what's the harm? What do we need to do? What's the decision?" And I like this latter case. It's more interesting to me than to just teach them how to do the algebra of partitioning chemistry.

Lifton's resituated scholarly learning—its move from research lab to public service setting—yields more than traditional disciplinary insight into the partitioning chemistry of pollutants: it assesses harm, needs for action, and decision options for policy and practice. It lays out the chemical content of the problem at issue, yet it also explores its effects on the larger environment in which it exists. In this view both the subject (the chemistry of water pollution) and its story (the settings and impacts of pollution) are part of an enlarged "problem" to be addressed. Lifton's moving her problem from lab to life, so to speak, let her see this larger picture of her problem. While influencing her research, that picture also touched her teaching: to teach the algebra of partitioning chemistry from the perspective of the natural environment in which one would find a water pollution problem yields a different image of that chemistry, for students, than does teaching it from the perspective solely of the research lab. The chemistry looks and feels different in these two sites—to students and to the researcher alike.

Although public outreach, like Lifton's, can provide rich opportunities for substantive learning, so may more traditional (internal) institutional service. A professor of policy studies working at a different university described substantive insights he gained through service on university-level curriculum review committees:

> The curriculum committees were very helpful to me, particularly as a teacher . . . The [university] has a diversity requirement where every student has to take a course that's diversity [oriented] . . . And I served on the committee that made the decision about whether those courses were gonna be approved. And I learned a lot about, how people construct syllabi . . . how they try and think about intellectual ideas . . .

> There was this one great course where this guy wanted to do a diversity course about [a specialized topic on ethnicity]. And . . . he would've done this thing for literally eight months. He gave us maybe seven versions [of his developing syllabus]. And I worked with him. We met on several occasions, and it was amazing to watch him . . . he basically started out with being a music guy who didn't know the literature on race and ethnicity, and at the end it's a great course. I mean, it's a really good course . . . Watching that . . . I learned a lot about how can you integrate [disparate subject matters]? What do you do? And it was fascinating to see how he did that. So, in that sense, yes, it was helpful.

As a member of the university's curriculum committee, the policy scholar advised a musician seeking to incorporate themes of diversity into a course he hoped to teach. Although the professor of music may well have learned a great deal, about ideas in his field and beyond, as he reworked his course, it seems that the policy scholar did as well—no doubt, about diversity and music but also, as he says, about how one goes about inquiring and creating teachable ideas across widely divergent fields of study. Although this learning did not contribute directly to the policy scholar's research, it contributed to his understandings of what it takes to bring together knowledge from diverse domains and to represent such knowledge meaningfully to others. Such understanding could, in the long run, matter in his scholarly learning.

These examples indicate that in some cases professors may gain substantively from engagement in faculty service. Directly or indirectly, their learning in service may bear on their scholarly learning. The scholarly learning of professors in applied and professional fields seemed especially responsive to their public and institutional service.

Service that Yields Community Resources for Substantive Learning Later On

At times engagement in service contributed to study participants' scholarly learning in less direct yet equally powerful ways: their service brought new sources of substantive knowledge—in the form of colleagues with subject matter expertise—their way. In other words, although their service did not provide opportunities for professors' learning in the moment (as in the preceding examples), it did open doors to the possibility of such learning in the future. Thus, professors and the new colleagues they met, initially through service, might engage in research or teaching, or they might connect, simply for scholarly conversation, at a later time. Thus, professors sometimes used service to identify stimulating scholars outside their own programs and departments, thereby broadening the base of relationships that in the future might support their scholarly work. A professor of finance described how service on a college committee led to this kind of research collaboration: "I've gotten to meet people in other departments [on committees] . . . which is . . . learning . . . So there are some [name of discipline] people . . . I knew they existed, but

I didn't know them, so I get to meet them this way . . . With [collaborator], I met him that way. But then it was really the research that got it going. The administration [service on committee] was, at most, the link." The scholar of finance gained a valuable source of substantive expertise through college committee service, but the two colleagues' intellectual colleagueship did not ensue until they took initiative, beyond committee work, to explore common interests. A social scientist described a similar discovery: committee colleagues who, he anticipated, could turn into research colleagues in the future: "I meet people on committees . . . who are interested in some of the same [disciplinary] issues that I am . . . in the [other social sciences departments, and] that I just didn't know before. We've talked about our research, and [that] may lead to some productive collaboration at some point. But they're people I never would have encountered . . . and may not have even known that they were interested in the same sets of issues that I was interested in." Engagement in faculty service alerted both these professors, and others like them, to possibilities for engagement in the future with new colleagues about subject matter issues of common interest.

Scholarly Learning in Faculty Service
Although often distanced from research and teaching, service can support professors' scholarly learning. Participating professors looked favorably on service that furthered their scholarly learning in the moments of service enactment. They also appreciated service that opened opportunities to relationships with stimulating colleagues and thereby promises of substantive collaboration in the future. Although service can at times get in the way of professors' scholarly learning, wisely positioned, it can offer intellectual support. The same is true of teaching and research.

What and Where: Toward Strategic Learning

In earlier chapters I claimed that conceptions of learning are incomplete without attention to what learners are learning. This chapter claims that where that learning happens is also important: certain features of the context in which a professor learns her subject of study mix with or otherwise shape that subject. As such, subject matter that is learned in a particular setting—for example, among a certain set of people, on a certain campus, at a certain time—may differ in meaning, to some extent, from similar content learned in another setting.[16]

This chapter also shows that context is complex, representing multiples of time, place, condition, or situation that frame the learning of any one person. The seemingly singular context is in effect plural—contexts. Assume, for example, a professor who, in conversation with a student, gains an alternative understanding of a substantive point with which he is deeply familiar. The professor learns something from this teacher-student interaction. Whereas that interaction is a primary context of the professor's learning, it is not the only context at play in this scholarly learning situation. Consider some of the other contexts that frame this teacher's learning. The talk between teacher and student is itself contextualized in a class full of other people and learning events that regulate what may be said in a teacher-student interaction: certain content enters, and other content is filtered out, depending on the aim of the class. That class is itself contextualized in a larger campus culture or climate that defines what counts as a class. The campus culture is further contextualized in distinctive regional, national, economic, and historic conditions that may further shape the culture and climate of classroom discourse and teacher-student interaction. Directly or indirectly, all these contexts shape the content of what the professor and student talk about, thus becoming "subject" to both their learning.

In addition, the conversation may further spur in the professor thoughts about a related conversation he had with a colleague two days earlier—or, for that matter, a talk he had with his own research mentor many years ago about a similar subject of study; both of those conversations, now the stuff of memory, were once as variously contextualized as the present-day interaction between the professor and his student. They also contextualize the professor's learning in the moment with his student. In this view the professor's learning of a single strand of his favored subject is situated, simultaneously, within multiple contexts, each bearing unique resources that constitute what the professor comes to know about his subject of study through the immediate context of his talk with the student.

A critic—perhaps an academic—might interrupt me at this point. "That's all fine," she might say, "but so what? What does all this context talk suggest for *my* scholarly learning—and for the scholarly learning of other professors?" Drawing on my presentation of study findings up to now, I would respond: "If we, as professors, want to expand our powers over *what we learn* so that we may more fully pursue our intellectual passions (thereby positioning ourselves to engage in scholarly learning), we must carefully choose, shape, or otherwise constitute the multiple sites of our learning of it, to the extent this is possible."

Becoming Strategic

Recently Tenured University Professors as Agents of Scholarly Learning

with KIMBERLEY B. PEREIRA

How can newly tenured university professors advance their scholarly learning amid the growing workloads—and learning loads—of the early post-tenure career? The answer to this question is both straightforward and complex: professors can advance their scholarly learning through this career phase by attending to it and by attending also to the contexts that sustain and shape it as well as those that thwart it. As chapter 4 indicates, the contexts that professors associate with their scholarly learning include academic activity (research, teaching, service), academic collectivity (community and colleague relations, locally or broadly), and personal life (personal reflection and memory, worldviews, personal relationships). This chapter takes this finding one step further to ask how professors may act within and on these contexts so as to advance their scholarly learning. What kinds of things can professors do—by way of constructing or reconstructing these contexts—to promote their work with the subject matters for which they care deeply, in effect to further their scholarly learning?

In an initial attempt to get at this question, Aimee LaPointe Terosky, Julie Schell, and I used *Four Universities Project* data to show that professors strive to resituate and advance their scholarly learning, after tenure, in very different ways. As evidence of this claim, Terosky, Schell, and I offered three contrasting images of professors' context construction (and reconstruction) efforts in support of their scholarly learning.[1] Building on this initial view, Kimberley B. Pereira and I analyzed the full range of actions that the project's forty professors said they took to build, rebuild, or improve the various contexts of their scholarly learning. We termed their largely self-willed and self-powered actions as acts of agency for scholarly learning.

Conceptualizing Agency for Professors' Scholarly Learning

Two terms help conceptualize how professors shape or otherwise arrange the contexts of their scholarly learning so as to maximize their pursuit of that learning: *agency* and *strategy*.

AGENCY FOR SCHOLARLY LEARNING

Agency, a term used by sociologists of the life course, responds to this question: how do individuals, who are themselves shaped by social-cultural forces, contribute to the "shaping back" of those forces, thereby taking part in the creation of the social contexts of their own development? The concept's analytic power lies in its melding of self and context, or in the words of Steven Hitlin and Glen H. Elder, in the bringing together of the "individual influences" and "structural pathways" that contribute to the shaping of a human life.[2] As Elder and Johnson put it, "Individuals construct their own life course through the choices and action they take within the opportunities and constraints of history and social circumstances."[3] But this intersection of person and place, self and context, is not mechanical. As Aaron M. Pallas explains, it must be understood as reflexive: individuals do not merely take social action; they take action that has meaning for them.[4] That meaning may be construed as what these individuals know already, what they want, what they value, and what they learn further as they act. Given the range of possibilities that this "subjectivity," as Pallas calls it, brings into play, professors, as producers of the contexts of their scholarly learning, are likely to vary in how they go about the task of context construction.

But why does it matter how professors construct their contexts—or even that they do? It matters because context often has the power to influence at least some of the content of professors' scholarly learning: something of context (be it a resource or a constraint) gets into the content to be learned. If a professor's selection of that content represents that individual's first step toward scholarly learning (as it must, given that scholarly learning is an expression of personal interest or desire to learn something in particular), then her selection of the contexts that help to constitute it cannot be too far behind.

A fair amount has been written to date about agency, but the term varies in meaning relative to whose agency is at stake and for what. As Pereira and I use the term in discussing newly tenured university professors' scholarly learning, agency entails a reflexive purposefulness, a thoughtful directedness born of personal desire and valuing. It entails an analytic awareness to possibility that professors propel reflectively, and often optimistically, into directed choice and action toward or within their scholarly learning. Agency may also reflect self-efficacy, a belief that one is able to act successfully toward one's intellectual desires, whether through substantive or instrumental action and whether with immediate or deferred rewards. Echoing the words of Victor W. Marshall, agency, broadly conceived, positions individuals as "not only produced by, but also produc[ing] their world," though in less than immediate or direct ways.[5] Rooted in learning, our view further assumes that the world that produces its actors is both availing and constrained, differentially so across time and in response to various events and actions; that the actors are themselves variously prepared and supported to produce their desired world, that they vary in the skills and insights they bring to their tasks of "world production"; and that both world and actors are subject to change in terms of what and how they produce and in how they are themselves produced.[6]

In sum, we define professors' *agency for scholarly learning* as their abilities and efforts to contribute productively to the construction or reconstruction of the contexts (environments, conditions, resources, activities, communities and collectives, opportunities, and so on) that situate and thereby shape their scholarly learning. In this view professors enact agency as they identify and bring into play research-, teaching-, mentoring-, service-, and outreach-based opportunities and resources for their scholarly learning or as they work at doing so.

STRATEGY

Strategy refers to professors' actions: paced, sequenced, and otherwise directed toward achieving specific desired ends, even as, at times, those ends shift. Strategy transforms professors' agency from abstract desire—to engage in scholarly learning—to specific action, thought through and pieced together yet revised as needed, so that professors may realize their desires concretely. Strategy emerges from desire, willful agency, and directed (ideally, reflective) action. It is proactive and optimistic, rooted in assumptions of self-efficacy and possibility. Thus, strategy activates agency.

In this view strategy assumes action and contemplation, forethought and retrospection, initiation and responsiveness. A strategy may be planful or created "in process," the product of "reflection in action," as Donald Schon calls it.[7] It is both analytic and creative, directed and flexible, forward-looking and considerate of past and current understanding. It experiments and evaluates; it involves risk. Much like narrative, strategy, once articulated, lets a professor look around and back and draw together what she sees to inform action; it is, therefore, watchful and synthetic. Targeted at university administrators and policy makers, studies of strategy in higher education have traditionally focused on how college and university organizations create their futures. But professors who strive to craft their own work lives in meaningful ways can also use it.[8] In this view strategy is part of a professor's story of her career in the making, with attention to all facets of narrative plot: valuing and desire, setting, character, relationship, event, challenge, risk, action, consequence, experience, reflection, realization, and voice.

QUALIFICATIONS

Although appealing, both agency and strategy must be put in perspective, their limitations noted. First, much like learning, agency and its enactment through strategy are incomplete without knowing what it is that they pertain to or are directed at. Thus, the question emphasized throughout this volume—"learning *what?*"—has its parallel in the questions of "agency for *what?*" and "strategy toward *what?*" For example, one may wield agency or strategy toward the creation of an administrative career or for that matter a personal life, inasmuch as for a scholarly one. This chapter's discussion is limited to agency and strategy in pursuit of scholarly learning in particular.

Second, this agency for scholarly learning, and its enactment through strategy, must be understood as a privileged good. As with particular literacies and skills, it is not distributed equally through the higher education community or in society. Some individuals may have been barred from it for much of their lives. Others may have had good access but little reason to use it.[9] Some may have been made well aware of its powers, others less so. Some individuals may, therefore, be more practiced in the uses of agency for their scholarly learning and in articulating their ways of using it. Professors' agency for their scholarly learning is hardly one thing; professors may enact it, strategically, in different ways.

Enactments of Agency for Scholarly Learning: Professors' Strategies

To define newly tenured university professors' enactments of agency in support of their scholarly learning, Pereira and I searched participants' descriptions of their subject matter commitments and scholarly learning for evidence of: involvement in the construction, reconstruction, or adjustment of the common contexts of professors' scholarly learning (teaching, research, service, outreach, colleague relations and community, and personal life); a purposefulness of action reflective of desire and valuing; and assumptions of self-efficacy in situations that avail and constrain opportunity for scholarly learning. We identified nine approaches that professors used to enact agency for their scholarly learning. We further grouped the nine approaches relative to the key thematic action implied, deriving three overarching strategies for enacting scholarly learning: creating space; containing attention; and connecting contexts. Approximately 80 percent of the participating professors used one or more of these strategies to pursue their scholarly learning.[10] The remainder of this chapter describes these strategies relative to the component approaches of each. Table 5.1 provides a summary overview.

STRATEGY: CREATING SPACE

Approximately three-quarters of the study's forty participants presented themselves as creating space for their scholarly learning. Use of this strategy entailed clearing out and revamping unsupportive workspaces or moving to new ones; engendering opportunities for substantive interchange; or building communities for substantive interchange over time.

TABLE 5.1 Strategies for Agentic Scholarly Learning and Approaches to Their Enactment

Strategy	Approaches to Enactment
Creating space	— Clearing out a workspace or distancing oneself from a workspace that diminishes scholarly learning or that does not adequately support it; revamping that workspace or relocating one's scholarly learning to a new one.
	— Engendering opportunities for interchange toward scholarly learning, for example, by building collaborative relationships with peers, students, mentors.
	— Building communities for interchange conducive to scholarly learning.
Containing attention	— Focusing on those facets of one's scholarly learning (usually in research or creative endeavor) that are most personally meaningful and viable, and setting aside, for some time, others that are less so.
	— Positioning oneself to engage in service or administration that supports scholarly learning and setting aside service/administrative work that does not.
	— Decentering one's career, including one's scholarly learning: attending to career, including scholarly learning, as but a single though valued strand of a broader, more complex life whose other contents are of equal or greater value.
Connecting contexts	— Using scholarly learning to connect teaching (or mentoring) with research, creative endeavor, or other scholarly activity, with the aim of enriching knowledge construction through work with students.
	— Using scholarly learning, alive in one's research or other scholarly study, to frame institutional, public, or professional service, so as to advance one's understanding of one's core subject of study.
	— Using scholarly learning to connect one's profession to one's life and possibly to the lives of others who may gain from that learning (e.g., one's readers, beneficiaries of service, colleagues, students). This may entail using learning drawn from one's life to enrich scholarly learning in research, teaching, service, or outreach. It also may entail using scholarly learning derived through research or other academic activities to enrich one's life.

Source: Four Universities Project interviews conducted in year 1 (*n* = 40) and year 3 (*n* = 39).

Clearing out a Workspace

Professors who sought to clear out and rebuild the spaces of their scholarly learning—uprooting distraction and irrelevance, revamping the infrastructure of their day-to-day work and sometimes that of their students and colleagues, or, alternatively, considering relocation to a more supportive workspace—focused on the organization of academic work. They spoke of taking actions such as redesigning the academic programs of which they were now senior members and leaders and focusing on strengthening the match between their work activities (research, teaching, service, and outreach) and the content of their scholarly learning. They moved their scholarly learning from its current less-than-productive positioning to a space that promised to be more conducive to it (for example, from research to teaching, from one colleague community to another, or from one employing university to another). They sought to improve the match between what they needed for their scholarly learning and what the environments in which they worked could provide. Professors' representations of clearing and revamping their work sites revealed an even greater variety of experiences.

Carmen Elias-Jones, the professor of music at Signal University featured in chapter 2, exemplifies the thoughtful use of the strategy of creating space. As Elias-Jones pursued beauty and feeling in musical performance and teaching, she also faced the very real—and demanding—calls of her job as a now-tenured associate professor. With her newly realized responsibility as a tenured member of the music faculty, Elias-Jones committed herself to improving the music program's capacity to fend off distractions to her own and her colleagues' and students' scholarly learning in music. She also sought to enrich the program's musical resources, thereby expanding opportunities for all its members' learning of music. To achieve these aims, Elias-Jones introduced an electronic platform, computer mediated, to support faculty and student communication and musical activity coordination. She also led in developing a new music fellowship and instituted a seasonal performance series to intensify program members' musical involvement. Through these actions Elias-Jones cleared out distracting workplace "noise" (communication and coordination mishaps) and set in place a much improved communication network (the electronic platform) and financial support opportunities (fellowships). At the same time, she added in substantive resources (performance series) toward program members' learning and creative activity. Thus, Elias-Jones cleared out space in the day-to-day functioning of her program while adding in resources (in the form of financial support and musical opportunities) to enhance music as the subject of shared community engagement.[11]

Matt Birand, a social scientist at Horizon University, also sought to create space for his scholarly learning. But rather than striving to improve his program's work flow, as did Elias-Jones, he changed what he did in the name of scholarship. He made this change out of intellectual interest and personal need: Birand's long-term program of research—and the scholarly learning that it has yielded for him—required that he travel internationally for extended periods of time. The travel pulled him away from home, a situation that, by the time of the interviews, had become untenable given changes in his family life. Birand felt caught between commitment to research-based scholarly learning and a desire to remain connected to his family, both deeply important to him. "When I'm here [in the United States,]" he said: "I'm thinking about this [the research and writing]. And when I'm there [in the field], I'm thinking about [my family life]."

Birand chose to stay home and to revamp his research but without giving up his scholarly learning. Hanging tight to its core substance—topics he had long pursued and wanted to continue studying—he created alternative ways to collect data abroad. In doing so, he indeed "cleared out" his obligations to extended international travel. Although it was challenging to coordinate, the approach promised success. Birand took a calculated risk, and worked at it.

Simultaneously, Birand rethought his approach to publication, which, in the past, had followed disciplinary tradition: submission of research articles to scholarly journals, writing academic books for social scientists. With tenure in hand, he turned to writing, in his words, "readable books," appealing to large sectors of an increasingly educated public. He taught himself to pitch his key ideas and findings to that public in ways its members could understand but without watering down content. In his final interview Birand referred to this new branch of his career as writing "science for the public," and he explained, "I think [there's now] an increased interest in [the] representation to the public of scientific knowledge." Thus, Birand identified a "lay" audience responsive to his scholarly learning and a publisher willing to promote it. Most important, Birand found that his new approach to writing—the creation of scientific meaning for a public that wants to understand it in depth—promoted his scholarly learning, unexpectedly, in "harder" and "more creative" ways than had his earlier, more traditional approach:

I got enthused about writing that way . . . Partly, it's a nice second income. But it was the challenge . . . it's just harder. It's . . . more creative, and it's simply harder . . . It [is] . . . taking a journal article, or taking fifty journal articles, and trying to distill the message [so] that a well-read interested person could read and really . . . get a lot out of. It was just really hard. It was the balance between being dry and technical and being fluffy and lightweight . . . really hard to strike . . . I'll write a page, and I'll look at it . . . on the screen, and I'll say, "This is just total crap . . . it just feels icky to write . . . You're pandering to the public." And so then I'll rip it up. I'll cut it out and then write it again. And then it sounds too technical . . . too many jargony [words]. And then [I'll] go back and have to find that balance . . . It's really tough . . . really hard, just plain hard.

As Birand wrote for his new audience, he challenged himself to talk about his long-term subject of study in new ways to people who wanted more than "fluffy" understanding. Those people sought new meanings, fresh thoughts, in words they could grasp—ideas for rethinking their worlds and lives. The task required Birand to engage in new and different talk and thought: he had to imagine and articulate his subject in novel, understandable, and as he said, intellectually honest ways—avoiding both jargon and fluff. He described the work as "just plain hard," as challenging his scholarly thought and thus spurring his learning.

Birand "cleared out" a research corner of his career, making room for new kinds of writing about his long-term subjects of study. As he said in his final interview, the change did not come easily; he worked hard at it. Neither was it risk-free. He worried at times how seriously his disciplinary peers would take his project of writing "readable books" about his subject of study. "It's really amazing," he said as we reviewed the niche into which he had steered his scholarly learning, and referring to his emergent "science for the public" effort, he added, "Everyone of us has colleagues who scorn that kind of thing." Drawing on the intense pleasure he found in this new approach to social science writing—in effect, a new context for his scholarly learning—and despite the risks of colleague critique that it augured, Birand created space for it in his dawning post-tenure career.

Nina Altman, the Libra State University professor of literary studies introduced in chapter 1, also made good use of the strategy of creating space for her scholarly learning but in ways that responded to her unique needs. Rather than revamping her academic program so as to make room for scholarly learning, as did Elias-Jones, or designing an altogether new approach to research, as did Birand, Altman did something even more basic: she revamped her teaching files. But revamping entailed a great deal more than moving around lecture notes or reorganizing journals and books to make them more accessible. Rather, Altman threw out her teaching notes—discarded most of her carefully worked-over teaching materials, all remnants of past work—positioning herself, post-tenure, to start out fresh. Although she was highly regarded for her intellectual accomplishments, Altman chose to remake the researcher identity she had cultivated purposefully at Libra State pre-tenure. After getting tenure, she became a teacher.

What of her scholarly learning? Post-tenure, Altman's scholarly learning continued full force. Other than the insights she continued to gain, on themes of literary translation, little about it changed, except its location: Altman moved her learning of the subjects she cared for deeply to her teaching. What was she up to? Altman had come to Libra State University years earlier as an experienced assistant professor, having taught in a four-year college that was strongly attentive to students' learning. Although responding successfully to the demands of the research university to which she had moved pre-tenure, she chose through her early post-tenure career to reverse, strategically, that earlier decision. She missed the teaching as well as the scholarly learning that the teaching had once inspired in her.

> One of the . . . things I did . . . [right after getting tenure] in addition to . . . clearing out my files and brainstorming about new projects, is I tried to focus in on . . . how to reclaim pleasure from teaching because I came from [a job in a teaching college several] years ago with a sense that teaching there really mattered and that students were passionately involved with teaching. And I came here, and before tenure, I felt like teaching always got second shrift—that it was always on borrowed time, that although teaching is valued here . . . what was most important was to get my

research done. And I couldn't devote as much time or care to my teaching as I'd like. That took away my sense of satisfaction and engagement with the students . . . I was so exhausted, I couldn't function well—I couldn't grade papers on time . . . I missed deadlines. It was very hard. I think I was just exhausted.

So last year [with tenure in hand,] I replenished . . . and I decided that my top priority was going to be to work with the graduate students because that was [where I would] reclaim the pleasure and the intensity that I had with [undergraduate students at my previous institution]. Because the graduate students here are very motivated and very smart, and they're getting better all the time. And so . . . this year, I've designed all new courses . . . I threw away a lot of my old materials and just started from scratch with new courses in order to force myself not to go through the routine. But [rather,] to . . . be involved in rediscovering something in the classroom. And so I'm not teaching my [previous] course anymore, although I have little bits [of it] here and there in my other classes.

As mundane—though risky—as Altman's space-clearing actions appear, they echo the larger scope of reconstructive action that Elias-Jones and Birand undertook: like them, she cleared away material she viewed as distracting to her scholarly learning. "I didn't go anywhere [through my recent research leave]," she said. "I stayed here and . . . spent time . . . clearing out my files . . . just trying to get . . . my life in order so that I can just do more of what I was already doing." Altman revamped the meaning of teaching in her career.

In each of these examples a scholar uproots and reconstructs long-established work practices: Elias-Jones uproots and remakes the infrastructure of her academic program; Birand replaces a long-familiar mode of research representation (writing for scholarly peers) with another riskier form (writing for educated nonspecialist audiences) as he also changes his approaches to data collection; and Altman uproots her pre-tenure teaching materials, recrafting them to align with the teaching-based scholarship in which she engaged years back. These three examples suggest that each scholar clears a space filled with activities that had served the scholar well for years but that, post-tenure, were failing to support scholarly learning.

Each professor strives to recreate the academic activities that contextualize their own (and sometimes their colleagues' and students') scholarly learning. In doing so, each scholar shapes her context to support or improve her scholarly learning, to render it meaningful. In a word, none of the three made changes simply for the sake of cleaning up and rebuilding their approaches to work. They clear out distraction and revamp the contexts of their scholarly learning so that they can engage their scholarly learning as directly as possible.

Engendering Opportunities for Interchange toward Scholarly Learning

In addition to clearing and revamping existing spaces, thereby re-creating them, professors may create brand new ones, for example by opening up opportunities for substantive collaboration. Within these "new" spaces, professors work with colleagues, students, and others who they define as colearners or as supporters of their scholarly development.

Les Thompson, a professor of business at Signal University, spoke at length about his research partnership with a campus colleague whose scholarly interests and expertise lie in a different but complementary business specialty. Their relationship, now several years in the making, has been fruitful for them both: they have taught each other through this period by drawing from the fields and specialties each knows well. They have also collaborated in learning about topics that neither has fully understood, for example, as they have stumbled across issues new to each of their fields. To learn Thompson and his colleague engaged in collaborative cross-field research. Thompson described how this collaborative relationship began and what it has yielded over time: "[A colleague] had a guest speaker [in] one of his classes. I showed up, and that's how the paper got started. That's how I met him because I was new . . . and he had been around for a while . . . It was a . . . topic that both of us wanted to research, but . . . (a), hadn't quite found the right way to do it, and (b), he needed [my specialty] to do the paper, and I clearly needed [his]. So . . . we couldn't have done it without the other person. So we got lucky. I learned a lot of [his subject matter] in the process. Hopefully, he learned some [of mine]." In joining up for collaboration, two colleagues representing different subfields created a work space, literally a new work environment, within which they could collaborate on research and, in doing so, support each other's scholarly learning.

Although most professors who used this approach to create space for their scholarly learning relied heavily on colleagues in their own institutions, as did Thompson, some sought out colleagues in other locations. An anthropologist at Libra State University spoke of her multiyear "great collaboration" with a disciplinary colleague at a university across the country. And a mathematician, also at Libra State, said, of her round-the-globe collaborations, "I'm very happy [collaborating] by email," comments echoed by numerous others: a chemist at Hope State University, a philosopher at Libra State, a social scientist at Signal, an engineer at Horizon. As expected, the majority described collaborative networks consisting of academic colleagues, but professors in applied and professional fields also included narratives of collaboration with practitioners: teachers in schools, managers and specialists in business and industry, leaders and policy makers in communities and government. As a professor of social work said of his engagement with community members and leaders, "I'm right in the thick of it."

Still others looked to their students for substantive colleagueship in support of their scholarly learning. A recently tenured professor of educational studies at Hope State University, William Alana, relishes the questions his students ask. Those questions, he said, "they stay with me. They're very provocative. Very provocative. [It's an] ongoing . . . regularly surprising source . . . Questions that I sometimes feel like I've forgotten to ask. Or that the whole [academic] community, in some ways, is forgetting to ask." Asked who he talks to about his scholarship, Alana responds: "The first two groups that come to mind would be definitely my peers in the field . . . And then the other—Where do I go to talk about the things I read, or live questions or conundrums even, or puzzles? I go to my students . . . I find myself doing that increasingly over these years." Alana relies on peers' reflections on his work, but he also turns to his students for insights, fresh turns of mind on ideas that, like them, he puzzles over, striving to understand deeply.

What is evident in each of these cases is that interaction around a subject of study constitutes the space, brief or long-lasting, within which scholarly learning can occur. Such interaction is, therefore, a primary context for professors' scholarly learning.

Building Communities for Interchange Conducive to Scholarly Learning

Recently tenured professors participating in the study occasionally identified spaces for their scholarly learning exceeding one-to-one interactions. Referred to as communities or groups, these larger spaces often promised greater continuity, protection, resources for substantive growth, and opportunities for relationship and identification. Although rarely built into the bureaucratic structure of the university (though some were), these collectives helped scholars to reimagine the social spaces in which they carried out their work and at times to expand their community affiliations, officially or not. For example, a professor organizationally associated with a comparative literature department might identify also as a member of a long-term but informal feminist reading and writing group offering her knowledge, inspiration, and friendship. She might value the group's offerings to her scholarly learning, and scholarly identity, as much or more so than those of her home department. As they entered a community, defined as a collective space, professors typically brought their scholarly learning into contact with that community's knowledge resources. Membership in the community offered a professor access to these resources, though requiring that the professor also provide access to co-members from her own. These continuing, sometimes complex communities worked when members felt that the collective's resources related to their own learning interests, when they sensed opportunities to build meaning within them.

Study participants described a variety of such communities that they and others created, often informally, though amid the demands of university organization, sometimes within departments and schools or beyond them. Serena Mandell, a historian at Libra State University, describes her experience in two such groups: a mixed-gender departmental reading group and a cross-departmental women's writing group:

> SM: [In the departmental] reading group I belong to . . . I like reading or hearing work that has nothing to do with my own interest . . . My research is important to me, [but] it's not . . . the only [subject] that I enjoy thinking about . . . I like learning new things . . . that I have no particular use for. So . . . when we're reading [in the departmental group, on *my* research topic], I think, "Aw, well, I'd

have to read that anyway. Make me read something [in a different field.]"

AN: You mentioned the reading group. Is that a —

SM: That's [a group associated with the history department]—although it's—held off campus, and is defiantly nonofficial, and began well before my time as a semi-secret, members-only, leftist reading group. Over time it's gotten looser, partly because people's politics have . . . shifted around . . . It's still . . . distinctly left . . . When it began, people felt more in opposition, and they don't necessarily anymore, so that it's more open . . . And it's not like a standing invitation that someone could just show up at [colleague's] house . . . on a Sunday night . . . But it's not exclusive, and they're bright . . . that's a really . . . fun group.

AN: So you've been a part of it for some time?

SM: Four years or five years now. And I'm in a small writing group with someone in [philosophy] and someone in [education]—all of us [in that group] are women, which is also lots of fun.

AN: That's [a] different [group]?

SM: Yeah, that's a writing group where we really read each other's works over and over, and you know [what an] improvement it can make—that people are willing to read your draft and then read the revised draft and read the revised-revised draft . . . Trying to be clear to people across disciplinary lines means that you really talk about the ideas as well as about the writing, rather than a writing group just of historians, [which is] less useful to me.

AN: So you can look at it from these different ——

SM: It brings the ideas to the fore because instead of being about "How is this position [taken up] within [my area of study]?" it's "What do you mean by [your use of the word] *agency?*" Or "What do you mean by your use of this argument?" or "How does the structure of this work ——?"

Mandell creates spaces for her own work, and the work of others with whom she aligns, by contributing to the efforts of two long-term colleague groups, one committed to understanding certain views of history (the group of historians) and another committed to improving individual members' knowledge construction (the group of women scholars).

Both groups offer a density of knowledge resources—here resources for knowing in particular scholarly ways—on which individual members can draw. This density of knowledge resources—contributed, created, and exchanged over time—marks each group as a community of practice.[12] Meetings are opportunities to focus group members' attention onto particular ideas or questions with which a member may be struggling. Individual members stand to gain from the effort as they bring to the group the puzzles, ideas, and questions on their minds.

Other examples of groups for scholarly learning stand out in the study sample. Stan Weaver, a political scientist at Horizon University, participates regularly in a small (8- to 10-member) monthly informal cross-departmental colleague reading group resembling that of Serena Mandell at Libra State. Ted Wilson, a philosopher at Libra State University, also participates in an interdisciplinary group—formally defined and funded and much larger (over 75 members)—assembling regularly to explore topics that bear closely on Wilson's scholarly learning. Groups such as those described by Mandell, Weaver, and Wilson support discussions, flows of thought, that over time respond to and inspire scholarly curiosity, imagination, and interest. In this sense they are spaces of knowledge creation, of scholarly learning. The scholar who brings her substantive puzzles to her group's attention stands to learn, as do those who think with her in group meetings.

STRATEGY: CONTAINING ATTENTION

To contain is to hold, bound, and frame judiciously in light of one's efforts to engage in scholarly learning. *Containment,* as we use the term, emphasizes *what* is to be contained and why, given one's scholarly goals. Usually what is contained is a strand or two of a profusion of activity, all of which cannot be held together at one time. In containment professors must choose which strands of their learning, service, and lives they will restrict their attention to, given the vast array of possibilities.

About two-thirds of the participating professors used this strategy for shaping their early post-tenure work, notably by containing their attention, judiciously, to: selected facets of research; selected facets of service and/or administrative work; and career, defined as but a single facet of a larger life, some of whose other facets merit far more attention than does career. Professors using this strategy struggled with these tasks: where to draw boundaries; what to keep within one's bounded span of attention, energy, and care; and what to attend to less fully.

Focusing on the Most Meaningful Facets of One's Scholarly Learning, Especially in Research

One of the more challenging career activities to contain is research, especially for professors who are deeply committed to their studies and whose identities are rooted in the learning of their subject matters. Consider, for example, what it takes to restrain attention to subjects that have for years stirred the kinds of passionate thought about which Carmen Elias-Jones, the musician, and David Mora, the astronomer, spoke in chapter 2. Research containment requires judicious withholding and focusing, including disciplined review of the "all-out" passionate pursuit of one's learning: it entails curtailing and shaping one's scholarly learning, or pacing it, deciding what one will not pursue at a certain point in time so that one can pursue something more meaningful. Such choices are never easy, especially so when "what's deferred" feels like it is part and parcel of "what's desired."

Taking on major program and college responsibilities right after receiving tenure, Benjamin Lucas, a social scientist at Signal University, worried about how to keep his scholarly learning alive amid rapidly escalating administrative responsibilities. Asked in study year 3 about increases in his university service, he quipped: "I wouldn't say that it went up. I would say that it landed like a piano on my back . . . I didn't feel that I was in a position to say no." Limiting service was not an option for Lucas, given his program's administrative design and his own sense of responsibility to it: it was his turn so he would do it. Lucas responded to the post-tenure challenge of increased service and administrative responsibility with a research containment strategy: he bounded his scholarly commitments, only taking on projects related to his core interest and methodological expertise. He pursued this contained research agenda with great energy. Lucas's research containment strategy led to success, even amid his growing administrative work. He completed several long-term research projects and initiated a new study that relied on frames and methods he had sharpened and polished over the years. But he was worried. Had he found a research "hammer," as he called it, that let him hit, perpetually, only the same kind of "nail"—namely, the bounded research questions and methods that he used time and again? In the face of narrow repetition, what kind of expertise was he developing? In his third post-tenure year Lucas pondered how to balance a strategy of research containment with his need to grow beyond what he already knew.[13]

Professor David Mora, the Libra State University astronomer who described the beauty of the stars and of beauty's meaning through his scientific career, spoke in his final interview of a need to contain his research agenda—but for a reason that differed from that of Benjamin Lucas. Mora's research ballooned as he moved into his early post-tenure years. Upon completing one of his key projects, he prepared to start up another, representing a related but new (and in his case different) line of work. Mora was well funded for both lines of work and at the time of the interviews felt no calls to service or administration.

Yet he wondered how wise it would be for him to take on the new work at this point in his career. Would he be able to handle it all without sacrificing one line of work to the other? Mora pondered the implications of committing full force to a brand new energy- and time-absorbing project, intimidating in scale, before fully completing previous undertakings. The older work, he worried, might never get done, or it might get done partially given the demands of the new research, itself a fascinating distraction from the old. How could he balance them so as to give his best to both? Mora addressed this challenge by positioning the older work as a "brake" on the unfolding of the new. To do this, he kept his students involved in the previous work while initiating on his own the newer line. In doing this, he ensured continuation of his learning in the older work while sensibly pacing his entry into the learning of the new.

> AN: You've moved from project to project . . . as you said, [you're] not . . . [wanting to make] major leaps and turns . . .
>
> DM: That's right . . . I think that's very clearly the strategy . . . you don't want to completely abandon everything that you've learned . . . one always feels maybe a little bit intimidated [by the new research possibilities] . . .
>
> AN: So what you're working on right now . . . ?
>
> DM: Pretty much all the above [i.e., old and new projects]. I really haven't dropped too many [of my previous projects] . . . Some stu-

dents of mine are working on those [older projects] . . . [I'm] very
actively working on the [new].

Like Lucas, Mora invoked a strategy of contained attention to research,
but he did so for a different end and a different reason: he sought to
control the process and pacing of substantive change in his research and,
more deeply, in his scholarly learning. Lucas, in contrast, sought continuity and, quite simply, scholarly survival.

Positioning Oneself to Engage in Service or Administration that Supports Scholarly Learning

Not surprisingly, many study participants sought to reduce their growing service responsibilities through the early post-tenure career.[14] Some,
however, took a different step, selecting themselves into service projects
that helped them organize their time so they could devote substantial
amounts of it to their scholarly learning. Or they chose new service that,
they sensed, would facilitate their accomplishment of still other service to
which they were already committed and that, in the longer run of their
careers, promised to let them devote more time to their scholarly learning.
Or they committed themselves to service whose content paralleled that
of their scholarly learning, thereby supporting their research or teaching
quite directly (see the discussion of scholarly learning in service in chap.
4). In these views expanding service responsibilities helped professors advance their careers rather than obstructing them. The cases of Serena
Mandell and Belinda Lessard illustrate these approaches.

The historian Serena Mandell, portrayed earlier as a contributor to
informal communities of scholarly practice, relied on the following approach to the management of her growing service load: she recast an
otherwise burdensome departmental service responsibly as a boon to her
research and indirectly to her scholarly learning. Partway through our
final interview Mandell began describing the gigantic labor entailed in
service on her department's personnel review committee, including the
thousands of pages of reading that this committee service required, for
example, through promotion and tenure reviews and faculty searches.
Although concerned about her rapidly expanding service workload,
Mandell reflected on what she was gaining from her experience on the
personnel review committee, which, she said, she took very seriously:

SM: In a twisted kind of way I like [service on the personnel commit-tee]. I like it because if you're doing it, you can't do anything else, so no one expects you to do anything else. If you're on it, you're not on six other trivial little committees. You're only doing the one big thing. And I also like it because it all matters. It's not . . . ad-ministration in the dull sense of the word. And I also like it because it's mostly stuff I'm reasonably competent at. I can read people's work and think about it and talk about it . . . I can . . . do a budget if I had to, but I don't have a talent for it, I'm not good at it, and I would really not feel confident at it. So . . . it's heavy service, but it's not the kind of service that I would hate. I'd much rather do this than be on . . . committee[s] where you deal with . . . restruc-turing graduate funding or things like that, that are perhaps also important but don't appeal to me. So that's like the big institutional involvement.

AN: So after tenure, [your] service responsibilities went up.

SM: Yeah. But it's okay.

For Mandell, like a number of other scholars in the study sample, service increases were hard ("heavy" as she said), but they felt "okay" because they addressed content that, as Mandell put it, she did not "hate." In fact, she gave several reasons for liking the particular service she had chosen: it displaced less desirable tasks ("if you're doing it, you can't do anything else"); it consolidated the energies she owed to service into one project (the personnel review committee work) rather than dispers-ing these across many ("you're not on six other . . . trivial little commit-tees . . . Only doing the one big thing"); service on the personnel review committee required use of her already developed talents and skills ("it's mostly stuff I'm reasonably competent at"); and the work felt important to her and to the university ("I also like it because it all matters").

Belinda Lessard, a professor in the humanities at Hope State Univer-sity, offered a similar strategy, yet in the context of her program coordi-nation responsibilities, it led her to a far broader band of institutional involvement than that described by Mandell. Asked how involved she was in campus-based service through her early post-tenure career, Les-sard replied: "I could best say . . . that I'm selfishly involved. Anything that involves [my academic] program I will be interested in. If it doesn't, I really can't say that I'm all that interested—unless it starts to impact work conditions for all of us . . . So the things that I volunteer for, and that I really want to do, have to do with [my] program. I begged to be put as the chair of this search committee [in my department] . . . I was two years on the graduate studies committee because I was intensely interested in being there . . . when the decisions are made for who to admit [to programs]." Although Mandell liked her service because "hard duty" on a single committee kept her energies from being overly dispersed, Lessard liked hers because the many (and diverse) tasks that she took on addressed her goal of program improvement. Both scholars arranged their service so as to make more room for their scholarly learning: Mandell by organizing her time, Lessard by organizing space for her own (and others') subject matter work to be realized. In this sense these two scholars' containment activities resonate, at least in tone, with the kinds of space-creating activities in which Carmen Elias-Jones engaged at Signal University: they made room for scholarly learning in their lives. Together, the examples of Mandell and Lessard suggest that to pursue a strategy of contained attention to service is to design one's service—to choose and shape it, to make sense of it, to use it—as carefully as one would research, shaving away the irrelevant and distracting, drawing in the meaningful.

Decentering One's Career and Scholarly Learning
Both men and women spoke of growing needs to contain their careers sensibly, not allowing them to overrun their personal lives. The concern about containing career was poignant in professors' comments about the birth and upbringing of children, desires to spend time with other family members, and, for some, regrouping after divorce.

Asked in her third post-tenure year to describe how important her research is to her, Katherine Winters, a scientist at Horizon University, briskly replied, "I have two small children, one is three and the other is five months, so at this moment . . . [research] is not particularly important to me." Surprised perhaps at her own candor in the interview, she added, with a laugh: "I said [that] somewhat tongue and cheek. It is, of course, [important]. I mean, the reason most people get into science and academia is that they love research, and I do, I do, I do love research, but it is not [like] initially a fresh young Ph.D. [whereby] 'Ah, research is everything!'" Asked two years later, in her fifth post-tenure year, how she thought about the place of her scholarly work in her life, she replied in much the same way, "It's one of four or five things that I value." "Are you able to say what some of those other ones are?" I asked. "Oh, yeah," she said, "My children. My broader family. Broader family and friends. Community things. And it may sound silly, but I exercise a lot . . . fitness is very important to me so that . . . definitely [is] one of the four."

Although family commitments, like those that Winters voiced, are often ascribed to women, a number of men in the study voiced them as well, in fact more openly so.[15] Asked how important his research is to him, David Mora, the astronomer at Libra State University who spoke in chapter 2 of his intense attraction to the night sky, said: "That's changed a lot over the years . . . because . . . I have different important features of my life now . . . I have my kids, and the time they take . . . that's a balancing act. I've realize[d] you can't be too over-consumed by the research aspect [of your career] because then you really will get into . . . a one-dimensional state. So there are just other outside interests . . . I think you have to have them as well." Although he is absorbed by his research, Mora wants to do more in his life than act "one-dimensionally" through research.

Like David Mora, George Bellanov, a professor of social work at Libra State University, has crafted a career that is deeply anchored in his life. As such, his professional efforts are sometimes hard to distinguish from the personal. Bellanov described the relation between his work and life:

> I think about it [my career, research and teaching especially] as an important part of my life. It . . . allows me to contribute in ways that I think are important. But do I hold work as [what's most important]? I guess there are different ways of thinking about work. Some people work to support their families. Some people work because that's what's most important. You know what I mean? So, I see work as an important part of my life, but it's not the most important. While I'm here [in the office,] I try to maximize it. I mean, I push it . . . [I] do the very best I can. I have certain policies . . . for example, I won't do work on the weekend. So, Friday night is, "Put everything aside," and maybe Sunday I may pick up something and say, "Okay, am I ready for Monday?" But if I'm not ready by Friday, sometimes I just say, "Okay, we'll see what happens"—but only because I want to focus on family.

Bellanov cherishes his career and the privilege it gives him to pursue, as fully as possible, professional work he values. Yet he also knows that to create a meaningful life he cannot focus on work alone. He respects other sides of his existence, notably by dedicating himself to a family life that expresses still greater meanings to him. Bellanov returns to his family and to himself personally for that.

A number of study participants with families, especially those with young children, portrayed themselves as feeling challenged in their efforts to advance their scholarly work while curbing its incursions into family life. Yet even those who said little or nothing about the complexities of raising children or caring for aging family members described efforts to temper the hold that career and learning could have on them personally. Asked how she thinks about scholarly learning in the broader context of her life, Marissa Velez, the psychologist in Hope State University's School of Business who used a year's leave to reconstitute her scholarly learning, explained, "It is my life," and in the same breath, "I don't want it to be" (see chap. 4) "I don't know how to relax," she said. "I think balance is what I need to achieve . . . [I need to] figure out things . . . in life that I want . . . I don't know what that is yet." And at Signal University Carmen Elias-Jones, caught up in the "gamut of emotions" that her music evokes in her, also spoke of distinct needs, "in the space of one week or two weeks, [to] have a music free day."

Scholars such as Winters, Mora, Bellanov, Velez, and Elias-Jones love their scholarly learning, whether it is situated in their research, creative effort, teaching, or something else. Yet they are learning, or have learned, that to have their scholarly loves, they must have larger lives—and larger loves—within which to situate their scholarly efforts. When career threatens to become larger than life itself, these scholars seek to contain it, shifting their attention to lives that, in their view, matter more and in fact make their careers possible.

STRATEGY: CONNECTING CONTEXTS

As discussed in chapter 4, professors feel the presence of their scholarly learning in various contexts, notably in the academic activities of teaching, research, service, and outreach. What that view did not consider, however, is whether and how a professor's scholarly learning connects across these activity contexts—for example, across research and teaching, outreach and research, service and research. About 80 percent of the professors participating in the study referred to such connection, describing it as tight in some cases (as when a professor's teaching openly advances her research) and in others as loose though palpable (as when a professor's subject matter learning, occurring in her teaching, expands her frame of reference but without touching on the specifics of her research existing at some distance from her teaching).

What might the strategy of *connecting contexts,* directed at enhancing a professor's scholarly learning, look like in the ideal? Professor Elizabeth Ferrara at Horizon University comes close. Ferrara uses her scholarly learning agenda, in policy studies, to frame and link her research, teaching, and outreach while striving to heighten the integrity and unique offerings of each of these activities for the diverse audiences toward which, by definition, they are directed. She threads consistently a single line of subject matter learning, in policy studies, through distinctive work activities while respecting, and even seeking to improve each activity for what it is uniquely. Ferrara's teaching, research, and outreach remain very much in the form of teaching, research, and outreach—none collapse into the other. But each reflects, distinctively, her particular policy interests. What emerges for Ferrara is a set of different work activities, held together, much like pearls on a necklace, by a common thread of scholarly learning.[16]

In brief Ferrara uses her scholarly learning to connect various professional activities, each conceptualized as a context of her scholarly learning. Most study participants tried to forge similar connections, but few did so as pervasively as she did. Most of them used this strategy more narrowly, striving to connect no more than two of their academic activities at a time (rather than three—research, teaching, public service—as Ferrara did). Many shaped their scholarly learning so as to connect the following pairings of context, or features thereof: teaching with research, or mentoring with research; internal or external service tasks, including outreach/community service, with scholarly study including research; or profession with life itself.

Connecting Teaching (or Mentoring) with Scholarly Activity
Professors participating in the *Four Universities Project* viewed their research and teaching (undergraduate and graduate, including substantive

mentoring) as being connected when their scholarly learning in one activity extended, supported, or simply resonated with scholarly learning in the other. To put it another way, scholars sensed cross-activity connection when the intellectual content of one activity (teaching or research) converged somehow with that of the other. Serena Mandell and Emily Lifton's experiences are prime examples.

Asked to describe the fit between her research and teaching (undergraduate in this case), Mandell, a historian at Libra State University, said that for her the two "go together well." Encouraged to say more, she explained that this happens because she treats her teaching, much as she does her research, as a site of her scholarly learning: "[A] reason why the two [teaching and research] . . . go together for me is that I see teaching as creative, and particularly lecturing or undergraduate teaching in general. [But] not just the lecturing . . .[rather,] the putting together [of] the readings and the shaping of a course feels to me like a creative intellectual act, or set of acts. When I write a lecture—maybe not every lecture, but a fair proportion of my lectures—I see [that] as intellectually engaging, and as creative, as writing my own stuff . . . So that I don't feel like in one part of my life, I'm a creative intellectual and in another part, I'm a . . . human tape recorder." Mandell said that what lets her teaching feel so linked to her research is that she herself uses the teaching to learn substance much as her students do. Mandell thus experiences herself as constructing subject matter knowledge in her teaching just as she does in her research. All the more intriguing is that Mandell teaches undergraduates, large classrooms filled with students reflecting diverse interests. She is not talking about her experiences in a doctoral seminar or lab.

Lifton, a professor of environmental engineering at Signal University, makes this point more strongly, possibly because she speaks about teaching that, by definition, is more closely aligned with research, namely the substantive mentoring of doctoral students. To Lifton doctoral mentoring and research, though distinctive, are intertwined: both require close attention to the construction of field-based knowledge, and both reflect substantive learning. Asked whether she views her doctoral students as influencing her scholarship, Lifton exclaimed, "Oh, sure, absolutely," then added:

For us [in the pure/applied sciences], we can't do our research without students. With us, it's—my God, our students are every-

thing. And even in [classroom] teaching . . . they'll ask me questions, and I'll never have thought of it that way. I'll think, "God,
that's so interesting. I never thought of it like that" . . . Have they
influenced me? . . . Sure, absolutely . . . I mean, every one of my
papers is coauthored with a student, and so they teach me things
all the time, absolutely, and . . . in fact, [the students] have to lead
a lot of this because otherwise . . . I have so much to do [that] if
they weren't leading and teaching me . . . But that's the nature of
doing research in the physical sciences . . . it's highly collaborative
with your students, and they're really on the front lines. I have the
big picture that they don't usually have. But while I give them the
big picture, they're giving me the . . . detailed picture of things.
So . . . it's very important.

Lifton points out that her learning in her research is closely aligned with
her learning through her doctoral mentoring (i.e., her learning in the
teaching of research to her doctoral students). Although the research and
doctoral mentoring overlap, they remain distinct activities with separate
aims. They connect on substance, in effect feeding each other.

Teaching (including substantive mentoring) and research may thus be
viewed as sites for professors' learning of their subjects of study. Lifton's
case suggests that, in substantive mentoring, students and instructor in-
habit research as the activity setting within which all learn their subject
together; they all engage in research. Yet even in this view Lifton guides
her students' learning; she teaches, for example, as she provides her students with "the big picture" that, as she says, "they don't usually have."
Mandell's teaching looks different: in contrast to Lifton's focus on palpable ("physical") problems in contemporary social and natural settings,
Mandell studies problems of human relation in times past. In contrast
to Lifton's lab- and field-based work with advanced doctoral students,
Mandell engages in the classroom-based teaching of undergraduates. Yet
as Mandell teaches, she learns—much as she does in research—though
in different ways and no doubt about different matters. Connection happens by virtue of the opportunities to learn that span research and teaching, regardless of whether what comes of both is one and the same (as it
is for Lifton, for example, a research article) or different (as it appears
to be for Mandell, whereby teaching yields insight, and research turns

it eventually into publication). Despite their differences, these scholars position their teaching or substantive mentoring toward advancement of their own scholarly learning while also advancing the learning of their students.

We have already seen this kind of strategic learning at play in chapter 4, in which professors described their experiences of scholarly learning within their teaching. We add now the observation that professors can purposefully build such learning, for themselves, into their teaching, or they may make the most of it as they spot it occurring in their everyday work with students. Such purpose speaks to agency.

Using Scholarly Learning to Frame Institutional, Public, or Professional Service

Professors often view faculty service, including institutional service (internal university upkeep) and outreach or public service (external work usually related to university aims), as quite separate from their more substantive research and teaching; that separation has been long engrained in the culture of the American research university. Although Ernest Boyer's scholarship of application has gone a long way toward bringing this arm of the faculty career—especially outreach—into the academic realm, faculty service is all too rarely construed as scholarly or learning oriented, a view that many study participants echoed.[17] Yet even as they took this position, most participating professors described opportunities they had had for priming their service for their scholarly learning. As described in chapter 4, a number of them described substantial gains from so doing: a professor of policy studies who enhanced his understanding of diversity through his service on a university-wide curriculum committee, a professor of finance and a social scientist who used their service on committees to meet future research collaborators, among others.[18] We view such "priming" as attempts to convert service or outreach into contexts within which professors can learn their subjects of study or otherwise advance their intellectual agendas. Service that is transformed into a site of scholarly learning readies it for connection with learning-infused research and at times teaching as well. What kinds of purposeful priming for scholarly learning were evident in participating professors' representations of their service or outreach?

Professor Amelia Artis, a social scientist, described her recent attempts, by way of faculty service, to direct the mission of a university-based institute for women's professional development:

> With the women's institute . . . I really wanted . . . to bring in
> extremely successful women and have them [be] available to
> [students]; I wanted to make networks between the undergraduates and the [accomplished] women in the business [school,] the
> women in the medical school, the women in the law school—
> and then have these high-powered women come in and talk to
> these . . . younger women, who are also networked with even
> younger women . . . [H]ad I had a chance to do what I wanted to,
> if I were the head of the institute, I'm sure I would've learned a lot
> from . . . those women . . . a lot of women who are leaders in cor-
> porations . . . [I]t's likely that having met those women, I might've
> been dragged off into different projects, and I would love to meet
> them . . . [T]here's . . . the fruits of thirty years of the feminist
> movement—[It] would be lots of fun to [explore]. And certainly,
> what I wanted my undergraduates to see [was] . . . the women's
> institute as a place . . . where . . . leaders in business and finance
> and law would come and talk about what the issues are [that]
> they've faced.

Artis wears her intellectual interests and values on her sleeve as she commits to institutional service. She takes on service projects directed purposefully at framing her campus's commitments to support women's professional development, a topic that is core to her own scholarly learning agenda. To prime her service for her own and her students' substantive learning, she aligns it with her research goals ("I'm sure I would've learned a lot from those women"). She also aligns it with her undergraduate teaching ("what I wanted my undergraduates to see").

What Artis does with internal service, other professors, mostly in applied/professional fields, do with external service—for example, service to the state or community (in the form of public service, or as it is sometimes called, outreach). George Bellanov, a professor of social work, says:

> Here at [Libra State University] . . . we're trained to think about
> our activities as fitting into either knowledge development, teaching, or service. In terms of . . . service, I try to think about . . . how
> can I become a part of a community that gives me new ideas, that

helps me understand a little bit more about what . . . the current issues are? I'll do things like visit sites, visit practicum sites, and I'll talk about what [the practitioners there are] doing, what some of the issues are they're struggling with. I'll read proposals and review them. I also do consulting with the . . . [community-based] clinic that works with assessment of [Bellanov's specific area of study]. So, I'm out there looking at some issues that are going on as a way of thinking about new ideas, new ways of thinking.

Bellanov actively moves his substantive learning into the external community. Whereas it is likely that practitioners at the community sites he visits benefit from his well-honed expertise in social work, we hear in Bellanov's words how he learns from them as well. He visits the sites purposefully to garner "new ideas, new ways of thinking" about "some issues that are going on" in social work that he can then more deeply explore in his research and teaching. In this way Bellanov aligns his outreach with his research and also with his teaching; these three "activity settings" frame the learning of subject matter that is important to him.

The cases of Artis and Bellanov, along with others presented in chapter 4, show that even in service, an activity typically cast as "not research" (and at times as antithetical to research), professors can position themselves to learn in meaningful scholarly ways. Those occasions, however, do not come easily. Nor are they likely to materialize without initiative and effort from professors because their careers are less than open to full free choice. In both the university and the field the "draft to service" is alive and well. Yet even under constraint, choice exists, as it does when a professor thinks through her service options, then strategizes choice with the aim of preserving or advancing her scholarly learning. Creatively and wisely made, such choice may yield opportunity.

Using Scholarly Learning to Connect One's Profession to One's Life

Study participants sought to link their academic activities by way of their scholarly learning. But many also sought to connect their scholarly learning with their lives personally. For most of them this meant more than finding livable balances between life and career, as important as that is.[19] It meant, rather, positioning life and career so that each serves as a substantive resource for learning occurring in the other. In this view a scholar's learning—and efforts to learn—in life might contribute to her scholarly learning. The converse applies as well: a professor's scholarly learning may help her pursue meaning in her personal life.[20]

I have already provided several examples of such learning. In interviews Nina Altman, the professor of literary studies at Libra State University, connected her childhood immigration experience to her growing appreciation of the nontranslatable in life, and she has pondered for years what it means to stand at the brink of the unexpressed. Altman's childhood experiences of immigration gave her entrée to a significant research topic. Her research, as an adult, lets her explore aspects of that experience that continue to hold great meaning for her. As a young boy, David Mora, the astronomer, was captivated by the glittering splendor of the night sky—he learned, visually, almost physically, of its grandeur. Years later, as a well-established astronomer at Libra State University, he devotes his career to strivings to understand that grandeur but now with the methods, tools, and theories of the science he has studied long and hard. Yet even now, as he peers into the night, he continues to feel, partly in remembrance of that first sighting, the magnificence of the night sky. Carmen Elias-Jones at Signal University literally felt her music as a child, making her dance around her parents' home. Now as an adult, and as a professional in the study of music, she struggles with the techniques of reproducing such sound, of understanding and mastering it ever more deeply, returning what she learns, technically, to the emotions that led her to it. The movement of such learning, and of the passionate thought it may yield, between personal lives and professional careers, is not the sole property of artists, humanists, and scientists. Social scientists and scholars of the professions experience connections between learning in life and learning in career as well.

Les Thompson, a professor of business at Signal University, described earlier as creating collaborative spaces for his scholarly learning, enacts that learning also in the interstices of career and life. In watching his young child explore his world, Thompson glimpses what it means to learn, much as he and his colleagues learn in their shared research.

I also like to watch this learning process in myself as well as others and—This isn't research. This is more personal. I've got two kids, a four-year-old and [an infant]. And one of the best things about the four-year-old is watching his mind work . . . watching him learn stuff because he'll put sentences together, and especially his language construction. He will say a lot of sentences that if you break them down into the individual word, they're completely, logically correct, but they're not the way I would ever say stuff. And sometimes I have to really stop and say, "Okay, [let's parse the] sentence into words because what he's done is [this]: I know what this word means. I know what this word means. I know what this word means. And if I string those sixty-eight words to-gether, that's the right idea." But because English is so idiomatic, it doesn't [require all those words in adult speech]. So he's given me a new perspective on thinking about the way we learn.

We may imagine Thompson wondering, in his professional work, how he and his collaborators and students bring ideas together, slowly and pains-takingly, as they engage in research, exploring what they do not yet know. He goes home then and watches his young son struggle to make mean-ing of what he does not yet know within a childhood world. As he sees his son naming discrete parts of his surrounding world, piecing words together, reaching for meaning among them, he is reminded of what goes on within himself as he uncovers a new reality bit by bit, trying to piece it together. As Thompson says, he "like[s] to watch this learning process in [himself] as well as others." The adult's learning at home—about his child's learning—parallels that adult's learning (about his own and oth-ers' scholarly learning) at work. This mirroring, from the personal to the professional, gives Thompson yet one more space in which to think about how he and others learn and what learning can mean in work as in life.

At Libra State University George Bellanov, the professor of social work, offered still another view of a scholar's learning from his personal life for his professional work and from that work for his life. In his first post-tenure year Bellanov described the former kind of learning, namely the personal learning (familial, cultural) that has framed his intellectual and professional endeavor:

There's another side of this I haven't shared, and that is that I'm the [number] oldest of [number] children. [Bellanov explains that he comes from a family of many children.] So children are very important. I see the benefits and the value of growing up in a family that's relatively intact . . . it's my reality. The other part—it's cultural—[is that] the value of children in my culture is important. So, when I see this kind of thing happening [e.g., court-ordered separations of children from family members], it raises some concern for me about, how is it that we can make these decisions, and do we really understand the impact of, for example, removing the child from their family? And then we know, for example, that was sort of the motive for [the new legislation I've been researching].

As this statement reveals, Bellanov's self-reflectiveness lets him see connections between his personal values, rooted in family and cultural life, and his professional choices today, both relative to the career he has chosen (professor of social work) and the particular subjects of study, within his career, that he pursues (child welfare practices and policies). Two years later, in his concluding interview, Bellanov repeats this central message (his personal life shapes his scholarly learning), but now couples it with his awareness of the reverse dynamic at play (his scholarly learning adds to his personal life). Asked how he came to be attracted to the study of social work in the first place, Bellanov says:

I think [my work as a scholar of social work] fits in well with . . . my general beliefs. So part of . . . my work is how I live . . . I see myself involved in a profession that is committed to working with, understanding, and making a difference around issues of disenfranchisement, oppression, discrimination . . . And my interest in children . . . there is this personal quality to it in that I'm the [number] of [number] children myself . . . I've grown up . . . valuing children. I have parents who are deeply committed to children. My experiences in working, for example, in Washington with [child welfare organizations] . . . validate the work that I'm doing. Feedback from others [who say to me], "Look, keep going." Some of the differences that I think I've made in the work I do [are] validating.

In this interview segment Bellanov says again that his personal values (growing up in a large family, valuing children) frame his professional endeavor (research toward improvement of child welfare practices). Yet he also says that his enactment of his personally rooted professional endeavor (social work attuned to children's welfare), along with encouraging "feedback from others," serves to validate him personally. Like the others, Bellanov's case shows that a professor may frame his personal life and scholarly profession in some proximity to one another, each drawing from and returning thought (the stuff of learning) to the other.

LEARNING ABOUT STRATEGY

Professors participating in the *Four Universities Project* assumed agency for their scholarly learning—in effect, activating it—in three strategic moves: (1) *creating space* by clearing out, revamping, or taking leave of a workspace that does not adequately support one's scholarly learning, by engendering opportunities for substantive interchange through collaboration, and by fostering communities for scholarly learning through time; (2) *containing attention* so as to emphasize those features of one's research and service that are most clearly aligned with scholarly learning while bounding the extent to which a career absorbs one's life; and (3) *connecting contexts* within which one's scholarly learning may grow, in particular, teaching (or mentoring) and research, service (including outreach) and scholarly study (including research), and profession and life.

Given the number of professors in this study who talked about using one strategy or the other (approximately 80%), along with several others' unrealized desires to do so, we may assume that strategy is on the professors' minds, at times intensely so. Saying it just that way, however, is tantamount to uttering an incomplete sentence because strategy, much like learning, is always *for something*. Strategy makes sense only in light of what it aims for. In the case of these professors, their strategy, like their agency, is for scholarly learning. Strategy, born of agency for scholarly learning, represents what professors themselves can do to situate their work, meaningfully, between passion and profession.

One can also wonder, "Why not just get to scholarly learning itself? Isn't all this strategizing—this creation of spaces, containment of attention, and context connection—just another set of processes that get between professors and their scholarly learning? Why bother with the processual distraction?" Contemporary scholars cannot engage their scholarly learning as directly as they might want because in modern-day society scholarly learning, in and of itself, is not a recognized "profession" in the same way that being a doctor or lawyer is. A state legislator, trustee, and tuition-paying parent will not understand scholarly learning as well as she will understand teaching, research, service, and outreach, the activities that situate it. These activities publicly define the occupational and social role of a university professor more so than does the scholarly learning that goes on within them. The dilemma at hand is that without the activities, and the occupational role that they comprise, scholarly learning cannot exist. Conversely, without scholarly learning, the role and activities are meaningless. To take one's scholarly learning seriously also requires taking one's professorial responsibilities seriously. To be serious about that role—to carry it out with integrity—requires serious attention to scholarly learning.

And finally, it must be realized that not just any strategy—even if directed at scholarly learning—will do. Although I did not collect data aimed at differentiating good strategy from strategy viewed as something other than good, I offer that "goodness" in professors' strategic pursuits of their scholarly learning, like goodness in any realm of human endeavor, is complex. Strategy can be well crafted and flawed, benevolent and heartless, authentic and insincere. It may proceed with kindness, dignity, and caring—being attentive to the lives it touches—or with callousness, even malevolence. It is thus as varied as the scholarly learning for which it strives.

Creating Professors as Agents of Their Learning

As this chapter shows, newly tenured university professors often work hard to advance, revise, or simply hold onto their scholarly learning. They draw on agency and activate strategy to plumb their subjects of study and teaching for understanding, creative realization, and insight. But why do they stick with their scholarly learning—with its sometimes tortuous pursuit—for as long as they do? I offer this hypothesis: that with tenure in hand, with long traditions of academic freedom on their side, with suitable salaries, often with comfortable homes and lives, newly tenured university professors nonetheless view their strivings as anything but complete. Like their instances of passionate thought, each research finding, scholarly insight, and artistic image that grows from their scholarly learning beckons still more. What pushes scholars through the "great middle" of their careers is this sense of incompleteness and of desires to address it as best they can through the subjects that they have come to know well but which they can never know deeply enough. If scholarly learning matters in higher education, so does its pursuit. We have seen in this chapter what professors can do to activate that pursuit. It is time now to explore what their employing academic organizations may offer toward it.

CHAPTER SIX

Organizing to Learn

What Universities Provide for Professors'
Scholarly Learning

The professors who were part of the *Four Universities Project* revised their jobs and workplaces strategically in order to pursue their scholarly learning. What did these professors' employing universities do, in turn, to support them? To understand how universities—and their leaders—can support professors' scholarly learning requires knowing which university structures, processes, and cultures engender professors' scholarly learning. This is because presidents and their staffs, deans, and department chairs cannot mandate professors' engagement in scholarly learning. That learning grows, instead, from the kinds of personal desires we heard in the voices of Richard Marin, Nina Altman, David Mora, Carmen Elias-Jones, and others. One thing that administrators can do is cultivate opportunities for scholarly desire to flourish. They may do that by leading in the creation of organizational settings that professors experience as encouraging of their scholarly learning—or at least, as not getting in its way. To support administrative effort of this sort, I identify and discuss features of university organization that professors participating in the *Four Universities Project* associated with their scholarly learning, whether supporting or thwarting it.

Academic Organization: Views from Outside In and Inside Out

I have purposefully avoided discussing the organizational contexts of scholarly learning up this point due to the power of organizational views to displace more detailed, person-centered considerations of what it means to live, grow, and age in those organizations. It is now time to take up the organizational discussion. I do so, however, with explicit attention to the more personalistic view laid out in preceding chapters. To highlight the distinction at issue, I present two organizational views: one that is "outside in" (drawn from studies of organizational psychology, sociology of organization, policy studies) and another that is "inside out" (based on interpretive views of scholarly learning and the contexts in which it occurs).[1]

Looking from the outside in—considering society's expectations of higher education—the organizational view casts the university as a collective social actor but with multiple identities: bureaucracy, political amalgam, communal culture, and anarchic assembly, among others. This outside-in view also portrays the university organization as an "open system" that searches out resources—people (matriculating students, new faculty), money and other social-economic benefits (tuition, grants, state funds), and knowledge (curricular knowledge, technologies)—within larger societal environments in which other organizations vie for similar "resources." At times those resources are plentiful; at other times they are scarce, and organizations, including universities, compete for them. Resource providers (such as state legislatures, private funders, communities) may make demands of the universities they support, holding them accountable for anticipated returns. University leaders strive to address such demands, reframe resource providers' expectations, or diversify their resource (and resource provider) base. As an open system dependent on its resource-bearing environment, the university strives to transform the resources it does acquire (e.g., students, tuition dollars, research grants) in ways that only academic organizations can by virtue of their distinctive social charters and identities (e.g., offer study opportunities defined uniquely as academic, engage in socially legitimated views of research). The university sends its transformed "products" (graduates, publications, useful knowledge) back out to an expectant, and scrutinizing, world as contributions to the social good. This outside-in view greatly enlarges the window that researchers of higher education have for thinking about the meaning of the contemporary university; its contributions to the study of higher education have been foundational.[2]

The conceptual start point for the outside-in view is external to the university. For the inside-out view, that starting point is internal to the university and internal to the people in it, in this case, professors. An inside-out view reveals people's experiences in learning and thinking within academic organizations constructed specifically to house that learning and thinking. An inside-out view reveals the human experience of such learning, including its emotion, even though scholarly emotion is rarely a topic of official university discourse. It reveals learners' strivings for substantive and personal meaning through professional endeavor—in their teaching, research, service, and outreach.[3] An inside-out view is deep but of necessity narrow. Although helpful, each of these views has its shortcomings: The outside-in view (targeting the massiveness of organization) misses what the view from inside out (human experience, including learning) provides, and vice versa. Both matter. I suggest that university leaders must use both, and that doing so involves letting each of these two views, conceptualized and deployed as well as possible, set the stage for the best that the other view can offer.

An outside-in view allows for broad organizational and environmental scanning. Attentive to organizational survival and development, this view allows administrators, policy makers, and professors in leadership positions to survey long distances—from their own organization to others nearby and far away, to the environment as a whole, now and in the future. This view lets university leaders see what lies beyond their own organization. It lets them glimpse social forces likely to shape their own, professors', and students' futures, including their learning. Alternatively, an inside-out view focuses on the experienced insides of university life. It also lets leaders see where in the university scholarly learning occurs— which structures, processes, and cultures situate it.[4]

On the assumption that the health and vitality of professors' scholarly learning is a priority for leaders of American higher education, I used these two very different perspectives to hone in on organizational settings and experiences that may bear on professors' scholarly learning. To construct initially a maplike outside-in view of each participating university, I relied on statistical and other indicators of organizational performance—for example, enrollment trends, financial health, shifts in educational and other knowledge offerings, productivity measures, and public image, to the extent these were available. To construct an inside-out view of the more specific within-organization locations of the scholarly learning discussed in previous chapters, I relied on year 3 interviews with thirty-nine participating professors. I therefore aimed for a bifocal view, broad in scope but trained on professors' scholarly learning.[5] This combined view features an outside-in lens that improves distance vision (laying out a broad organizational and environmental view) and an inside-out lens for looking closely at aspects deemed worthy of such scrutiny (scholarly learning specifically). Like the view from behind my own bifocals, that combined view is imperfect—and it takes time to learn to use to good effect.

The Four Universities as Social Organizations: An Outside-In View

I used an open-systems model to build profiles of the institutions participating in the *Four Universities Project*—Signal University, Horizon University, Hope State University, and Libra State University[6]—portraying each as a societal organism that pursues and draws in resources, transforms them internally, and projects them, re-formed, into an external environment that may further support that organization's function, strive to change it, or limit its power. In this view the details of organizational-environmental interaction—instrumental, political, and symbolic—are front and center, given that the organization depends on its external environment for survival.

To construct this outside-in view of the university as a resource-dependent open system, I rely on a number of commonly used organizational descriptors of colleges and universities: institutional identity and mission with attention to relative emphasis on research and undergraduate teaching, urban/suburban/rural location and foci, and historical roots and patterns of development; institutional control, type, size, student base, funding bases, strategic positioning, and key clientele; governance; distinctive cultural features; and key challenges and opportunities defined in terms of resource acquisition.

The four campuses where *the Four Universities Project* participants worked and where they sought also to learn their post-tenure work have been classified historically at the top ranks of the American higher education system as Research I, Doctoral/Research-Extensive, and Research University–Very High Research Activity (RU/VH).[7] All but one (Hope State University) claimed membership in the elite Association of American Universities (AAU). The two public institutions (Hope State University and Libra State University) belong to the National Association of State Universities and Land-Grant Colleges (NASULGC). These labels tell but part of an institutional story, for within the bounds of institutional type the campuses vary still more: by control (two public and two private), institutional size (one large, one small for each subset of public and private), geographic location (located across three states), and regional characteristics (one urban and one suburban for each public/private pair).

Still other patterns of similarity and difference characterized the four sites. They shared in their emphasis on research, strivings for excellence in graduate and undergraduate education, curricular attention to the liberal arts and professional education, incorporation of major medical schools and/or law schools, and established or growing interest in outreach or public service. They differed, however, in their approaches to organizing research and teaching, interdepartmental openness, emphasis on undergraduate learning, leanings toward basic or applied research, sensed obligations to address regional and state needs, financial concerns and strategies, among others. Although they all sought to achieve respected public status, they varied in their achievement of this goal by both popular and professional measures.[8] Here I describe how these and other institutional features coalesced to form the unique campuses on which the participating professors worked and endeavored to learn. What emerges for each organization is, of course, limited to what the outside-in view can provide and without much attention to what life—and learning—really are like on the inside.

SIGNAL UNIVERSITY

Signal University stands as a compact powerhouse of scientific research, professional preparation, and cross-disciplinary liberal arts undergraduate study. A small, elite, private university of sectarian origins, founded in the 1800s, modern-day Signal University is simultaneously global, national, and local in its reach. Its well-tended suburban "ivory tower appearance" belies its intense, research-based contributions to the nearby sprawling urban center. The university's byword in every endeavor is excellence, and this is reflected in in-house conversations and public image. Professionally and publicly, Signal is consistently ranked as among the "top ten" in various fields, disciplinary and applied. Signal University's enrollment of about fifteen thousand, divided fairly evenly between graduate/professional and undergraduate students, is heavily out-of-state. The university asserts strong interest in undergraduate learning but has made its name, nationally and internationally, in leading-edge rescarch.

Although it has been defined historically as a center of intense intellectual endeavor, Signal University came into being well after the East Coast "Ivies" appeared. Yet it views itself, and is viewed by others, as being among them. Still, it strives for more. The desire to stand with the best while crafting itself uniquely is, in fact, a historic theme for Signal: paradoxically, this striving, mentioned by a number of interviewees, is part of its character as an identity-seeking institution. Pursuing that identity in the present day has involved the university's openly favoring some academic areas, deemed excellent, over others and its forging of intersections among still others. Given this push for focus and convergence, the campus resounds of creative tension between commitments to "world-class" research and thoughtful undergraduate teaching, attention to human growth in the liberal arts tradition and support for knowledge growth through "big science," valuing of college education as a preparation for life and as a priming for professional engagement, dedication to disciplinary rigor and to cross-disciplinary experimentation in research and teaching, and desires for institutional reputation and needs for identity. Amid such tensions Signal presents itself as intellectually nimble and as alert to changes in the world and in itself. It keeps its eye on possible futures and positions itself, internally and externally, as still "becoming."

Having broken ties with its church-based beginnings, modern-day Signal University is governed by a relatively large board of trustees described as financially conservative. Its president and several other chief officers had taken office within two years of the study's start-up, and other mid-level administrative transitions had recently taken place. Some key issues in the news through the time of the study included creative teaching arrangements, technological improvements in university teaching, challenges in the management of a developing athletic program, and closing of a major academic unit, among others.

Located within a major American metropolitan center, Horizon University, a dynamic private university founded in the 1800s, aims to create informed and thoughtful citizens, enrich community life, enhance industrial vitality, and deepen cultural understanding for the surrounding city, state, nation, and world. In contemporary times the university has focused on educational approaches to improving life in twenty-first-century urban centers. Although relying historically on teaching to address its historic mission, the university has, in modern times devoted its research function toward this end. Horizon is a private institution pursuing a prominent public mission, attuned to social service that is simultaneously local and global, and enacted through research and teaching.

At the time of the study Horizon enrolled about thirty thousand students, approximately half of them undergraduate. About two-thirds of the student body was in-state and largely commuter; a strong majority were people of color. A number of the university's programs and schools, especially those offering professional education, had excelled in the academic rankings competition, achieving an enviable top-ten listing. Life on campus was diverse and energetic—intellectually, culturally, athletically, and aesthetically. Many faculty were struggling to understand difference as they confronted it and to use it pedagogically to best advantage.

Despite the clear identity that its urban mission proclaims, Horizon was immersed in numerous challenging tensions at the time of the study. To improve its standing, for example, Horizon's leaders had tightened undergraduate admissions criteria, in part by stepping up out-of-state recruitment, even as in doing so they ratcheted up concerns about the university's responsibility to the residents of its own neighborhood. Second, university leaders' commitment to professional education, its primary vehicle for enacting its urban commitments, had clashed recently with some professors' commitments to liberal studies as the core of undergraduate education. Third, as Horizon pursued academic improvement, it encountered tensions between the cohorts of academically devoted students it had proactively recruited and others who had themselves chosen Horizon for the social culture that college often provides. Fourth, in committing to educational excellence, the university emphasized disciplinary study, yet its efforts to boost cross-disciplinary teaching and research required downplaying traditional disciplinarity when it blocked efforts toward cross-disciplinarity.

The university is governed by a large board of trustees and expansive administrative team working together in a financially conservative climate to ensure that each year ends "in the black." Top administrators do not usually intervene in school and department decision making. Yet the faculty do sometimes feel pressed to support top-level initiatives. Faculty view Horizon's faculty senate as active but often as ineffective. Headlines in the news at the time of the study included: philanthropic successes, the university's athletic prowess, public service activities, and academic personnel concerns, among others.

HOPE STATE UNIVERSITY

Hope State University is a hard-hitting, "rough around the edges," center-city public university. On first glance it is a fortress, walled off from the surrounding urban sprawl. "Is this the postmodern version of the secluded ivory tower?" a campus visitor wonders. Yet things at Hope State are not what they seem. Talks with faculty and administrators reveal that the campus's urban surround flows right into and through it, defining and sustaining it. Hope State is anything but secluded or walled off. It is of the city.

The youngest of the study sites, Hope State University was founded in the twentieth century through an institutional merger. Its sense of academic self is still taking shape, and in its struggling youthful spirit Hope State seems captivated by its own development and by possibility. That said, the university, though short on history, has made great strides into its future, claiming impressive top-ten rankings for some of its professional and applied programs. But the arts and humanities have also fared well in academic rankings and are poised for growth.

Interviewees cited Hope State's size as a comparative advantage. For a public university it is small, young, and flexible enough to maneuver and adapt in ways that larger, older, more established institutions cannot. Its largely in-state commuter enrollment of twenty-five thousand, two-thirds of which is undergraduate, is composed predominantly of first-generation college-goers. As an administrator pointed out, the university reflects no clear demographic majority; it is among the most diverse of American universities.

Although still developing, portions of Hope State's identity are well defined. Its strong allegiance to the city in which it is located is expressed through service enacted largely through teaching, professional preparation, and increasingly, applied research. But Hope State wants more: it is striving to become a world-class institution of far broader reach. To do this, it positions its work in the surrounding city as a template for similar work in other large American cities. This attempt—to turn the local into the cosmopolitan—stands as a work-in-progress. That it exists is a sign of aspiration and possibility, though often accompanied by tension: between teaching and research, service and research, professional and humanistic education, interests in disciplinary development and interdisciplinary professional endeavor, dreams of becoming elite and commitments to nonelite working-class populations, and not least, desires to build a vigorous faculty and awareness of many newly tenured professors' interests in leaving. "Expectations are high," said a university leader, but at this time in its history Hope State is not a "warm, cuddly place" for faculty.

Hope State University, designated as land-grant, belongs to a complex state higher education system and is, therefore, well buffered from direct state intrusion. But there are downsides to this arrangement: in sharing system membership with other institutions, Hope State, as a newer campus, can be overshadowed by them. And in competing with peers for scarce state funds, finances are unstable at best. The full university system is governed by a small board of trustees, most of whose members are appointed by the governor. Hope State is administered by a leadership team headed by a president who reports to the state system's chief officer. Top news through the period of the study included student access policies, academic hires, research capacities, and assumption of office by Hope State's new president.

LIBRA STATE UNIVERSITY

Libra State University, a premier American public research university, celebrates its expansiveness and excellence in both research and teaching—a surprising combination in modern-day academe and possibly the university's most generative tension. Among the largest of U.S. public institutions, Libra State's student enrollment at the time of the study was forty thousand, about two-thirds of which was undergraduate; about one-third was out-of-state. Libra State University is located in a small yet cosmopolitan, progressive college town; the university is the town's intellectual, cultural, and economic center. Located within a short drive of a major urban center, Libra State University takes seriously the challenges of twenty-first-century metropolitan life, nearby and worldwide. Although designated as the state's flagship university, Libra State's "public-ness" is national and global. Its contributions in the sciences, social sciences, arts and humanities, and professions are renowned. Many of its programs are repeatedly ranked in professional and popular sources as among their fields' top ten. Clearly, the university has managed well the strains that can emerge between size and quality.

A number of the ideas that germinated through the university's founding, in the 1800s, have resonated through to the present day, among them a staunch dual commitment to scholarship (and later research) and excellent undergraduate teaching; dedication to tolerance and democracy in thought and practice; valuing of curricular breadth spanning the arts and humanities, social sciences, sciences, and professional studies; standpoints on knowledge as enacted "in practice" and as teachable from the stance of practice; dedication to the creation of informed and active citizens and leaders; and respect for the faculty's intellectual freedom and critical debate. Not surprisingly, various instantiations of these themes were challenged as they evolved historically. As such, tensions arose over the years between: commitments to national and international research and thoughtful, locally oriented undergraduate teaching; dedication to disciplinary study and calls for cross-disciplinarity; desires for selectivity and for breadth; views of knowledge construction as locally situated and as "bubbling up" on campus, and felt needs to orchestrate and review the quality of local efforts in centralized ways; and faculty power and administrative responsibility. The university, in modern times, holds to the following touchstones: academic excellence achieved through disciplined inquiry, openness to diversity in thought and practice, cross-disciplinary mindfulness, and learning in practice. These are, of course, ideals, yet in university publications and in my own campus conversations, their power in the framing of campus identity was unequivocal.

Libra State University reflects a strong tradition of decentralization tempered by the connectedness that its trustee, administrative, faculty, and student leadership provides. The university, part of a state system, is governed by a small, university-appointed board of trustees, a president, and a cabinet of key administrators. A new administration had taken office a few years before my study. A key feature of university governance at the time of the study was its top leaders' clear involvement in academic life. Administrators saw themselves, and were seen, as "of the faculty," and virtually all of them taught or worked with doctoral students. Although characterized as "fragile" due to its dependence on the public purse, Libra State's long-term financial diversification strategy, and its positioning as a valued national resource well worth supporting, has garnered substantial autonomy for the university. At the turn of the twenty-first century headline news focused on campus racial and gender diversity, athletic accomplishments, intellectual property, student drinking on campus, and corporate relationships, among others.

UNIVERSITY ORGANIZATION: SINGULAR OR PLURAL?

The participating professors' employing universities were broadly and deeply diverse. One might argue that their vast internal differences crystallized into a distinctive organizational character for each (or "culture," as it is sometimes called) and that that character now contextualizes, and infuses, professors' scholarly learning. But this claim is hard to back up. A campus's character, or culture, is not a single thing, nor does it ever fully crystallize. Rather, it embodies innumerable meanings, and it can shift and change momentarily or over long stretches of time. Given the manifold meanings alive on any one campus, it is impossible for any one professor to bring the fullness of her university (literally, an academic universe of activity and meaning) into her scholarly learning. The human mind is not omniscient. It functions on a principle of selection: learning and simply perceiving occur within the span of a person's bounded cognition and equally bounded personal meaning. What happens, instead, is that particular facets of the university—selected slivers of meaning that professors take in, consciously or unconsciously, as the "realities" of their work lives—frame those professors' learning, scholarly and otherwise. Thus, in any one university, and in any one department or program, different professors may engage in quite different contexts. Much depends on what they themselves bring into view as mattering to their work and, therefore, to their learning as well.[9] I suspect that this was the case for professors participating in both research projects.

Bearing these qualifications in mind, I asked: Which facets of university organization got through consistently to professors' scholarly learning—that is, as they felt it? To what extent did one or another "sliver of organization" consistently frame the scholarly learning of participating professors, as they described it to me? And did one or another subgroup of professors (women, disciplinary groupings, faculty on a particular campus) feel more influenced, in their scholarly learning, by some of those organizational slivers than others? How did such "contextual effects" differ by campus? Questions such as these, which favor attention to selected, but nonetheless shared, organizational experiences, shrink under the gaze of an outside-in view of academic organization. The telescopic features of the outside-in view simply cannot visualize these features. To get at them requires a view that grows, alternatively, from the inside out, privileging professors' unique experiences in the construction of an organizational landscape.[10]

From Inside Out: University Organization as Part of Professors' Experiences of Scholarly Learning

Assuming an inside-out perspective, I note three facets of academic organization that professors participating in the *Four Universities Project* consistently associated with their scholarly learning, whether supportively or not: the nature of their local intellectual colleagueship; the campus's openness to cross-disciplinarity in teaching, research, outreach, and service; and the campus's ability to provide alternative locations for professors' scholarly learning external to the campus and in some cases to academe itself.[11] Although an outside-in view might discuss these features of academic organization, that view cannot dredge up evidence that may matter to professors' scholarly learning. Doing that falls to a view that grows from inside the university and also from inside professors' experiences of their campus work lives.

PROFESSORS' ORGANIZATIONAL COLLEAGUESHIP: THE INTELLECTUAL AS LOCAL

I define *faculty colleagueship* as the patterning and quality of peer relationships that professors experience locally. My discussion only takes campus-based colleagueship into account. Colleagueship comes in different forms, from highly visible, day-to-day colleague relations to diffuse patterns of interrelation fading into a background campus culture. Professors themselves vary in their consciousness of it. I only considered colleagueship that was out in the open of a professor's awareness and in her interview talk; typically, this included references to colleagues down the hall or in other departments or colleagues with varying expertise—for example, in methodological issues, teaching, or institutional politics.[12]

For this analysis I only consider forms of professorial colleagueship that speak to professors' substantive (intellectual) endeavor. Thus, I focus on colleague relationships that anchor professors' scholarly learning rather than on their other campus experiences. Much can grow among colleagues besides scholarly learning. They may collaborate on program coordination issues, faculty salary negotiations, grievance reviews, and human resources policies that have no bearing on their substantive thought. Much as the words *learning* and *strategy* demand specification of the "objects being learned" or "objects being strategized" in order to be meaningful, so does colleagueship require an object to clarify its unique meaning. Colleagueship for what? Here I limit my discussion to colleagueship that situates or that somehow bears on professors' experiences of their scholarly learning.

Images of Colleagueship

Thirty-two of the thirty-nine professors (approximately 80%) participating in year 3 interviews of the *Four Universities Project* referred to relationships with local colleagues—their academic coworkers—as they spoke, in interviews, about their scholarly learning. Ted Wilson, a philosopher at Libra State, described a recent and memorable experience of colleagueship with another philosopher in his department:

> I was in our commons room . . . talking to a colleague . . . explaining this idea [at the center of my research]. And he said,

"Oh, I had that idea ten years ago." He gave me a paper of his which is on a completely . . . different topic. But he did have the idea . . . ten years ago . . . And it turned out that this paper of his . . . fit perfectly into my view . . . I made a lot of use of that . . . because I now understand something I didn't understand before. Something . . . pretty important . . . I hadn't read it—I hadn't even heard of it. But he's right. And his view fits just perfectly in mine. So I did learn that. That was a really, really important thing for me to learn.

This interaction emblematizes an ideal colleagueship, an experience of intellectual sharing, local but disciplinary in nature, that many professors long for. It is positive and memorable. But sometimes colleagueship—indeed, the configuration and experienced quality of peer professorial relations in a particular work site—is memorable in hurtful or thwarting ways. Sometimes colleagueship obstructs professors' learning. Consider the situation of Jeannette Parsons, a newly tenured scientist, at one of the four study institutions:

As a member of a committee desiring to improve the conditions of women's work on campus, [Jeannette Parsons] had devoted extended time and energy to bring a particular feminist speaker to her campus. The task was arduous: she and others had to make a case to a difficult committee . . . [and] they had to . . . raise [the] funds . . . While [Parsons] worked hard at this effort . . . her male departmental colleagues engaged in important substantive work in which she did not participate. [Her male colleagues thus] learned something, in their shared science, in which she had no part because she was otherwise occupied—struggling to bring in a feminist speaker for women in the sciences: "And I would get into these great debates [on the committee selecting the feminist speaker] . . . What really annoyed me was that my male colleagues would be [engaged in tasks more closely related to their research than I was,] and they were . . . finding out how to [decipher an interesting/important formula,] while I was arguing about who was more feminist than the other . . . that was probably the only committee I've ever served on where aside from learning some interesting things in [general education/liberal arts,] I basically didn't learn very much." . . . By working for the good of the order, this scientist missed out on an opportunity to advance her scholarly learning while her male colleagues engaged more directly and continuously than she did in their scholarly learning. [As a professor, Parsons] was clearly engaged in important work on behalf of other women scientists, but . . . [it] cost her in terms of her scholarly learning. Such instances, repeated, reflect an erosion of opportunities for women to learn in substantive and meaningful ways.[13]

The case of the scientist Jeannette Parsons makes several important points: (1) the scholar devoted herself to service for others' benefit (advancement of campus women in the sciences); (2) to do so, she gave up time from her research; (3) her male colleagues persisted in their scholarly learning, in research, while she worked with a challenging committee to bring her faculty service into being; (4) and her male colleagues appear to have offered no direct help, and it is not evident that they expressed appreciation for Parsons's service to women in the sciences. Nor did these colleagues try to involve Parsons as a research colleague in work that collectively they deemed important. Parsons's colleagues' action toward her smacked of the politics of exclusion by way of omission (compared to the open and very positive interaction between the two male philosophers previously described). The male scientists failed to attend to their female colleague's scholarly interest in their collaborative work. Their act, like that of the philosopher colleague, was memorable but in a very different way.

These examples reflect definitive acts: one person touching another's scholarly learning, directly and helpfully among the male philosophers and indirectly and harmfully among the mixed-gender group of scientists. Both acts make impressions, though of different kinds. Most colleagueship, however, is not so memorable; it makes little, if any, impression, directly or indirectly. It hangs in the air, ghostlike by virtue of its absence, and in professors' wishes for it. Asked what kinds of situations help her to learn best about those subjects that she studies or teaches, Esther Sharan, a professor in the humanities at Hope State, exclaimed, "Conversations with colleagues." But in the same breath, she added that in her experience such conversation "doesn't happen very often." Time is tight: "My schedule doesn't coincide with that of my colleagues and none of us stays around on campus. We're not, any of us, here more than two or three days a week. We plan the occasional lunch, but by the time we've caught up on . . . general things and talked some shop about issues in the department, [you] don't mostly get around to actually talking about your work." As Sharan indicates, the very absence of colleagueship, as a context for her scholarly learning, serves to accent her desire for it.

These examples present different forms of colleagueship emerging from the *Four Universities Project*—generous or self-interested, vividly fore-grounded in professors' consciousness or recalled from faint background awareness. Most notably, the colleagueship of professors is particularistic and often quite concrete. Although it does contribute to a more expansive communal character, sometimes referred to as an organizational culture (visible from the outside in), it refers, at base, to what goes on *between individuals* in dyadic and small group relationships as they interact with one another or as they reflect on their interaction after the fact (visible only from inside out).[14] Another quality of colleagueship emerging from this project is the distinction between *colleagueship* and *collegiality,* the former representing diverse, interaction-based relationships and the latter a normative ideal (thereby relatively consistent) toward which such rela-tionships may occasionally strive.[15] Colleagueship may thus exist among people bound by an ideal of collegiality, or not. At the risk of oversim-plifying, colleagues may be "nice" to one another—helpful to and sup-portive of each other's efforts—or not. Colleagues can provide for and sustain each other's attempts to engage in one or another activity—here scholarly learning—or impede, even foil, such efforts. All these interac-tions redound to colleagueship.

Colleagueship and Scholarly Learning
What do study data reveal about how colleagueship, generative or thwart-ing, can get into professors' scholarly learning? Some professors partici-pating in the *Four Universities Project* argued, sometimes forcefully, that it did not—only to turn around later in the interview with vivid examples of how certain local colleagues had touched their scholarly learning, help-fully or not. Consider the experience of Les Thompson, the professor of business at Signal University who describes a generative intellectual rela-tionship with a local colleague. Asked if he thought that the content of his core research would be different at another university, where his col-

leagueship would likely differ, Thompson responded, "Not really . . . the market for [my] research isn't Signal University [in particular,] although the people here judge it . . . it's . . . national or global."

In light of his response I assumed that Thompson did not interact much with his colleagues, that he kept to himself to do his scholarly work. But later in the interview I asked Thompson about the kinds of situations that help him learn best about the subjects in business that he studies and teaches. "When people push you or question you," he responded. "There's no reason I can't work at home . . . with a high speed connection . . . Yet almost all these fifteen people [in my area] come in [to the university] every day." And with but a second's pause he added: "Because it's very nice to have [Mark] down two doors . . . If I'm working on a refereed report I don't get, I walk down, I say, '[Mark], I don't get blah, blah, blah.'"

Thompson paused to reflect on what he had just said. "Part of it's social," he explained, 'cause I love to watch [Mark] think. He's just unbelievably smart, and it's really interesting to get his perspective . . . And part of it is it's much more efficient if I ask [Mark, or John for that matter] a question, and he explains it in ten minutes [instead of me] beating my head against the wall for an hour. So . . . it's all about . . . the people, whether it's teaching or whether it's research."

The example of Les Thompson makes two points. First, colleagues can, and occasionally do, learn their subjects of study and teaching from one another; they are (or at least can be) each other's teachers and learners. And second, despite this reality, colleague-based teaching and learning are quite invisible, even to the professors who are drawn to and involved in them; those professors often take what happens in their exchanges, learning wise, for granted. They assert their individuality in learning, yet in discussing their favorite instances of learning, they often refer to interactions with others.

Suffice it to say that Les Thompson learned in the context of his colleagueship with Mark. What did his learning look and sound like? How did it work? As Thompson explains:

There's a professor in our organizational studies department . . . what he does is very similar to what I do. And he's done a lot of [work on financial lending]. Now, in one dimension the question he asks is identical to the question I ask. But the way he thinks about the world, and the way I think about the world are about as different as you could get.

And we've become good friends, and we meet a couple times a month socially, just to have lunch—but we end up talking about our research. And we spend most of the time arguing about, "Well, no, that can't be true," I'll say to him, because my view of these transactions, they're financial [unlike his, which are organizational].

"I lend you one hundred dollars, and the reason I'm lending you one hundred dollars is you're gonna give me more than that back. And if you're not gonna give it back, I won't lend to you, and if you are gonna give it back, then I will."

Whereas [my colleague's] perspective is [like this]. "This lending relationship is part of a broader social relationship. In fact, these lending officers don't just lend money; they also take these guys out to ballgames. They also attend the same churches."

And I say, "Yes, but they're doing that because they collect information."

I always gotta stuff it into my model, my view of the world—which he finds hysterical. But you know, anything he says I'm gonna shove into my little box even if it doesn't fit.

Les Thompson lays out a narrative of colleague-with-colleague interaction that portrays him as doing two things simultaneously—defending his own long-held and well-established view (the concept of "transaction," which he then equates with "my little box") and while taking in his colleague's very different sense of the same phenomenon ("a broader social relationship")—to muster the best defense he can to preserve, as he says, the contours of his own "little box." One could argue that Thompson did not learn much. After all, he resists his colleague's interpretation. He may well reject it. As he says, "Anything he [my colleague] says, I'm gonna shove into my little box even if it doesn't' fit."

What makes this learning, as I use the term? Thompson makes an effort to probe, understand, and respond to his colleague's very different view on a topic of interest to both. To have this conversation, Thompson has to travel to places in his thinking that he would not otherwise go.

Out of interest Thompson moves to places of substantive thought that without his colleague he would not likely access. He may or may not accept what he finds in those places; he may treat the thought that he finds there differently than his colleague does. A strict reading of this narrative suggests that Thompson's colleagueship with the organizational scholar did not lead him to change his mind. Instead, this colleagueship helped him do a better job of defending his own well-entrenched thought—by exposing him to competing views that he then incorporated into his own, rather than testing his own against them.

But through this interaction, or later upon reflection, Thompson's thoughts about financial lending did grow in some directions that were new to him, even if only in defense of his core ideas. "I think [that this relationship with my organizational colleague] hasn't changed my research as such, I don't—" he hesitated, "I don't know if I want to say it that strongly." With a few seconds' pause, he added: "It's not obvious how it's changed my research. It's clearly changed the way I think about the process. It's clearly changed when I discuss stuff."

Thompson says that in interacting with his colleague, he has changed somewhat in how he thinks about a professional practice that he already knows deeply and well—expertly. Thus, in his view he has learned. Without firsthand data showing where his thinking was about the lending topic early in his relationship with the colleague, compared to where it was later on, I take his own self-analytic word for it. Maybe it changed, truly, through his talk with his colleague, or maybe not. What does come through is that, in Thompson's experience, colleagueship (with the organizational scholar) presses against what Thompson thinks he knows, encouraging him to try out other views, opening a door to further questioning, now or later.

"None of my evolution as a [scholar] was influenced . . . in the slightest by anyone working [at the university]," Iris Galina asserted without being asked. "Nothing really affects my work as a scholar. I almost think of it as a separate life from my job here. I mean, it really, really is . . . What I do in my [scholarship] is . . . very separate from my job as professor here." Throughout both project interviews Galina positioned her creative endeavors, and her learning in them, as being fully separate from her institutional work as a professor. But in her year 3 interview Galina revealed a major—and with tenure, recent—change in her professional life:

> Because the world of [our academic program] is so small, I automatically had a mentor as soon as I came in [years back, as a beginning professor], a self-assigned mentor. And I very stupidly didn't listen to anyone else. I just let the facts, quote unquote, facts of reality of the [larger department] be told to me by [that] one person. And I . . . shouldn't have done that. I should've listened to a lot of people . . .
>
> Some of the things he . . . taught me were very important. But one of the things he taught me over the seven years . . . was to come to work with a great deal of hostility and chip on my shoulder . . . When he was in my office, it was all hatred and hostility—who's stupid, and . . . That was what he was talking about.
>
> And I decided that's not working for me anymore. It shouldn't have ever been part of what I did. I shouldn't have just listened to that. And I don't want that anymore . . . because when I came not expecting hostility, I didn't get any.
>
> And when I tried to express that to him, he responded like it was a huge betrayal . . . He probably felt like I was chastising him and that I had no right to do that . . . even though my communication all had to do with myself . . .
>
> This was met [by him] as betrayal . . . [that] he had done so much for me, that I should be grateful . . . [that] once you have somebody who supports you, you're just supposed to be beholden forever, and continue to be that apprentice.
>
> That's what I've been thinking about for months now.

Here Galina describes not only a change in her colleagueship but a change also in her understandings of it, including what she now would like it to be. Years ago, she said, she felt that she had nothing to learn from colleagues beyond her "self-assigned mentor"—that the world revolved around the "facts" this mentor shared in discussions they kept to themselves. And clearly, she succeeded in garnering her mentor's professional support through her pre-tenure years—though just as clearly (and based on the record of scholarly accomplishments she shared with me), she won her tenure by virtue of her own scholarly achievement.

As Galina moved on post-tenure—exerting leadership as she redesigned the institutional sites of her own and her students' work—things changed. She awoke to what she had to gain, and learn, from others beyond her mentor: colleagues who could help her refashion the academic program she now oversaw in ways that would heighten participants' learning. At the point that I left her, Galina still divided her scholarship from her institutional work; to her they were separate. But she had also begun to sense that her local colleagueship—now opening up—could be helpful to her, certainly in her teaching and possibly in other parts of her work as well. She learned this as she distanced herself from her longtime mentor, increasingly working with others in the context of her teaching and service. "This semester," she said, "I've found that I'm getting a great deal done on the graduate studies committee [that] . . . I'm on, working with people who are not in [my] program." Separating herself from her mentor, she awoke to a colleague world in which "everybody [is] cooperative, everybody else in the department . . . treat[s] me like a colleague . . . cooperating with me and working with me . . . I was getting so much done."

As Galina awoke, literally, to the colleagueship surrounding her, she grasped its value to her: her campus colleagues could help her recast the world in which she and her students worked and learned. In turning away from the mentor who had kept her from others and joining with them, she changed her colleagueship. In doing so, she changed a significant part of the context of her scholarly learning, thereby enlarging the spaces in which that learning could flourish—the resources and opportunities on which she, as a learner, could draw.

Colleagueship as a Feature of University Organization

Given the diverse forms it may take, how may colleagueship be manifest organizationally in major research universities? The preceding examples suggest that colleagueship, as a force in professors' scholarly learning, may be embedded in the most basic locales of university functioning, its departments and programs as reflections of academic bureaucracy (as it is for Iris Galina, Jeannette Parsons, and Ted Wilson), and also amid the informal and friendship dynamics of the university as a community of experts (as it is for Les Thompson). Colleagueship may surface as a planned and recurring ritual (consider the regularity and purposefulness of Thompson's interactions with his colleagues) or as an incidental but not unusual occurrence (as is Wilson's fortuitous meeting with his philosophy colleague), both viewed as parts of a campus culture. Defined as a feature of the university as a political amalgam, colleagueship can perpetuate a cultural status quo, resisting change in how people relate to each other (as it did for years for Esther Sharan and until recently for Iris Galina), or alternatively, it may help spur public action and policy-level change (actions that Parsons and Sharan could consider). Colleagueship might focus on research and scholarship (as it does in positive ways for Thompson and Wilson and in negative ways for Parsons), or on teaching, outreach, service, administration, and other core institutional duties (as it does for Sharan and Galina).

The range, and in some cases intensity, of these examples suggests that colleagueship can be a powerful context of professors' scholarly learning, meriting the attention of university leaders who strive to create the university as a place where scholarly learning can occur at its best.

Patterns of Experience: Colleagueship and Professors' Scholarly Learning

How did study participants experience their colleagueship—and through it, their organization—as a setting for their scholarly learning? As previously noted, thirty-two of the thirty-nine professors participating in year 3 interviews (about 80% of the sample) linked their scholarly learning to their colleagueship. Ten of them (a quarter of the sample) portrayed their colleagueship as in some part ineffectual in or detrimental to their scholarly learning. It will come as no surprise that of these ten, eight were women, three of whose voices I have already included: Esther Sharan, Jeannette Parsons, and Iris Galina. The numbers reveal that just under half the women participating in the study (n = 20) reported problematic relationships with colleagues. I must point out, however, that those problematic relationships were not always with men, nor were they always with senior or peer males; other women and junior males sometimes posed obstacles as well. Further, seven of the eight women reporting negative experiences located their colleague difficulties as organizationally proximal to themselves (e.g., within their program or department). Their colleague challenges were thus located within or quite close to their key workplaces, probably shaping their day-to-day experiences. Only a fifth as many male participants voiced comparable negative colleague experiences (2 of 19).

Institutionally, interviewees at Horizon University (large, private) and Libra State University (very large, public) reflected the fewest concerns about negative colleague experiences (one each); Signal University (small, private, aspiring) and Hope State University (small, public, aspiring), together, represented eight (of 10 total) cases of negative colleagueship experience; seven of these eight were women.

An analysis by disciplinary sector revealed several patterns. Less than a third of study participants in each of the following fields—applied/professional, sciences, and social sciences—reported negative experiences (1 of 11 in the first group, 2 of 11 in the second, and 2 of 8 in the third); in contrast, half of the sample participants in the arts and humanities indicated some version of negative colleagueship (5 of 9 total, 4 of the 5 were women).

Although small-scale findings warrant a larger, more broadly generalizing survey, within-sample generalizations such as those previously cited merit attention in light of the propositions that they yield.[16] First, colleagueship matters in university professors' attempts to engage in scholarly learning, certainly through the early post-tenure career. It is a prominent location for such learning and needs to be viewed as such. Previous studies have not named colleagueship as a context of professors' efforts to learn in this way.

Second, colleagueship appears to pose challenges to newly tenured women's scholarly advancement in the nation's central sites of knowledge production, namely its major research universities. Colleagueship may be especially problematic for women in the arts and humanities.[17]

Third, the colleagueship that appears most problematic for women's intellectual pursuits and, by extension, their scholarly development exists very close to them professionally—in programs and departments, arenas of colleague interaction that administrative policy rarely touches but that serve nonetheless as the sites of professors' day-to-day work.

Fourth, colleagueship, as a location of professors' intellectual development, may be more challenging in smaller universities than it is in larger institutions (where professors may have more places to turn when a particular relationship fails to work). An alternative interpretation is that intellectual colleagueship may be problematic on campuses reflecting strong "cultures of aspiration," or as KerryAnn O'Meara calls them, "striving" institutions.[18]

CROSS-DISCIPLINARY OPPORTUNITIES

Sixteen of the thirty-nine professors (approximately 40%) participating in the year 3 interviews associated their scholarly learning with cross-disciplinary engagement portrayed in two ways: (1) as *social interaction* with colleagues from scholarly communities beyond their own (e.g., attending a conference to advance one's scholarly learning in a field of study different from one's own), or (2) as *challenges to habits of mind* (e.g., engaging in a thought experiment inspired by reading in a discipline outside one's own).[19] Professors used at least one of these two approaches to define their cross-disciplinary efforts; a number of them used both. This pairing—social interaction and challenges to habits of mind—suggests that simply bringing together people from diverse fields does not ensure cross-disciplinary engagement in depth; attention to scholars' interactions with one another is only part of what matters. To understand cross-disciplinary endeavor one must take a harder look at what can go on within it by way of scholarly learning—for example, as scholars encounter habits of mind different from their own, examining them deeply, reconsidering their own in light of them. For that kind of "hard look" I turn to professors' experiences of cross-disciplinary scholarly learning.

From within professors' views *cross-disciplinarity* refers to changing dynamics of thought as stirred, typically, by interaction with the thoughts of disciplinary others. It involves looking hard into the thoughts of other minds, newly encountered, taking seriously the subject matter contents of those minds, struggling to connect one's own subject matter thoughts to theirs, or simply reflecting seriously on the meaning and validity of one's own thoughts relative to theirs. Cross-disciplinarity involves acts of boundary crossing—possibly boundary blurring—among people, thoughts, disciplinary and other knowledge communities, departments and other organizational units, and other social groupings. As a mode of thought, cross-disciplinarity involves questioning lines of intellectual division among individuals and groups and the knowledge that these individuals and groups define as valid or important. Increasingly popular in professors' research, cross-disciplinarity is also a subject of interest in professors' teaching and in other academic work that involves sharing knowledge (e.g., outreach, service, and mentoring). At their best—amid the flow of Socratic talk, for instance—teaching, mentoring, and other forms of academic discourse involve the stirring around of knowledge that otherwise may settle into immovable text or crystallized belief. Possibly more so than research, teaching and teaching-based mentoring, outreach, and service may elicit cross-boundary thought, cross-field imagining. Finally, though looked to by many as helping to open up thought frontiers that otherwise might be shut tight, cross-disciplinarity does not always lead to positive results. It may lead to nothing of import. It can even go bad. Like any human endeavor that calls for opening doors to new thought, cross-disciplinary endeavor provides entrée to both selfless and selfish impulses, just and unjust images, opportunities equally to give and take; or it may have no effect at all.

Images of Cross-Disciplinarity

"In the last couple of years, [I have been] reading research . . . by people who don't work in the part of the world where I work," Anthony Marco, a social scientist at Signal University, said. His reference to "parts of the world" was metaphorical: "the world," to which Marco refers is academe, and its "parts" are disciplines and fields. "And when I read a piece of research or hear a talk, a colloquium in another part of [that academic world], and the particular kind of analysis they're doing [there] . . . I think, 'Wow, I'd really like to try that out [in the part of the academic world] where I work to see if that works [in my own field].'" When he feels this way, Marco adds, "that tells me it's a good idea." Marco describes his cross-disciplinarity as efforts to question or otherwise challenge his own established habits of mind. Whether through reading or listening, he seeks out analytic lenses from other disciplines and fields to apply to subjects of interest within his own which he has come to view in set ways. Reflecting back on what he just said to me, Marco mused: "What is it that T. S. Eliot said? Bad poets borrow. Good poets steal. And [the] idea of—if it's a really profound insight, it ought to work in other places [of the academic world] as well . . . That always impresses me." For Anthony Marco cross-disciplinarity grows from a practice of intellectual border crossing that he conducts as he reads, plays out thought experiments, listens to and reflects on talks, or participates in colloquia. His most productive thoughts occur along such boundaries.

As noted in chapter 4, I use the term *cross-disciplinarity* to refer to "expeditions out of one's own field" aimed expressly at learning something new to "bring home" to one's own work and often to one's scholarly community. That something new may include alternate lenses for rethinking long-familiar thoughts or new data about a development of interest, fresh theoretical constructs for examining a lingering problem, among other possibilities. As a political scientist at Horizon University said, learning through cross-disciplinarity requires "pick[ing] . . . pull[in g] . . . that corner of . . . the university" that can spur a scholar "to think of things that are slightly different . . . things that hadn't occurred to people to integrate before." From an organizational perspective professors' frequent engagement in cross-disciplinary learning suggests the presence of norms and bureaucratic incentives that encourage departmental and related forms of boundary crossing or that at least do not thwart them. Some institutions encourage cross-disciplinarity far more than others.

Although some professors portrayed their cross-disciplinary learning as an individual experience and others as shared, all of them portrayed it as interactive: one mind interacting with one or more others, in instances of cross-field exchange. Not surprisingly, professors referred to such interaction as they talked about cross-disciplinary collaboration, usually in research. Richard Marin, the physicist at Hope State introduced in chapter 1, exemplifies this point as he talks about the origins, development, and outcomes of his collaboration with a philosopher across campus.

> About two years ago a philosopher here at Hope State asked this common friend, who's a professor in physics, whether . . . he knew of anybody who worked in this particular area of physics because . . . his work in philosophy had focused on this area. And it turned out to be exactly what I was working on . . . almost to the word. [And so] we got in contact, and he [philosopher] showed me some of his papers, which were just right in line with what I was working on. So, it was very bizarre to see this. But of course, his point of view was completely different, and his goals were completely different. But it was the same topic [as mine]. We were both working on the same topic.

And so we started to talk, to have discussions, meetings and discussions. And . . . after a few months we realized that we could put our points of view together into something kind of unique . . . [and we wondered if] maybe it was worth exploring whether . . . we should put that point of view out there in a more formal way . . . That's developed dramatically over the last two years. And [we] now have biweekly meetings. We meet once or twice a week, and we have a couple of papers in progress.

We really have developed a point of view that is sort of half-physics and half-philosophy about certain topics. And it's . . . good work in its own right. It's fed back into how I think about my . . . physics. So I think it's . . . had a big impact on [my other lines of research]. It really has changed my outlook on some things.

The physicist and his new collaborator, a philosopher, join together through a third colleague's "intellectual matchmaking." The match took hold, and as the two colleagues worked together, their ideas evolved—as Marin says, "dramatically"—as did their colleagueship. Their understanding of their shared area of study grew in a space they created, on the disciplinary (and in this case departmental) border between them.

Some professors cast the net of their cross-disciplinary thought still farther, well beyond dyadic interaction yet retaining its flavor. Asked where ideas that are new to her come from, Nina Altman, the professor of literary studies at Libra State University, said: "Things that are really alien to me, that I haven't figured out on my own, I absorb from other people. I don't really go out and seek—start reading up on—something that's entirely new to me unless I can figure out why it matters to someone else. If I notice that . . . my colleagues are really interested in social theory—although I don't know much about social theory, it's because they're talking about it and they're getting me engaged with their interest—then I will go out and try to learn more [about it]. So it's . . . gregarious." For Altman scholarly learning is social, woven into webs of discourse.

In light of these images of social engagement even the solo scholar who reads more than talks—who interacts with texts more than with their live readers—cannot be viewed as learning alone. As a member of scholarly communities, formal and informal, this solo scholar reflects on thoughts that others perhaps shaped long ago and that still others will continue to shape in the future. The inescapably social nature of even the most text-bound scholarly learning, stretching back centuries—and of efforts then to extend that learning further among individuals who will work with it more in the future—is captured by William Alana, newly tenured professor in education at Hope State University. Alana describes how he works between two fields, education and philosophy, to bring his students, many of whom are "in-service" practitioners in urban schools, to some of the richest writings that exist on education:

> I sort of feel like . . . Dewey and Socrates [and other philosophers on whose work I draw]—whomsoever—is with me in a strange sort of way. My sense of [such reading] is that it brings voices to the present. And the way I try and teach Dewey is to make his voice right by our own, next to our own. It's almost like he's coming into our ears, he's sitting in the circle [in class]. I try and really take that very seriously, and so [I say to students:] "Listen to him as we listen to each other. Don't judge him any differently than we would judge each other. Don't say, 'Oh, well, he wrote in 1916 so he must be—.'" I really work with students not starting with those presuppositions. Just saying, "Well, he talks different, but let's see what he's got to say," and [then] bringing our questions in.
>
> I feel that [same thing also] as an inquirer . . . when I think about questions [in education] and draw on Dewey. I mean [that within my teaching and my scholarship] I really feel like he is so alive and well . . . I'm not studying Dewey, qua Dewey. Some people do [that], but that's not what I do. He, rather, helps with studying what I'm interested in [in the field of education]. If that makes sense.

Alana, who conducts his work on boundaries between the fields of education and philosophy, makes an important point: in learning—truly learning—even the most secluded of scholars is deeply engaged with others, mindfully so, even across fields that differ from that scholar's own or across historical times long past. Authors enter into the presentness of this scholar's thought through his research, and they then travel through him, into a future with others, through teaching. None of this speaks to experiences of scholarly aloneness; the experience is deeply interactive—

even "gregarious," as Altman put it—but now among people who think and strive to know in the past, present, and future.

Several inferences follow. First, the explicitly interactive features of cross-disciplinarity—people talking in the moment or sharing thoughts over centuries of study—define it as social: an interaction within relationship, between colleague and colleague or author and reader, often is at play. Second, to portray such cross-disciplinarity as social is to link it to colleagueship which is also social. Although I treat the terms *colleagueship* and *cross-disciplinarity* separately (though interrelated, they are distinct) it is noteworthy that a third (14 of 39) of the professors participating in the study in year 3 spoke of them as overlapping, defining cross-disciplinarity as a unique form of colleagueship.[20] Third, I have referred heavily to cross-disciplinarity as inspiring professors' scholarly learning through research. As William Alana, professor of education at Hope State University, makes plain, however, such learning can also happen through teaching. It can happen, too, in the context of faculty service, as it did for a number of professors highlighted in chapter 4.

Exploring Some Challenges of Cross-Disciplinarity
Although higher education leaders and writers usually portray cross-disciplinarity as being good for professors and also good for their institutions[21]—and indeed, participating professors echoed this assumption—disciplinary boundary-crossing does not always go as well as one might like. For one thing it may not come easily. It may not always "feel good," developmentally, to those who take it on. Misused, it can be a career mistake. While typically cast as collegial sharing, cross-disciplinary endeavor may take the form of knowledge "poaching" in anything but collegial ways. Some examples follow.

WHEN NORMS OF SCHOLARLY ENGAGEMENT ARE MISSING. Asked what the "feel of a good idea" is in her field, Emily Lifton, professor of environmental engineering at Signal University, replied in thoughtful detail, merging images of colleagueship and cross-disciplinarity at their best. "A light goes on," she said. "You think, 'Oh, that might explain it.' A lot of times that happens just in having a discussion . . . my work tends to be collaborative . . . the central feature now in almost all my work is that it's collaborative." She explained, "I do the chemistry, but I'm interested in understanding how the chemistry and the biology work within the [environmental] system."

"Oftentimes," Lifton continued, "when I'm trying to discuss something with a person in the field that's not close to mine—trying to explain it to them, and they explain something [to me] . . . I say something that makes me think of something. Or sometimes it's listening to . . . a seminar in a different field . . . and I just think I see a parallel with my work, or I'll learn something that suddenly provides an explanation for why I'm seeing something so bizarre in my own particular [area]."

"So, clarity," she said, "you just have this moment of clarity. You go, 'Oh, my gosh. That could be it.' Now, I don't know if it will be . . . important. It just stimulates you to go down a different path . . . or a door unlocks. You know, you're at a dead end, and you think 'Ugh, why can't I figure this out?' And then—"

"What I find interesting," she reflected further," is that . . . [scholarly learning] happens, at least for me, in a discussion or in listening to someone in a really different field [than mine]. And those are the two things, I think, in engineering that are not typical, at least in [our program here]. Very few discussions, very, very few discussions. And not enough of this going to seminars and listening to other people. I think that [happens] more often in other fields. Engineers don't like to talk," she said. "I mean, they just don't like to talk."

Thinking about what she had just said, I asked if she found this difficult.

"Oh, sure," she replied but immediately challenged herself, "[but] I can understand when you have a very demanding [project] . . . you can't have something highly social [like talking, get in the way]."

Spinning right back again, she retorted, "But it wouldn't hurt once in a while if I'd have someone to go to lunch with, or to have some discussions and stuff . . . We miss a lot of opportunities in not having more discussions because you can learn so much when you listen to other people."

Referring to her own experiences, Lifton laid out the contributions that cross-disciplinary colleagueship had made, and could further make, to her scholarly learning in engineering. But she followed with a critique. Her field, and its crystallization at Signal as department and as local culture, offered few opportunities for the kind of substantive talk that would bring her ideals to life. She knew what she wanted in the way of cross-disciplinary exchange, but her professional workspaces, field based and local, did not provide it as fully as she envisioned.

WHEN CROSS-DISCIPLINARITY TRUMPS DISCIPLINARITY. As in the case of Emily Lifton, some of the professors participating in the *Four Universities Project* complained that their program, department, or field did not invite cross-disciplinary exchange. Others, however, worried about something quite different: that their colleagues, or the university overall, had overdone cross-disciplinarity to the point of nullifying the disciplinarity at its base. In so doing, the scholarly development of professors, still young in their careers, could be shortchanged—something that may not dawn on them until years later as they assess their future career options in light of their work in the past.

Jack Redrick, a chemist at Libra State, defined his own developmental trajectory in this way: "What . . . I was given at Libra State University was a climate of interdisciplinary work with no expectations that I would . . . make my mark in any particular field . . . what I was given here was the freedom to explore anything I wanted to explore. There was no sense that I had to prove myself as a chemist, for instance, and I took that as carte blanche to do anything I wanted to do. I know at other places there might've been more pressure on me to make my mark in the field [chemistry] represented by that department [to which I belonged]. That's not what I felt here." He concluded that in having the freedom to explore "anything I wanted to explore" within a "climate of interdisciplinary work," he lost his focus and possibly his positioning in his field. Post-tenure, he wished that in years past the university had circumscribed his cross-disciplinary explorations by forcing him to focus in his own discipline, chemistry, rather than wandering in surrounding fields. Although Redrick's critique—of being brought to cross-disciplinarity prematurely—deserves attention, another may apply as well: that he may not have been adequately guided in learning what cross-disciplinary effort entails— how to cross a boundary, when, and for what reasons; how to position oneself as a visitor and learner in a new field; how to work there in focused and disciplined ways; how to bring back to one's own field what one has learned in another; and when to say no to cross-disciplinary engagement.

WHEN TAKING SUPERSEDES LEARNING AND SHARING. Still other study participants voiced concerns that cross-disciplinary effort, like any effort, might occasionally lose its moral ballast—as when one field of study reaches out to appropriate—or, as an archaeologist says, "consume"— the stuff of another, rather than enjoining scholars to explore their neighboring fields respectfully, learn deeply what they find there, and then leave, enriched and appreciative, with offers to share and reciprocate. Regina Keishin, an archaeologist recently tenured at Libra State, explained: "I guess archaeologists are famous consumers of theories of other disciplines . . . so a lot of trends in humanistic studies more generally get filtered into archaeology [from] cultural anthropology . . . sociology . . . ecology and environmental studies . . . So, we consume a lot of other people's ideas . . . Archaeology has always defined itself as interdisciplinary, but [in] a lot of ways, in the sense of consuming other disciplines versus what I think of as true interdisciplinary—which is giving back and forth between them." Keishin wondered whether disciplinary boundary crossing entails a respectful opening up of disciplinary specialists' minds to others or the outright swallowing of others' ideas purely for their own benefit.

As Lifton, Redrick, and Keishin indicate, cross-disciplinarity, like many academic and organizational innovations, cannot be viewed as inherently good: introducing cross-disciplinary endeavor to a university will not necessarily make it a good place to work and learn. These three scholars point out three significant features of cross-disciplinarity that can render it problematic. Lifton points out the cultural challenges it may pose: cross-disciplinarity may be inconsistent with long developed ways of "how we do things here in this department" and "how we do things in our field." Redrick points out that cross-disciplinarity, as a career-long endeavor, should be a subject of mentoring, especially for pre-tenure professors; it may be mislearned, risking a loss of the "disciplinarity" at its base in fields where that matters. Keishin makes a point too easily overlooked: that like all features of human relationship, cross-disciplinarity can yield both human good and harm. Its moral content, like that of colleagueship, must be thoughtfully shaped. Sadly, the newness and promise of an innovation such as cross-disciplinarity can "tune out" challenging features such as those that Lifton, Redrick, and Keishin described. Leaders and senior members of communities that encourage cross-disciplinary endeavors would be wise to recall both the promises and challenges of cross-disciplinary endeavor as a site for professors' scholarly learning.

Cross-Disciplinarity as a Feature of University Organization
Although nontraditional institutions have always claimed membership in the American "knowledge enterprise," more so now than in the past,[22] major research universities continue to play a lead role in defining the kinds of knowledge that matter, including what can count as knowledge and as knowledge production. Three of the universities (Signal, Libra State, and Horizon) participating in the *Four Universities Project* have existed since the nineteenth century, and their internal structures—departments, programs, and institutes as key sites of academic knowledge—are long on history. Many of these core organizational units have been literally "frozen" in place—crystallized bureaucratically—for a long time. In such sites some unfreezing, or liquefying, of structures may be helpful in advancing knowledge flows. Professors' cross-disciplinary engagement can at times spur that, or it can simply express the fact that efforts to unfreeze old structures are in play.

Although directed primarily at individuals (at least in the public discourses of the university), cross-disciplinarity may be directed also at the university as itself a knowledge construction, even a knowledge "product." From an organizational perspective cross-disciplinarity signals efforts to liquefy at least some portions of a university's long crystallized departmental core, rendering it as somewhat more amenable to reform than it otherwise would be.[23] In this view an inside-out perspective on cross-disciplinarity invites images of human learning, while an outside-in perspective yields thoughts primarily about organizational change.

Patterns of Experience: Cross-Disciplinarity in Professors'
Scholarly Learning
Cross-disciplinarity emerges as a promising but not unproblematic site for professors' scholarly learning on campus. How did the four study institutions line up with regard to participating professors' involvement in cross-disciplinary endeavors? Approximately half of the study participants at Signal (5 of 10), Libra State (5 of 10), and Horizon (4 of 10) spoke to involvement in and desire for cross-disciplinary experiences;

most of them commented on the benefits of such experiences to their scholarly learning. Under a third of Hope State's participants (2 of 9) referred to involvement in cross-disciplinary effort.

It is hard to know, of course, whether Hope State's lesser involvement in cross-disciplinary endeavor is meaningful, given the small sample sizes, yet the more substantial involvement in cross-field involvement at Signal, Libra, and Horizon is noteworthy. As discussed earlier, the long-term departmental and programmatic crystallization of knowledge in these universities (since their founding in the 1800s) may make cross-disciplinarity desirable there. This observation does not apply in the same way to Hope State, which is quite a bit younger (founded in the 1900s and thus reflecting, perhaps, areas of study that are less crystallized). It is conceivable that Hope State's academic structure has not yet "gelled" enough to warrant significant refashioning. It is also possible that cross-disciplinary behavior was built into many of Hope State's departments and programs, rendering professors' "crossing out" from them as less than necessary. The role of cross-disciplinarity in institutional life cycles—as well as professors' life cycles—is a topic worthy of future consideration.

The preceding views of disciplinary boundary crossing call for two forms of future organizational and policy study for higher education. First, studies of organizational life courses are few and far between in American higher education (histories of colleges and universities aside). A deep understanding of cross-disciplinary endeavor and of resistance to it, cast as developmental features of the university's life course, could usefully illuminate challenges within a university's knowledge production efforts. University leaders need to understand at what point in their institution's history cross-disciplinarity is meaningful and when it is not. A university's knowledge production function (viewed from the outside in) is but another way to talk about its collective scholarly learning (which an inside-out perspective can highlight). Institutional readiness for large-scale cross-disciplinary effort needs to be thought through from both these views. Second, analyses of cross-disciplinarity and resistance to it, as events in academic careers, might be equally yielding of insights about the "prime career time" for cross-disciplinary engagement as well as when such engagement may not be appropriate.

I turn now to a third facet of university organization that can define newly tenured professors' scholarly learning: university-supported opportunities to step outside the campus to pursue a subject of study that is situated amid the events and conditions of "the world out there"—or alternatively, to make pertinent features of "the world out there" part of the scholarly learning occurring "in here" (within academe). Such efforts go by many names: outreach, public service, community service, applied work, clinical effort, professional activity, practice, research on practice, policy research, action research, consultancy, and advisory responsibility, among others. I define such activities as *externalized opportunities for professors' scholarly learning* if those activities accomplish two ends: advance professors' pursuits of their passionate thought and address the learning of others beyond the university. Externalizing efforts can be university-initiated and sponsored, or they may be propelled by professors themselves, with or without external funding.

Such externalizing opportunities allow a professor to move her subject of study out of familiar academic locations (a campus office, lab, classroom, conference room) to sites outside academe where others put knowledge to work. A move of this sort may help a professor think about her subject of study in new ways, with new intellectual materials, and with new collaborators. Half of the professors participating in year 3 interviews of the *Four Universities Project* (20 of 39) portrayed their scholarly learning as occurring through externalizing opportunities such as university outreach programs, community service, or national advisory service.

Externalization as an Opportunity to Learn
One offshoot of the myth of post-tenure decline, equally mythical, is that aging professors lose "the edge" to learn that research provides. Thus, they turn to teaching or service, where they are less burdened to learn rigorously. I suggest a different story line: that professors in advanced career may turn to teaching, outreach, or service because they want to bring their scholarly learning closer to the problems they study, as those problems exist in the natural or social world. A professor who moves her

learning outside academe—or to her students, assuming their connectedness to that outside world—is not necessarily turning down or turning off her scholarly learning. She may be turning it up. With access to a site replete with live versions of the problems and topics she pursues, and with her past research-based knowledge and skills primed to pursue them, that professor continues to engage in scholarly learning but from fresh perspectives. Such learning can in fact occur through the early post-tenure career, even in fields typically distant from "applied" work (mathematics, literature) as well as those where knowledge application is central (engineering, education, social work).

But many newly tenured university professors, well socialized into disciplinary research, do not expect the learning that externalized opportunity can bring. They stumble on it, often quite by surprise. Jennifer Oldak, a renowned mathematician recently tenured at Libra State, described her unexpected learning while preparing to teach in a campus-based summer outreach program for local high school students:

JO: I have taught for a couple of summers some high school students here. There's a [summer] program [for talented high school students]. And I had a couple courses [through] that, on the same topic each time—knots and polyhedrons—and that somehow cut across different levels. There was [mathematical] material in there that you wouldn't find in the standard undergraduate curriculum . . . [The mathematics] was devoid of all the complexities, but it was still there. You wouldn't find [that] in a standard [undergraduate] course. The aim was to go very deep but without using very much [mathematical] background. And it's quite possible to do if you [as teacher] choose your path carefully. That may have had more impact [on my own learning] . . . The construction of the course may have had more impact on my thinking about [the mathematics] than standard undergraduate courses [do] . . . more impact [on me].

AN: Really.

JO: Yes, surprising.

AN: Can you give me an example of what it might have done [for you]?

JO: It makes you realize that various things are connected. Because you're having to pick your way carefully to find things that could be understood with the minimum of background—and are still interesting—[this] brings things together which you didn't really think about. [This experience] hasn't actually resulted in my thinking of a new theorem . . . But it's certainly giving me a new perspective on this theory.

Oldak describes a common "outreach through teaching" activity: a classically trained mathematician, she agrees to teach a brief summer unit in mathematical theory to a group of highly motivated and talented high school students living nearby. But because the course is brief and because Oldak has no control over her summer students' previous exposure to foundational mathematical ideas, she must teach her subject in ways that differ from what she usually does with her undergraduates. She packages the mathematics content of her summer outreach teaching with care, positioning herself, as she says, to "go very deep . . . somehow cut[ting] across different levels" of mathematics but "without using very much [mathematical] background" to do so. She thus positions herself to "pick [her] way carefully" through a landscape of mathematical ideas, traversing it, for teaching, in ways she has not done before. In doing so, she finds that she "bring[s] [mathematical] things together which [otherwise] you didn't really think about," leading her to realize, by surprise, "that various [mathematical] things are connected"—ideas that previously she had kept apart. Although the experience did not lead Oldak to a new theory, it did give her "a new perspective on . . . theory." It positioned her to move through and around her subject, see it in new ways, and collect insights and exercise thought toward her future scholarly work.

I could have included Oldak's experience in chapter 4 as an example of a professor's scholarly learning in the context of service, in this case public service or outreach or for that matter teaching. Both these images of scholarly learning assume an inside-out perspective, for they take what goes on, inside teaching and learning, as the starting point of analysis. But how does Oldak's experience of learning in teaching, or learning in outreach, fit into the kind of outside-in organizational view to which Libra State administrators and policy makers would expect to attend? From an outside-in perspective Oldak's scholarly learning happens in the context of an environmentally attuned organizational initiative (the outreach math program at Libra State) that seeks to intensify the flow of university knowledge out into the surrounding community, external to the university, while bringing in valued community resources (possibly future students). It does so by offering local high school students a taste of world-class mathematics learning. That offering to local students and their families may further generate good feelings about the university, thereby leveraging community-based support (social, monetary, political) for the university's larger efforts.

Thus, in the context of service within an organizational effort to build up community support (viewable from an outside-in perspective), a professor just happens to heighten her scholarly learning (viewable from an inside-out perspective). It is possible to think through Oldak's work from both these perspectives. Clearly, in order to heighten opportunities for students' and professors' substantive learning, it is essential for university leaders to do so.

Images of Scholarly Learning External to the University

Other than teaching-through-outreach activities, what can count as externalized opportunities for professors' scholarly learning and, simultaneously, for the university's own organizational advancement? We have already seen several such examples in earlier chapters, though I did not call them by that name. In chapter 5 I introduced George Bellanov, a recently tenured professor of social work at Libra State, who, as part of his larger connecting career strategy, used his service to families and agencies in the community as sites of his learning. Although some universities frame such activity formally as university outreach, Libra State University has not defined faculty members' public service in this way. Bellanov's connective career strategy grows from his own interests and career needs. Through his service-oriented professional work in the community he gains insights for his research and teaching, identifies topics and sites for future studies, and fulfills service obligations that his department, college, and field expect of him. Whether the leaders of Libra State realize it or not, they gain much from Bellanov, for as he works "out there" on his scholarly agenda, he also directs cutting-edge knowledge to a local community in need of it. That casts Bellanov—and by association, his employing university—as making a significant community contribution. For decades, university leaders have sought to promote the image of the university as contributing directly to real, local needs and thus as being worthy of the community's (and society's) continued support.[24]

In chapter 5 I presented Emily Lifton, an environmental engineer at Signal University who moved her thinking about the chemistry of water pollution from her university-based lab—her primary work site up to this point in her career—into landscapes and communities where those chemistries were problematic, ecologically and health-wise. During our last interview she was feeling torn. Career wise, should she take the secure route—sticking with science as it was traditionally pursued in the lab and scientific community—or turn instead to the riskier study of community practices and policies for water use, framed in light of chemistries she understands deeply? I left the interview wondering how Lifton would address this challenging question in future years, for at the time she felt very much alone in pondering it. Where would she seek out advice and assistance—or simply space and time—to figure out the best possible response to the decision she faced? One might imagine that the university that had tenured her for life might help out: aiding her directly or through connections to funders who might support her work at the intersection of multiple fields of study, protected thereby from the winds of traditional science threatening to sweep her back into the normative career or outwardly away from academic work. When I last spoke with Lifton, she had identified no such source of decision support, institutional or otherwise.

Although not counting as university outreach explicitly, Bellanov's and Lifton's externalized scholarly learning experiences are packaged as clear-cut public service projects. Scholarly learning through externalization may also occur within activities that are more diffuse: expert consulting or advising; writing journalistic commentary on local or statewide challenges; interacting with students whose jobs as practitioners promise to enlarge academic understanding; or simply attending to the flow of themes, relevant to one's work, in life itself, in activities as basic as reading the morning newspaper. Asked where he finds the problems or questions on which he works, a recently tenured political scientist at Horizon University said: "Lots of different places. From, obviously, the morning newspapers." Asked the same question, a policy studies professor, also at Horizon but in a different department, quickly replied: "It's always been [the scholarly] literature. You're reading literature in your Ph.D. training, the journals you read." But this policy scholar suddenly shifted his tone. "Now it's still my main source," he said, "but I'm looking more and more to the phenomena—to what's happening in the world to identify problems . . . reading the business press . . . talking to people, listening to my students." Like the political scientist, the policy scholar looks outside academe for his research problems. He also finds that his post-tenure writing about his research is "in terms of who I perceive I'm talking to." "Prior to tenure," he said, "my audience was mainly academics. I wanted my research to be accepted, to be considered credible . . . Now I feel I should be talking to multiple audiences."

Professors in the other participating universities echoed these professors' statements, though more sparingly. "I read the popular press," said a professor of business at Hope State University, "Even the *Wall Street Journal* [can] talk about issues [applicable to my work]." Another source of research questions, he said, is "daily experiences . . . I started off just price matching guarantees, primarily based on my experience of buying a microwave and getting [a] thirty dollars refund . . . That incident started [me] thinking about this idea of price matching guarantees [as a topic of research.] Why do companies do that? How can they do it? . . . Sometimes it's like that." As he shopped for a microwave oven for his home, this professor happened upon a question that he later worked into his research.

Bellanov, Lifton, and others position the "world out there" as sites to which they carry their scholarly learning and also as sites to which they can return the fruits of their learning. In doing so, they may learn, as may the external communities they serve. Their employing university may benefit as well as it associates its name with their contributions.

On the Internalization of Externalized Scholarly Learning

Although helping to clarify the organizational locations of professors' scholarly learning, externalization is anything but clear-cut in academe. At times that which seems "outside the university" turns into the stuff of its "insides." Such turns in the social reality of university life can show up, forcibly, in classrooms—thereby in professors' teaching—as when the stuff of books gives way to the stuff of students' lives as "texts" for learning, by students and professors alike. The experiences of Wayne Acker, professor of policy studies at Horizon University, provide a picture of such learning.

"When I came here, I was going to teach a class . . . [using] a book on black and white relationships." Acker sat at his desk, and I sat across from him, surrounded by shelf upon shelf of books, daylight streaming in the windows around us. "I grew up in a city . . . [that] was black and white," he said, reaching back to our earlier conversation about his past in rural and suburban America, far removed from the bustling and diverse urban center that now occupied his professional thought. "I was taught by every . . . teacher I ever had in my life [growing up, going to college, that] race in America is about black and white."

Acker described himself as infatuated by the "here and now" of life in the sprawling metropolis in which he teaches—its colliding languages, races and ethnicities, cultures and folkways, technologies, economies, occupational streams, and legends. He also acknowledged the autobiographical knowledge that, he said, often stands him well in his teaching but that at other times gets in the way of what his students seem to know far better—lessons that he, as their teacher, has yet to learn. The simplistic black-white dichotomization of his own past learning has been one such example.

"So, I walk into this classroom," he said, "I'm all prepared to teach black and white. And it doesn't work. I'm in [this] city. [This city] isn't black and white. "It's brown. It's yellow, it's white, it's black, it's green, it's blue. It don't work . . . [I was] using this book. [Its author is a] very smart guy, very good book—I got halfway through this class with this book, and I looked at [my students,] and said, 'I'm sorry. This was a mistake.'"

Turning toward me, Acker explained: "The class itself . . . really just clarified for me that you can't do this in [this city]. You cannot teach it in what has been, for my entire scholarly life, the conventional way of thinking about race in America."

"You get halfway through [the book]—" I started to ask.

"Halfway through, I just looked at them and said, 'There's no Latinos in here, right? There's no Asians . . . This is just—this is nonsense. We can't do this.'"

"And you'd read the book before?" I queried.

"Oh, yeah, sure. I had read the book, I had prepared."

"So, what did you do at that point?"

"What we did . . . was we spent time thinking about why was it that this very smart [author] . . . could write a book in [the mid-1990s] like this? How could [the author] do it? . . . And it was a great discussion. I mean, we had a really interesting discussion . . . In the short term that's what I did. In the long term I just completely changed the way I teach the course. I mean, including not using that book again."

Reflecting on his own words, Acker added, "So, that's the best example of how the teaching, and indeed everything now, [is affected]. I don't teach anything, I don't think about anything as a scholar, where *that's* not present—[with] *that* being in [*this* city] compared to being in [a white smaller college town]."

"That's kind of [the name of city] effect," I tried out.

"Yeah," he said, but corrected me, "But it's also the classes, right? . . . I'm sure it's happening in New York, and certainly . . . other places. I mean, my classes . . . we're talking about race, and I'm looking at the class, and I'm trying to get their attention because they don't like talking about race. And I said [to them], 'Look around the classroom. There are . . . three people in this room who are African-American. They wouldn't be here in 1960s, right? . . . Look around the room. There's nine Asians. Would they be here? There's five Latinas. Would they be here? Think about who's around you.'"

"It's inescapable," Acker explained. "That's gonna be true everywhere in academia soon. But it's certainly true here. And you can't teach a story of America and just ignore them. I mean, how can you, as a teacher? . . . [It's] half-nonwhite, non-African-American, non-European . . . if not more. I can't teach [a class about this city] that's 'Oh, well, that's not important.' This is *their* [city]."[25]

Acker's experience broadens and blurs conventional images of "what's in and out of the university" and also who and what moves in and out. As such, his experience blurs my previously posed views of externalized opportunities for professors' scholarly learning. Externalization, as I said earlier, involves a professor's taking her research out into the community or a university's formal sponsoring of such efforts (e.g., through an outreach mission). Drawing on the preceding inside-out analysis of Acker's experience, I add now that externalization can occur in reverse: the external community can enter the university, flooding its classrooms, even overtaking its subject matters. Acker indicates that traditional academic sources (e.g., the textbook he had selected) had little to do directly with the learning he experienced in class. Acker himself had little to do with it.

Rather, he and his learning were at the mercy of externalized knowledge that "came at him" in his class on campus. The city in which he taught, he said—its people—positioned themselves as learners in that class—and also as the subject matter that they and he would learn.

Now what if Acker had studied and then taken a professorial position in a university located in a part of the country much like the one he came from, secluded from the massive cultural, economic, and political changes of the modern-day urban culture that he experiences in his current job? What (if anything) could that far-flung university have done to bring Acker's classroom, and his own learning in it, to the curriculum of twenty-first-century urban America—its changing peoples and families, neighborhoods and communities, challenges and aspirations, its needs to understand its changing sense of collective self? In this day and age university leaders may need to rethink where they and their institutions fit into and how they relate to the world about them—but not simply in response to vague goals of fiscal accountability and educational responsiveness (accountable for what specifically? responsive to what specifically?). Rather, these leaders need to articulate where they and their campuses stand with regard to more substantive goals such as supporting professors' learning of those subjects they claim as their own, and doing so in the new cultural, demographic, and economic contexts in which they (and their students) find themselves—much as Wayne Acker did. To lend substance to their goals, university leaders must do much more than invent new academic incentive systems, introduce post-tenure reviews, or rethink tenure altogether. They need to take professors' scholarly learning for what it is: a serious endeavor that faculties and leaders must position—and successively reposition—in contexts that help professors turn their learning into the best it can be, for the university and all its learners, professors included. University professors can and should themselves lead in this endeavor, but their institutions and fields can certainly help.

Externalization as a Feature of University Organization
Externalization may be envisioned as academics' attempts to do good in the world while sharpening further their own academic expertise (an inside-out view). It may also be envisioned as concrete, outwardly directed efforts made by university leaders to contribute to broad social aims while advancing the university's status, heightening its legitimacy,

or broadening its resource base (an outside-in view). Externalization draws attention to the boundary that separates internal university functioning from environmental dynamics outside it. It highlights both the defining nature of that boundary (marking off what constitutes academic endeavor uniquely) and significantly, its permeability (letting streams of its "academic core" out of the university, bringing in resources critical to the life of its core). Allowing for such breathing space at the boundary after an institution has achieved maturity (as Libra State, Horizon, and Signal clearly have), allows it to move and grow from inside. Much the same may be said for professors: freed from overly restrictive academic norms, freed to engage with live problems, midcareer professors may engage in scholarly learning that grows both from and beyond what they know already.

Patterns of Experience: Scholarly Learning through Externalization

As indicated earlier, half of the professors participating in year 3 interviews of the *Four Universities Project* (20 of 39) referred to pursuits of externalized scholarly learning. But what was it about professors, or about their universities and fields, that contributed to their so doing? Professors' gender did not: equal numbers of men and women (10 each) engaged in externalized scholarly learning. Professors' affiliation with a particular disciplinary sector and institution mattered more. Not surprisingly, all professors associated with applied and professional fields, in all four universities ($n = 11$), indicated engagements in scholarly learning in externalized settings. Half the professors in the social sciences (4 of 8) also did, as did three of the nine humanists and two of the eleven scientists. A substantial number of Horizon participants (8 of 10) indicated such learning, as did half of those at Signal (5 of 10). Three of nine participants at Hope State and four of ten at Libra State did too.

This pattern can be read in two ways: that not nearly enough of these newly tenured professors are "out there," attending, through their deeply honed subjects of study, to "real-world problems"; or alternatively, that a surprisingly large proportion of the sample are. I prefer the latter, more generous reading. Ongoing discussions of university outreach aside,[26] researchers and policy makers have not historically talked about professors' academic learning occurring outside academe. That one-third of the study participants affiliated with nonapplied fields (9 of 28) sought to externalize their scholarly learning is a sign that this kind of learning can happen—and that it does, with or without institutional assistance—in a variety of fields whose traditional interests may not include external activities.

I do not mean to suggest that all humanists, social scientists, and scientists ought to pursue opportunities to externalize their scholarly learning—rather, that universities may wish to avail scholars of such opportunities should those scholars deem it relevant to their learning. I say this carefully: the lure of public support and increased access to external resources, among other things, could lead university leaders to direct externalized efforts, such as those described here, toward their own interests. Although nodding at professors' scholarly learning, those leaders may not strategize authentically toward it. They may, for example, implement externalizing initiatives in ways that do more harm than good to professors' scholarly learning in the long run.

As evidence, I return to Sandra Covington, the professor of public health at People's State University, whose responsiveness to a campuswide externalizing imperative (grant writing toward high-priority and significant funding availabilities) unhinged her, professionally, from the scholarly learning that meant a great deal to her. Fascinated by the epidemiology of a benign bacterium commonly found in hospital and community settings, Covington had hoped to devote good portions of her post-tenure career to understanding it. Yet due to her expanding responsibilities within others' agendas—to pursue collaborative research on a far more threatening and indeed more important organism—Covington set aside her favored studies. By her third post-tenure year Covington had dedicated herself, almost fully, to the new agenda. To do this, she let her attention to her favored research lapse until but a "thread" of that earlier work remained. She thus watched herself grow distant from learning that she continued to refer to as "her core." Although engaged in socially important work, Covington wondered if soon she might "burn out." How might we explain Covington's predicament, and how might it have been averted? Sandra Covington responded to her university's social action priorities selflessly, but her university did not reciprocate in kind, for example, by helping her find time to attend, even briefly, to the earlier work. Doing so might have fueled her work on other less personal (but nonetheless socially important) projects, thereby lessening the sense of impending "burn-out" that she increasingly sensed and worried about.

Providing for Professors' Scholarly Learning: A University Imperative

Following on the message of chapter 5, that professors can do a fair amount to ensure that their scholarly learning continues, this chapter presents a complementary point: the universities and colleges in which professors work—their administrative and faculty leaders, colleague networks and communities, the university's staff—can and should help in this effort. To help requires being aware of what scholarly learning is and of how much it can matter to professors. To help also means listening to professors closely to discern where, in the university, they are trying to position their scholarly learning and the extent to which their efforts to do so are bearing fruit—or not. To help is also to be aware of which professors manage to position their scholarly learning successfully in the university and which of them struggle, in undue ways, to do so. Not least, to help involves building up those features of academic organization that professors rely on to support their scholarly learning.

The Middle Remapped

*Toward an Ecology of Learning in
the Early Post-Tenure Career*

What happened to the scholarly learning of the newly tenured university professors whom I followed—some through their fifth post-tenure year—through the *Four Universities Project?* First and foremost, these professors continued to pursue their scholarly learning in new or revised form. Indeed, some struggled to do so. Not surprisingly, many pursued their scholarly learning through research or creative endeavors. Some pursued it through their faculty service. Virtually all pursued it through their teaching of both graduate and undergraduate students.

By their final interview—three to five years post-tenure—most professors participating in the *Four Universities Project* engaged their scholarly learning through at least two of the following academic activities: research, teaching, or service (internal or external). I infer that career-wise, their scholarly learning was spreading out beyond the research on which most had focused pre-tenure, to other professional activities. As their professional activities diversified, so did the locations of their scholarly learning. It is hard to know exactly when that spreading out began. It is possible that for some professors it started before they were tenured. But because so many pre-tenure professors concentrate on research—given the intense research expectations of most university tenure reviews—it is likely that most could not move their scholarly learning to teaching, service, or outreach until after they were tenured. The literary scholar Nina Altman delayed such a move until she had tenure in hand: although deeply attracted to teaching as a way to engage her students' and her own scholarly learning, Altman purposefully played down her love of teaching during her pre-tenure years at Libra State University. As an assistant untenured professor, she knew that the tenure review process at her university would strongly favor an accomplished researcher over an accomplished teacher. Things changed post-tenure, at which time Altman openly asserted her teacher identity, though without loss to her scholarly learning. She restarted a long dormant scholarly agenda, still on her favored theme of translation, but now did so openly amid her classroom teaching.

The post-tenure spread of scholarly learning—from professors' research into their other work roles (e.g., teaching, institutional service, and public outreach)—did not proceed unchecked. As professors moved their scholarly learning into these new professional activities, many tried to keep it rooted at its personal source: in their lives as locations of unique personal meaning. Several study participants wove stories of childhood fascination with the sounds and sights and "feelings" of subjects that, years later, they transposed into scholarly study, most often in their research but increasingly, in teaching, outreach, and occasionally institutional service.[1] These sights and sounds and feelings are no doubt what kept many of these professors engaged in their scholarly learning as they moved that learning from research to other professional activities. Doubtless, too, these sensations shaped the content and scope of what professors selected for their scholarly study, amid the multiple other possibilities they encountered in their daily work.

Given that little has been written in higher education, and elsewhere, about the stream of experience to which I refer as "scholarly learning," one might wonder how real it is, independent of the research, teaching, outreach, and service activities in which it is embedded. Those professional activities are, after all, so much more palpable (discernable, assessable, even countable) than is scholarly learning. Administrators, policy makers, and members of the general public usually accept words such as *teaching, research,* and *service* as representing the "real" work of professors. In saying them, one imagines concrete activities in concrete spaces: a professor in front of a classroom of freshman students or in a lab with post-docs and technicians nearby or in a committee poring over a newly drafted curriculum. In contrast, scholarly learning is amorphous; it is an experience of mind that is hard for disciplinary outsiders to visualize. "Scholarly learning—what's that?" they might wonder. Indeed, my own colleagues might ask as well: how did I, as researcher, know that what I heard in interviews was indeed scholarly learning as opposed to something else? How, they might ask, would I recognize such scholarly learning if I heard it again today with the *Four Universities Project* behind me?

Drawing on what I learned through the two studies, I would recognize professors' scholarly learning if and when I tripped across signs, however brief or infrequent, of their *passionate thought*. Professors typically portray their passionate thought as intense feeling for their subjects of intellectual study: high excitement or exuberance at its realization, sadness or despair at its loss, frustration at its delay, desire in its absence. They also portray pursuits of passionate thought as transgressions of common academic boundaries: between personal and professional, subjective and objective, emotional and cognitive, aesthetic and scientific, life and career.

I would therefore expect to hear professors speak emotionally about their scholarly learning. I would also expect to hear them refer to the blurring of self and subject of study. But passionate thought does not come easily; it is usually accessed through struggle. I would then expect to hear professors talk about the intensity of effort they devote to scholarly learning: culling through theories and findings in a field's literatures; juxtaposing old and new thoughts; bringing together images previously held apart to experiment with new meanings; replaying long-accepted ideas against new knowledge backgrounds; rethinking long-accepted meanings while verbalizing them to audiences previously unexposed to them.

Virtually all the professors I interviewed through the *Four Universities Project* referred to having experienced passionate thought. They also portrayed themselves as mobilizing the tools and methods of their fields to cultivate the scholarly learning in which, they hoped, they would realize such thought. Despite their differences—disciplinary, perspectival, methodological, professional, personal—professors readied themselves for scholarly learning in a number of ways: positioning themselves to expand on what they know already (extending their subject matter knowledge); reorganizing their well-established knowledge so as to yield otherwise unseen meaning (reforming it); poising themselves to explore an idea transferred from one site to another (recontextualizing that knowledge); and pondering images that, quite by surprise, they invoke in class or in other public settings while struggling to translate important disciplinary ideas in terms that newcomers to the discipline can grasp. I defined activities such as these as the mindwork in which professors engaged within scholarly learning—that is, as they pursued their passionate thought.

Scholarly learning aside, what else did professors in the *Four Universities Project* try to learn—or view themselves as learning—and how did they orchestrate that other learning with the scholarly? To be sure, professors were trying to learn much more broadly than in the scholarly realm alone and portrayed themselves as pursuing a range of skills and activities: engaging subject matters that had little or no bearing on their scholarly learning but which they took on nonetheless; gaining skills in key academic practices, including teaching, research, outreach, service, mentoring, and so on; unearthing resources and constraints built into their university and disciplinary communities; discerning limitations on the practices in which they and their colleagues engaged (the bounded nature of reform); defining or refining their identities as persons and scholars; trying out practices of selective inaction and restraint; and disengaging from one or another academic practice that they experienced as distracting from meaningful endeavor.

To manage this broad-ranging learning of the early post-tenure career, the professors drew on their own and on their communities' resources to invoke one or more career strategies, including *creating space* for their scholarly learning (clearing out and building relationships and communities); *containing attention* (focusing professional energy on matters of personal meaning); and *connecting contexts* of work and life so as to enhance their scholarly learning while also gaining personally from it.

Yet professors were not fully on their own, and many of them reported campus-based support for their scholarly learning. This support came from the colleagueship they developed with campus peers; the university's openness to cross-disciplinary engagement; and opportunities for scholarly learning that were available off-campus and outside traditional conceptions of research, for example, in various forms of public service. Yet one person's support can be another's constraint, and opportunities for growth and learning vary, sometimes in unfair and hurtful ways. Patterns of difference, by gender and field of study, mediated professors' experiences of scholarly learning, including whether or not they felt supported on campus in their learning. A number of the women in the study struggled, their intellectual growth seemingly at risk compared to that of their male colleagues.[2] As such, a number of study participants—disproportionately women—spoke of support for their scholarly learning as being largely nonexistent (e.g., Esther Sharan, who found no time at all for collegial conversation). Other women portrayed such support as ineffectual (Emily Lifton, who relished supportive collegial exchange but found herself in a culture that did not value it). Others referred to outright obstacles to it (Jeannette Parsons, who sought to advance feminist interests on campus by working to bring in a speaker, while her male colleagues persisted in their research without sharing much with her).

Newly tenured professors' experiences of scholarly learning varied relative to who and where they were when I interviewed them, what they were (and were not) doing, how close they felt they were to work that spurred their passionate thought, and how they saw their future prospects. "What happened" through their early post-tenure careers is that most professors awoke to new possibilities for and constraints on their scholarly learning—even as their campuses awoke to the potential of those professors' learning. Tenure may have signaled the forging of a new awareness of and relationship between person and place.

Insights

The two studies I conducted yielded several insights.

Learning is a central experience of the early post-tenure career, and *professors care deeply about their scholarly learning.* Throughout the early years of their post-tenure careers professors' attempts to engage in scholarly learning, and to realize its personal meanings to them, can be intense and powerful. Although references to such personal meaning in scholarship are rare in the literature of higher education (evident mainly in autobiographical works), most professors in my studies treated it as a familiar topic. None were surprised by my interest in this aspect of their work, though some did struggle for words when asked to talk about it. Most struck me as practiced at least in their thoughts about personal meaning, as evidenced by the variety and vividness of the images and feelings they shared.

I was surprised at the prominence of learning, and of desire for scholarly learning especially, in the interviews. Such experiences are uncharted in research-based writings about higher education. They also are absent in policy makers' and faculty development specialists' talk about the faculty's vitality and engagement, and incentives to heighten these. Policy makers and academic administrators rarely talk about the kinds of learning struggles and desires that professors talked about in interviews. In creating university policy and setting the university's direction, these leaders often overlook experiences that are key to the academic life: notably, professors' scholarly learning in personally meaningful subjects of study, agency toward such pursuit, passionate thought as high points of its realization. Given this absence—of talk and thought about professors' scholarly learning—institutional leaders and policy makers may fail to consider ways to preserve and foster it as central to the faculty's work.

Scholarly learning exists, but too often its *where* and *when* are misunderstood and its *what* (that which is learned) is ignored. Most outsiders to academe assume the *where* of scholarly learning to be research (overlooking teaching, outreach, and service). They may view good portions of its *when* as early career (leaving out the learning that occurs post-tenure). They often fail to consider its *what* and the fact that this can change over time (alongside changes in its where and when). Extrapolating from the findings of my studies, I posit that learning may well go on through the full length of the academic career—that most professors do not stop learning and that what may appear as stalled learning is really learning whose *what* has changed.

I suggest then that professors generally do not stop learning. Rather, what they learn changes. Thus, a professor who appears to have stopped learning, or caring about learning, about her long-term subject of study— for example, in mathematics, engineering, literature—may in fact have turned her attention to learning other features of her academic and personal life, including how to juggle them: how to help a network of research colleagues work together productively given interpersonal tensions among some members; how to turn a department, long incoherent in its intellectual content and values, into a functional unit; how to work with ten advanced doctoral students, several newly inherited from departing colleagues but few of whose dissertations bear directly on one's own expertise; how to share the fascinations of scientific discovery with a required freshman science class that seats six hundred; how to balance a major commute, demanding family life, academic marriage, and care of ailing family members with rising program coordination duties, growing committee responsibilities, and intensified mentoring and teaching loads. These tasks require learning that absorbs time—often long stretches of it—that one could otherwise allot to scholarly learning.

Learning does go on as professors age—but of an increasing array of things in their careers and lives. But even if a professor succeeds in juggling broad learning in diverse areas of life and career so that she can devote energy to pursuing subjects that hold great meaning for her, it is likely that over time aspects of those subjects will change, as might the subjects themselves. To learn something is to change it in one's mind, often bit by bit.

Scholarly learning matters a great deal to professors; it is a beacon of meaning in their careers and lives. The recently tenured professors I interviewed portrayed themselves as striving to learn things in particular because they wanted to learn those things and not because they were induced to by forces beyond themselves. Such wanting to learn something, from within oneself, may well override the power of coaching, prodding, motivating, engaging, leading, or for that matter "incentivizing." Professors' desires to learn subjects that matter to them personally, and their strivings to do so, are important but largely undiscussed (and underused) resources that higher education leaders could more fully deploy—for the good of students, the university, society, and indeed, humanity. It is conceivable that policy makers might not need to push their faculties toward "productivity" and "engagement" quite as strenuously as some, these days, think they should if they attend more openly to what professors already want to do, bringing it around to the university's benefit.

To establish scholarly learning as real in professors' lives requires more than assessment of its outcomes: it requires hard looks at what goes on in that learning. To learn is not the same as to produce. To learn is to see and ponder, sense and approach, create and grasp—an idea, question, image, or problem—that promises insight. Such learning takes time and effort as well as an awareness that sometimes nothing can be learned, that the learning may be false, or that it may hit a dead end. Experiences of learning need not be grand or magical. They need not be countable or publishable or even connected to research. They need not be "right" or "complete" on each try. That said, not every idea, publication, countable project, and research activity counts as a learning experience. It is important to distinguish those that do from those that do not. What then counts as scholarly learning?

Scholarly learning can be viewed as a person positioning herself to work with subject matter knowledge, to move it around, to explore it, to seek some insight into it that may or may not materialize. Learning—as attempting to know something of significance to the learner—is personal, for when it does materialize, the learner experiences it as memorable, beautiful, or deeply touching, prompting desires for more such mental engagement. Such learning can hold a learner to her path, even during unproductive times, for its memory reminds the learner of "what's possible" by way of insight. Learning viewed more distantly, as something achieved or as a product, misses the fullness of the experience of getting there, of wanting and struggling to do that. Both views matter. To speak of learning without specifying what is sought or gained (as product) is indeed meaningless. But to attend solely to the products of learning, without appreciating what it was like to discern or create them, is to miss the wholeness of what the learner experienced—and to lose the sense of what an instance of coming to know implies for future knowledge production.

Commitment to the advancement of scholarly learning requires university leaders' and others' attention to where it can happen, what professors can do to ignite and maintain it, and what universities can offer toward its support. A major finding of the *Four Universities* study is that newly tenured professors are likely to be learning continually and across multiple strands of their work. Virtually every feature of their workplace can turn into a place for learning something. Whether that something is useful or not—whether it relates to a professor's intellectual passions—is, however, quite another matter.

What is central is that professors' learning, certainly in the scholarly realm, does not and cannot occur without a location. In describing features of their workplaces that shape their scholarly learning, for better or for worse, professors participating in the *Four Universities Project* referred to their colleagueship, cross-disciplinary resources for learning, and opportunities to move their studies outside conventional academic spaces (externalization). As noted earlier, study participants named their own teaching as well as their research, outreach, and institutional service as important locations of their scholarly learning.

But this discussion is incomplete. Professors and their learning, their scholarly learning especially, do not sit at the end of a one-way street: Scholarly learning involves far more than a context impressing itself, unidirectionally, on its professors; it involves far more than professors absorbing key elements of context into themselves. Scholarly learning, when it happens in busy, demanding, and complex universities, entails action in two directions. Diverse contexts may act on professors, offering them new or unusual resources and opportunities for thought (e.g., in the form of colleagues' expertise) as well as new constraints. But professors can also act on contexts by nudging, shaping, or otherwise maneuvering their workplaces, for example, so as to support engagements with knowledge that they desire. Professors can work at clearing away and revamping features of an environment that does not adequately support their scholarly learning, or when possible, they may move their learning to new and more supportive locations. They can also contain some of the attention they give to that environment's undesirable features, thus limiting portions of their learning purposefully. In doing so, they can keep their minds and hearts on the learning that matters most to them. Not least, professors can reorganize and connect contexts to enhance meaning and thereby initiate, support, or elaborate meaningful learning. Professors may then take a hand in crafting the contexts of their scholarly learning so as to engage and nourish such learning. While professors can take such action in support of their scholarly learning, university leaders can support them by cultivating open and generative colleagueship, norms of cross-disciplinary collaboration, and opportunities for externalized learning (e.g., public service conducive to scholarly learning).

Implications

Based on the study findings, what should newly tenured professors do to promote their learning now and in the future? What should university leaders and policy makers bear in mind as they strive to enhance professors' scholarly learning? Not least, what should higher education researchers study to improve on extant understandings of professors' learning—and how should they do so? I respond by speaking directly to these individuals and communities.

≫→ Find or create your subject of study, or reconstruct it, so that it is meaningful to you even as it bears import for others. Both of these sides matter; both speak to the significance of scholarly learning. Having several subjects of study is fine, especially if you can identify meaningful linkages among them: such linkages—among subjects that are truly meaningful to you—may let you use the insights of one subject to advance others. Know what your subject is. Be prepared to explain it publicly, including why it matters and what you hope to learn from it. Remember that searching for a subject is part and parcel of having one; both are essential elements of scholarly learning.

≫→ Despite its public presence in your life as a statement of what you know and what you can share with others, the subject you study is a statement to yourself of who you are, what you care about, and what you want to know. Your subject also is a space in which you can explore ideas and questions that mean a great deal to you now and that may launch you into future study in unexpected ways.

≫→ You will be invited, requested, or pulled to learn in subjects beyond those that you declare as your own. You will need to decide how much attention to give those other subjects, including the extent to which you believe they can advance efforts that are closer to your heart. Doing that is not easy. As a professor and scholar who has gained from the support of various communities, you will want to "give back" to those communities, and otherwise fulfill your professional obligations to them. You should do that but without sacrificing the scholarly agenda and identity to which these communities gave you access in the first place. To give to others in self-abnegating ways shuts down what you can give to anyone, now and in the future. Serve yourself and others in equal and healthy measure, searching for balance over time.

≫→ The emotional matter of scholarly learning—its high points—are gems to be sought and treasured, remembered, and pursued time and again. But they cannot be realized without the *ground* of scholarly learning from which they grow. Be sure to care for that scholarly ground, even through times of seeming intellectual drought, for that is the only space within which high thought will grow. That said, scholarly learning may itself take root in many corners of one's professorial career: in teaching, service, and outreach inasmuch as in research. Position it and care for it in all these career places. Learn, too, from what you see across these places of learning. Look for passionate thought within and across them.

⫸ Search the university for colleagues, for cross-disciplinary relationships and events, and for scholarly learning opportunities that extend beyond the university, as they may move your scholarly learning forward in fruitful ways. In doings so, consider how you might reframe those parts of the university in which you do your work in ways that will support your scholarly learning.

TO UNIVERSITY LEADERS, INCLUDING POLICY MAKERS COMMITTED TO EDUCATIONAL IMPROVEMENT

⫸ In considering the university's welfare, attend equally to the campus's societal (including economic and political) existence and the human life of its insides. Members of a campus community attuned to one of the two organizational sides are likely to differ, in their agendas for learning and action, from members attuned to the other. It is crucial to deal fully with both. Find ways to bring the best that each side can yield, by way of insight, to the other. When possible, position persons knowledgeable of one side to collaborate with those knowledgeable of the other in ways that will encourage them to educate each other.

⫸ Avoid thinking of leadership as a dynamic that generalizes across the multiple concerns and functions of the university. Leadership should be framed in more specialized ways, as attuned to the specific "stuff" of the leading at issue. Rather than applying a generalized image of leadership, presumably applicable to diverse university functions and specialties, develop leadership within and for those specialties specifically: one form distinctively for the undergraduate curriculum, one tailored toward oversight of university budgets, one attuned to the specialized work of the university's promotion and tenure process, one that understands fully the insides of the university's student activities functions. What it takes to lead in one area is likely to differ from what it takes to lead in another. Leadership in various substantive areas assumes different forms. This suggestion rests on the hypothesis that leadership, much like teaching, is sensitive to the subject that it treats. To work as well as it can, leadership needs to be situated in that subject, much as is teaching.

≫→ Recall that the scholarly work and learning in which professors engage represent far more to them than do "work for pay" and "work for advancement." Asked to describe the work they love, none of the professors I interviewed through my second study referred to pay or advancement. Although these kinds of inducements may spur some professors to respond to administrative initiatives, it is not what they think about or reach for. As such, it is unlikely that such promised "rewards" can spur professors to action that is as thoughtful and imaginative as the promised opportunity to advance one's scholarly learning.

TO RESEARCHERS WHO STUDY HIGHER EDUCATION

≫→ The field of higher education should acknowledge the centrality of subject matter to professors' work as well as to institutions' larger educating efforts. To talk about professors' teaching, research, outreach, and even service without closely considering *what* these professors teach, study, and otherwise share leaves too much of their experience unsurveyed and undiscussed. Professors act in and on their subjects inasmuch as they act in and on organizational matters that everyone can plainly see. If we want to understand professors, as scholars, as deeply as we need to—including how they go about their educating tasks and what some of them do to grow as educators—then we need to hear their thoughts about the subjects they study and teach, in the name of education.

A higher education researcher might not understand a theoretical physicist's discussion of a challenging physical concept or how to teach it. But in eliciting subject matter explanation from that professor, the higher education researcher positions herself to see more of that scholar's struggles than she would without such an explanation. University-based physicists, mathematicians, engineers, and others whose subjects strike laypersons as esoteric do learn over time how to talk about the content and value of their work to nonacademics—they become, in effect, teachers to nonmajor students, funders, university administrators, colleagues in other fields, government officials, and the public. How these scholars connect to people who are outside their immediate disciplinary sphere, but who want to understand their work, can also be applied to conversations they have with higher education researchers. The field of higher education needs to develop research designs and methods for exploring professors' work with, and experiences of, the subject matters they teach and learn. We can do that without infringing on professors' expertise. Indeed, by opening up that expertise for broader appreciation, we may strengthen its social position.

⮞ The field also would benefit from bringing together two modes of thought and talk in higher education: that which focuses on organization (emphasizing largely an outside-in perspective) and that which considers faculty lives, teaching, and learning (from the inside out). At the present time scholars in these separate areas cluster within their own subcommunities. Certainly, they interact at annual conferences and publish in common journals, but when it comes to their interest and engagement with specific subject matter, they often go separate ways. Organizational scholars write about faculty but within organizational frames; scholars of faculty careers employ their own frames to define the faculty's experience of organizational life. Although the substance of their work intersects (both communities acknowledge the value of organizational study and of faculty careers), their conceptual framing diverges in ways that set them apart from each other, and as a result, cross-subcommunity talk lapses. Bringing different communities of scholars together is a long-term project but one that could be profitably begun.

⮞ The field needs to develop further the qualitative research in which its members increasingly engage, especially so in studies of teaching and learning. To understand what goes on in classrooms, researchers need to sit, watch, listen, and think with the teachers and students in them. They need to hear and explore how teachers and learners talk and otherwise share the subjects—substantive and otherwise—in those classrooms. They need to be with those teachers and learners, in class, in the moments of their work together. Toward that end, the field needs improved classroom ethnographic (observational and interview) designs and methods. The field also needs to foster virtues of persistence, close study, analysis attuned to subtleties—all are required for such study. The field also needs to learn how to engage subject matter specialists collaboratively in research on students' and teachers' subject matter change.

Coda: Why Learning?

I chose to explore university professors' experiences of learning, especially scholarly learning, because I view those experiences as central to the promise—of heightened opportunities to learn—that higher education extends to all who enter its doors. I view professors as the central carriers and cultivators of that promise and the tenured professorial career as its primary path for growing into something more than a promise. We still have much to learn about the learning toward which we all aspire.

Study Designs and Background Data

In the *People's State University Project* and *Four Universities Project* I explored newly tenured university professors' learning—especially their scholarly learning—as an experience in their careers and lives. Given the emphasis on experience, the studies called for designs and methods that could reach into professors' consciousness with attention to: *what* the professors pursued in the name of learning; what their scholarly learning (their learning of their favored subject matters) meant to them, including how they experienced instances of such learning; *where* they conducted their scholarly learning and how these sites joined experientially with the substance of their learning; the extent to which professors chose and directed their learning, especially scholarly learning, and how they did so; and the extent to which professors felt supported, challenged, or blocked in learning. Here I describe the study designs and methods that allowed me to pursue this study agenda.

The *People's State University Project*

In the *People's State University Project* I explored how newly tenured university professors experienced their work and workplaces and the extent to which they cast their academic identities in light of these experiences.

Study Design

Conducted in the early and middle 1990s, the study involved thirty-eight professors (22 men, 58%; 16 women, 42%) in diverse disciplines and fields, working at a major public research university with a prominent land-grant mission.

I followed twenty of the thirty-eight participating professors from the first through the third post-tenure year (cohort 1), and eighteen from the year of the tenure review through the second post-tenure year (cohort 2). Breakdown by disciplinary/field sector for the full sample was as follows: arts and humanities, three (8%); social sciences, three (8%); sciences, eleven (29%); and applied/professional fields, twenty-one (55%).[1] Ten of the twenty-one professors appointed to applied/

professional departments had substantial expertise in the sciences; others were aligned with the social sciences and arts or humanities. All areas of the university active in the tenuring process in year 1 of the study, and in the preceding year, were represented, except for selected professional schools (medical, dental, veterinary, law) where the faculty role differs from other areas. To ensure representativeness of disciplinary/field affiliations, gender, age, ethnicity and race, countries of origin, and related features of the university's early post-tenure faculty corps, I used a random selection process to identify potential participants from the approximately one hundred people tenured by People's State University in year 1 of the study. Yet, given the small number of racial/ethnic minorities holding senior-level faculty appointments in major research universities through this period of American history, I over-sampled tenured professors of color whenever possible, bringing minority representation to 13 percent (5 of 38) of the sample.[2]

Rate of agreement to participate in the three-year study was 81% for the full sample (47 individuals, confirmed as qualified for study participation, were invited); participation agreement rate for cohort 1 was 91% and 72% for cohort 2. The thirty-eight participants indicated willingness, year by year, over three years, to continue in the study; for logistical reasons, however, one participant was away on sabbatical in each of project years 2 and 3 and could not be reinterviewed. As such, participation rates for the three years were: 100% in study year 1, 97% in year 2, and 97% in year 3. By project year 3 three individuals had left People's State University for employment elsewhere; I conducted final interviews with each of these three by long-distance telephone.

With the aid of a semistructured protocol, I conducted interviews with all study participants, usually in their offices, for two hours in the first year, an hour in the second year, and an hour and a half in the third. I tape-recorded all interviews except for one in which I took notes by hand at participant's request. When possible, I also took descriptive notes of the interview setting. All recorded interviews were transcribed in preparation for analysis. I also collected the following data from study participants: curriculum vitae, narrative statements for the tenure review (if available), publications and other manuscripts, and course syllabi. I used these materials to clarify and/or amplify interview data. Through the three years of the study I also collected and reviewed data on People's State University's history and mission, key campus events, enrollment, research and service performance, programs of study, planning efforts, and public self-representation. These and other campus materials (collected in project archives) were summarized in an extensive campus case study that provided contextual perspective for the primary analysis of newly tenured professors' interview data. As noted in chapter 1 (see n. 5), I promised all study participants strict research confidentiality and have limited data displays to abide by this promise.

Data analysis included identifying, grounding, and confirming themes of experienced change through professors' early post-tenure careers. Analysis proceeded iteratively: multiple rounds of data review allowed insights to build on one another and provided opportunities for comparative checking, thereby permitting correction, revision, addition, and confirmation, cycle to cycle. Any one analytic round might involve identifying a pattern of interest, responsive to the study's aim and evident (though diversely) across multiple cases; formulating a propositional claim for that pattern's existence, possible meanings, and significance in the context of People's State University; testing the claim against the data that initially gave rise to it and then against other data from other sample cases; rewriting the claim in light of the data drawn from the rest of the sample; and tacking back to the data that had originated the claim for retest. In searching for data-based patterns, I attended consistently to negative (discrepant) data, using such data to interrogate further the meaning of the proposed pattern and the certainty of the claim at issue. In brief the *People's State University Project* helped me discern a conceptual door that the later *Four Universities Project* then opened.[3]

Background Information

People's State University, a major public land-grant institution, is located in a mid-sized American town about a two-hour drive from a major urban center, yet its research centers are distributed widely throughout the state. Over 75% of the university's forty thousand student enrollment is undergraduate, heavily in-state, with many students housed in massive residential complexes. Over the years the Carnegie Commission on Higher Education and the Carnegie Foundation for the Advancement of Teaching have classified People's State University as Research University-Very High Research Activity (RU/VH), Doctoral/Research-Extensive, and Research I. People's State University is listed among the top universities in the nation, and many of its academic programs—notably in professional/applied fields but also some disciplines—stand out in professional and popular rankings as being among their field's "top ten."[4]

As this public image indicates, People's State University is a campus "of the people" and "for the people," striving to bring the best of academe to communities and individuals throughout the state and, increasingly, the nation and the world. The university espouses dual commitments, historically rooted in its two-pronged mission: to create and share useful knowledge in the spirit of its prominent National Association of State Universities and Land-Grant Colleges (NASULGC) identity and to contribute to "pure" research, notably in the sciences, in the spirit of its American Association of Universities (AAU) status. People's

State University's land-grant ideal emerged from its founding in the 1800s as an agricultural college and gained power after World War II through the university's contributions to statewide industrial and technological development. This historic identity undergirds the university's strong interest in applied work, generally, and in scientific research supportive of agricultural, industrial, and technological development, in particular.

The academic and applied strands of the university's mission, however, have not intertwined easily. Such was the case at the time of the study: sensing the growing tension between these strands, university leaders launched several campus-wide efforts to bring them together—symbolically at upper university levels and concretely in academic departments. A new president and chief academic officer, both devoted to public service, had recently taken office. The university's Office of Public Service actively facilitated their goals to turn faculty research toward the university's public service goals.

Although many American public universities have, historically, felt such presses toward public service, a number belong to state systems, supra-organizations that may mediate a state's reach into the academic core of campus life. People's State University is not part of such a state system, and thus its relationship to its state legislature is unmediated; it "feels" the state's presence keenly and is highly responsive to changing state priorities as these bear on university funding. This posture has led some campus members to portray the university's financial character as unstable. Compared to other universities, faculty governance and voice at People's State University was weak at the time of my study, and administrative power (at all levels, including by a small elected board of trustees) was quite strong. Campus news of note around that time included state budget cuts to higher education, efforts to frame the university's public service, faculty diversification, athletic successes and problems, and symbolic campus-wide unification efforts, among others.

In sum, through the years of my visits to People's State University, I came to view the boundary around its "academic core" as relatively permeable and the core itself as responsive to external demands; this pattern of responsiveness, and concern about it, was audible in the interviews I conducted.

The *Four Universities Project*

The aim of the *Four Universities Project*, which I carried out over three years starting in the late 1990s, was to elucidate the intellectual, professional, and personal learning of a new sample of forty professors working at four major American research universities. Through the study I sought to identify professors' experiences of their learning, especially their scholarly learning, with attention to what, in particular, they were trying to learn. I also sought to define where they carried out their scholarly learning as well as how they positioned themselves strategically to pursue it. Later I also considered universities' responsiveness to professors' pursuits of scholarly learning.

The forty professors (20 men, 20 women) participating in the *Four Universities Project* claimed primary membership in one of the following four disciplinary sectors: the arts and humanities (9, 23%), the social sciences (9, 23%), the sciences (11, 28%), and professional/applied fields (11, 28%).[5] On a per campus basis I included two professors for each of these disciplinary sectors and added between one and three additional professors reflective of prominent institutional tenuring patterns. Therefore, each site included between nine and eleven professors, split fairly evenly between men and women. As in the *People's State University Project*, professors with appointments in medical, dental, veterinary, and law schools were excluded from the study due to distinctiveness of the faculty role in these units. In their first project year fourteen of the forty participating professors (35%) were in their first post-tenure year, twelve (30%) were in their second post-tenure year, and fourteen (35%) were in their third. Two years later, by project year 3, these participants were between three and five years post-tenure. The study therefore yielded a five-year window on the early post-tenure careers of professors whose research, teaching, and service contributed to the breadth of knowledge offered by the American research university at the turn of the twenty-first century.

Other features of the sample merit attention as well. In study year 1 all participating professors carried the rank of associate professor; by study year 3 a few of them had been promoted to full professor, and a number indicated they would likely "come up for review to full" during the next year or two. As in the *People's State University Project*, I actively sought out participants from underrepresented minority groups. University tenuring patterns continued to favor whites, however, perhaps especially in the sciences and selected applied/professional domains, making study recruitment a challenge. Of the forty participants six (15%) were people of color, three of whom were foreign born; of the thirty-four (85%) white participants, six were foreign born. In year 3 of the study the age range of participants was twenty-nine through sixty.

To identify study participants, I asked the high-level university official granting me institutional access to connect me with the campus office that could provide me with a list of professors who had been tenured and promoted to the rank of associate professor through the three preceding years, excluding those with appointments in medical, dental, veterinary, and law schools.[6] The number of professors meeting this criterion were: approximately sixty at Signal University, ninety at Horizon University, ninety at Hope State University, and one hundred at Libra State University. I analyzed the four lists relative to field of study, gender, ethnicity (when this could be identified), and other characteristics that might reflect meaningful variations in professors' learning experiences. Based on this preliminary examination, I invited eighty-four individuals from across the four study sites to participate in the study via letter and follow-up telephone and email conversations; I sent out these invitations in waves, such that after a first wave, I sent out a second and then a third until forty slots were filled. Of the eighty-four initial conversations revealed that eleven (13%) did not qualify for the study (e.g., appointed to a medical school). Of the remaining seventy-three, forty-two agreed to participate (58%). Seventeen (23%) declined, and fourteen (19%) did not respond to letters, telephone calls, and email follow-ups; I do not know whether these thirty-one nonparticipants qualified for the study. Given this base, rates of agreement to participate, by institution, were: Signal University, 67% (10/15); Horizon University, 43% (12/28); Hope State University, 75% (9/12); and Libra State University, 61% (11/18). Total sample rate of agreement to participate was 58%.[7] I interviewed study participants initially in year 1 of the study and then again in year 3. Participant retention through the full course of the study was 98%; one person, on extended leave from campus, was not available for the year 3 interview. As such, sample size for study year 1 is forty, and for study year 3, it is thirty-nine.

To encourage study participation that threatened to falter due to concerns about research privacy (a concern I identified through the *People's State University Project*), I crafted a comprehensive participant confidentiality protocol that allowed potential participants to consider and choose between two levels of identity masking for final study reports: one that would provide standard masking (by using pseudonyms and masking other fundamental markers of identity) yet retain salient features of identity (e.g., discipline or field, subjects of study and teaching, biographical and other background data) and another, heavier approach that would blur or exclude these features of scholarly identity (present a professor as a member of a broad disciplinary sector rather than a specific discipline or field, refer to an individual's teaching, research, and background in general terms) (see app. B). For year 1 interviews thirty participants (75%) elected standard identity masking, and ten (25%) elected the heavier masking. For year 3 interviews thirty-four participants (85%) preferred standard identity masking, and five (13%) opted for the heavier. None of the requests for change in identity masking involved movement from standard to heavier masking. As in the prior study, I limited displays of data, from the *Four Universities Project,* to abide by promises of confidentiality included in this protocol (see chap. 1, n. 5, for additional details). To do this, I removed revealing data, referred to scholars as belonging to disciplinary sectors as opposed to specific fields (e.g., humanities as opposed to comparative literature, sciences rather than microbiology, and so on), and in three cases changed scholars' areas of study and field affiliation. For longer excerpts I favored use of data provided by participants requesting standard masking, as opposed to heavier identity coverage.[8]

Project interviews, each about two hours in length, occurred during three- to five-day visits to each university. In four instances (all in study year 1) at least part of an interview occurred via long-distance telephone. Through study year 1 a research assistant and I used a shared semistructured interview protocol to conduct interviews through one or two campus visits. I conducted all year 3 interviews myself through the course of two to four visits to each campus. Although I retained several key interview questions between the two data collection time points, I added a number of new questions, derived from year 1 analysis, to the year 3 protocol (see app. B). All interviews were tape-recorded, with the exception of one, at the interviewee's request (handwritten notes were substituted).

To supplement the interview data, researchers recorded observational notes of the interview setting (usually the professor's office) and public campus spaces and collected a number of documents from study participants: a curriculum vita, tenure narrative (if available), published works and other writing, and syllabi. Over the years project staff also conducted numerous Web-based and library searches for public information on the forty professors participating in the study. They assisted also in transcribing observational notes. To understand the institutional setting, I collected additional institutional documents while on site and in advance of the campus visit (view books, catalogs, accreditation reports, planning documents, and campus and city newspapers). Further, during study year 1 I conducted interviews, each an hour in length, with a top-level university administrator and a senior faculty leader knowledgeable about academic cultures, work norms and conditions, tenure review processes, and recent campus history relative to professors' work and careers. During study years 2 and 3 project staff developed extended data archives for each institutional site, drawing on public information (institutional Web sites, catalogs and campus viewbooks, campus histories, *Chronicle of Higher Education,* the *New York Times,* National Research Council departmental rankings, *U.S. News and World Reports* rankings, and other sources) pertaining to the university's history and mission, recent campus-based events, and financial status.

The core study data—the seventy-nine interviews with recently tenured professors conducted in years 1 and 3 of the study—were immediately transcribed in full and later checked against tape recording and notes for accuracy. Interviews with administrators and senior faculty were also transcribed in full. Average annual interview transcript length was about forty-five single-spaced pages. Participant data files containing interviews, documents, observational notes, and related materials were then readied for analysis. Campus materials were organized into extensive campus case studies to help guide analysis of the core project interviews.

Although no two analyses proceeded in exactly the same way, I followed a general approach. For each major research question I designated several specific analytic questions to which the study data, fully assembled, could usefully respond. In reviewing the data, I successively reframed the analytic questions to position them increasingly closer to what the data could yield in the way of response and also to fine-tune them conceptually. As I reviewed responses to any one analytic question (typically drawn from all interviews and often generating several hundred pages of excerpted text segments per analytic question), I identified data-based categories of response and sorted the data accordingly. I re-sorted repeatedly, however, as categorical improvements became evident. Iterative data review led to multiple such sortings and re-sortings, collapsing and separating out of new data categories, and categorical sequencing and re-sequencing so as to "tell the story" meaningfully and validly, from and with data, that best and most clearly responded to the study's aim. Throughout this process I checked and rechecked the evidentiary warrants for the themes proposed, often revising those themes in the process; this involved remaining open to discrepant messages in the data and being willing to rethink and revise "working ideas." The approach reflects an effort to build a grounded theory, though one anchored in my own view, as conditioned by existent theory.[9]

Notes

1. The term *sciences* refers to all branches of the sciences and mathematics but not engineering, which I designated as a professional and applied field. Professional and applied fields may be science based (e.g., engineering), social science based (e.g., business management, social work), or arts based (architecture).

2. At the time of the study People's State University was tenuring approximately fifty faculty members per year university-wide, 80 percent of whom qualified for the initial invitation to participate in the study (excluding tenured professors in medical and law schools). Given the design stipulation that cohort 1 members be one year post-tenure, and that cohort 2 members be "under review" during study year 1, eighty professors, from across the two cohorts, qualified for invitation (pending confirmation of positive tenure decisions for members of cohort 2, along with further verification that professors did not work in the medical school and other units not included in the study). The random selection process yielded a study sample reflective of People's State University's unique programmatic focus and tenuring pattern. As such, the study included more scientists and scholars in applied/professional areas than in arts, humanities, and social sciences. Because study results called for greater attention in future inquiry into the role of subject matter in professors' careers, I revised the sample construction

strategy for the *Four Universities Project* that followed so as to better represent key disciplinary sectors.

Lists of the two targeted faculty cohorts provided by People's State University did not include social characteristics (e.g., race/ethnicity, gender, country of origin, age, and disability status). I relied on other sources (e.g., campus-based faculty associations) to identify potential participants on the basis of these characteristics. I was usually unaware of individuals' backgrounds, however, until I met them for interviews. I did not distinguish native from foreign-born minority scholars through this study.

For data on the career progress of faculty of color in all types of U.S. higher education institutions at about the time of study start-up, see "Characteristics of Full-Time Faculty . . . 1992." Over a decade later the number of tenured faculty of color in American higher education remains low; see "Number of Full-Time Faculty . . . 2005." Data are indicated by rank only, and thus tenure status is inferred.

3. For the final report of the *People's State University Project*, see Neumann, "Between the Work I Love and the Work I Do."

4. The Carnegie Foundation for the Advancement of Teaching, "Basic Classification Description," www.carnegiefoundation.org/classifications/index.asp?key =791 (accessed December 28, 2007). Also refers to measures popularized by *U.S. News and World Report*, *America's Best Graduate Schools,* and *America's Best Colleges* and by the National Research Council.

5. For definition of sciences and applied/professional fields, see n. 1.

6. The official was usually the chief academic officer or a representative designated by that officer.

7. Due to availability constraints (e.g., professor was willing to participate in the study but was unable to schedule an interview during study year 1), two professors, both at Horizon University, were dropped from the study, reducing the initial participant total from forty-two to forty. If rate of qualification to participate among the thirty-one nonparticipants (individuals declining and failing to respond) were to be viewed as comparable to that of those agreeing to participate (87%), then the adjusted response rate would be 63 percent.

8. I typically identify study participants by campus to provide insight into individual professors' understandings and experiences of institutional functioning and culture. For individuals facing particularly challenging situations or requesting coverage for selected features of their campus experience, however, I omitted institutional affiliation; doing so enhanced participants' local confidentiality in ways that the standard global confidentiality could not. *Local confidentiality* responds to the possibility that a participant's institutional (local) colleagues may be able to identify each other in a research report, given shared local meanings, even

though outsiders to the institution may not. While shielding the basics of identity, *global confidentiality* is not as attuned to possibilities of local identifiability.

9. For interested readers the analytic approach herein summarized has been presented in greater detail in other publications of the *Four Universities Project*. See Neumann, "Professing Passion." Related methodological sources include Glaser and Strauss, *Discovery of Grounded Theory;* Kvale, *Interviews;* Maxwell, *Qualitative Research Design;* and Schatzman and Strauss, *Field Research*. For background information on the campuses, comparable to that presented previously on People's State University, see chap. 6.

Interview Protocols and Consent Forms
for the *Four Universities Project*

Interview Guide, Project Year 1 *(Abbreviated)*

Background

I would like to start by getting some background information about you.

— It is my understanding that your academic title is [Associate Professor] in _____. Is _____ your home department (program)? (Clarify) Do you teach or have other responsibilities in other departments, programs, institutes, or other university units?

— How long have you been at _____? Where were you previously? What were you doing there?

— When did you complete your doctoral work? In what field? From what university?

— So, your first academic term here was _____? What was your title when you came here?

— Was that a tenure-track appointment?

— Why did you come here?

Research and scholarship

Some academics find that their scholarly, research, or creative interests change over the years. Others find that these remain the same.

— I would like to get a sense as to how your [research / scholarship / creative work, writing] has developed over the years since you were a graduate student. Could you tell me about that.

— What are you working on now?

— Where do you see your scholarly work [research, writing, creative work, other] going over the next few years? In the future more generally?
— How has the *way* in which you [do research, carry out your scholarship, write, engage in creative effort] changed over the years?
— How have your ideas about what research [scholarship] is changed over the years?

Or: You're an [artist, writer], and you have certain ideas about the nature of your work. How have your ideas about what this work is changed over the years?

— What do you see as the greatest challenges in your [research / scholarship / writing / creative effort] at this time?
— How important is your research [scholarship] to you personally?

Teaching

I would now like to ask you some questions about your teaching.

— Do you think that you have changed as a teacher since you first became a professor?
— Thinking back over your own teaching, what challenges have you faced through the years?
— Would you say that the subjects you would prefer to teach have remained the same—or have they changed over the years?
— Do you think that your students have influenced your thinking as a teacher or as a scholar?
— How important is your teaching to you personally?

Scholarship more broadly

— Beyond this research and teaching, are there any other ways in which you express your scholarly interests and commitments? How important is [name of activity] to you personally?

Love of work

There are many different ways to experience the work of being a professor. In this next set of questions I want to focus on your experiences of work that are especially meaningful for you.

— What is it about your work that you love? Sometimes it's hard to talk about what's going on inside us when we have experiences like the kind you're describing. However, I'm wondering if you could spend a moment and try to put into words what might be going on inside you at such times as _____.

— Looking back at your life, do you have a sense as to where this _____ may have come from, or when did it start for you?

— Do you feel that your current work situation supports _____?

— Have you ever noticed this _____ [name of interest] surfacing outside your academic work?

— To what extent do you see others—for example, your students or colleagues—as having similar experiences of _____?

If interviewee indicates that there are no features of work s/he loves:

— Is there something that you truly love to do—or that you feel deeply personally committed to—but existing outside your academic work?

Learning and boredom

The word "learning" is often associated with professors' work. I'd like to ask you some questions now about your own learning.

— We often think of our learning in terms of our successes and achievements. However, learning is also often a struggle. Can you give me an example of a time in your life when you have struggled with learning something?

— What kinds of situations help you to learn best?

— Where do ideas that are new to you come from?

— One thing professors sometimes talk about is the subject of boredom in their own work, and what to do about it. Has boredom ever been an issue for you in your work?

Relationship to discipline or field of study

I'd now like to ask you (briefly) about your membership in professional organizations.

— To which professional organizations do you now belong? How long have you belonged to these? How important are these to you at this time? (Probe for nonimportance.)

— Professional organizations aside, do you see yourself as belonging to some community, or maybe informal grouping of scholars who study things similar to your own interests?

— So, how would you describe your relationship to your field(s) of study at this time?

Scholarly identity

We often come to be known in particular ways by our colleagues in our fields. That is, our colleagues may see us as having particular "scholarly identities."

— How do you think that your colleagues in your field see you? In other words, what is your scholarly identity in their eyes? How does this compare to how you see yourself?
— You are making a career for yourself in the area of _____. Why do you think you became attracted to this particular area of study in the first place?

Colleagueship

Colleagueship is a very real but not often discussed aspect of professors' work lives, so I'd like to ask you a bit about your relationships with colleagues.

— What makes someone a colleague for you?
— Who do you think of as your primary colleagues? (local, external, changes over the years)

Institutional issues and experiences

— How involved are you in institutional affairs and issues at this time? What are these? Does this feel like the right level or kind of involvement to you? Would you say that this is more or less or about the same level of involvement in campus affairs as you've had in past years?
— I understand that you were tenured in _____ (year). What was the tenure review process like for you?
— It is sometimes said that the granting of tenure gives professors more power, or perhaps more opportunity, to determine the course of their intellectual work than they had at earlier times in their careers. Do you think this is (will be) true for you? What has changed most for you since you were granted tenure?

Well-being in the workplace

— When you're asked by colleagues at other universities, what it is like to be on the faculty of _____ at _____, what do you say? (What is it like for you to work here?)

— What do you worry about in your work?

— Academia is sometimes referred to as a stressful place in which to work, and some academics find themselves worrying about their health or their general well-being. To what extent has this been an issue for you?

— What do you most look forward to in your work?

A professorial career within a life

— How do you think about the place of your work in your life?

— What is your *personal ideal* of what it means to be a professor? What should a professor be? What should a professor do?

Interview Guide, Project Year 3 *(Abbreviated)*

Background

I'd like to start by being sure that I've got your title and position right.

— It is my understanding that your academic title is Associate Professor in _____. Is _____ still your home department? Are you appointed in any other programs, departments, or institutes? Have there been any [other] changes in your faculty appointment over the last two years?

— For clarification, my notes indicate that you received your undergraduate degree, which was a [name of degree] in [field of study] from [institution]. And that was in [year]. Is that correct?

— In what year were you born?

Research/scholarship

I would like to start out with some questions about your research and scholarship generally.

— Do you think that your scholarly or intellectual interests have changed over the past year or two? What are you working on now in your [research, scholarship, writing]?

— Do you think that you yourself have changed as a [researcher, scholar, writer, artist, musician] over the past few years?

— Looking back on your years in scholarship, do you think your conception of what research is has changed over time?

— Where do you see your scholarly work [research, writing, creative work, other] going over the next few years?

— I'd be interested to know whether there have been any changes in your professional or personal situation over the past two or three years that have affected your work as a professor or as a scholar. Have there been any such changes?

Teaching

I would now like to ask you some questions about your teaching.

— Clarify: Do you teach doctoral students? Master's students? Undergraduate students?
— Do you think that you have changed as a teacher since you first became a professor? Do you think that your teaching has changed just over the past year or two?
— How would you describe the fit between your teaching responsibilities and your areas of specialization or interest?
— Do you think that your students have influenced your thinking as a teacher, as a researcher [artist, writer], or as a scholar more generally?
— I would like to ask about what goes on in class: There are times when we have to teach ideas, methods, techniques, or simply, ways of thinking that are really quite challenging for students to grasp. Can you tell me how you might go about teaching an idea, perspective, or method in [subject] that is likely to be challenging for your students?
— I'd like for you to think about the best teacher(s) you've ever had. This can be at any point in your education or your life. Who would you say that is or was? What made her/him such a good teacher in your experience?
— Sometimes as we're teaching or preparing to teach, we find that we ourselves are learning something new about our subjects of study. Can you give me an example of something that you have learned, or maybe realized, about [subject] from your classroom-based teaching?
— Do you think that any of your teaching contributes to your [research, scholarly, writing, artistic] career in any way? In other words—what, if anything, do you get out of your teaching for your own work?

Epistemologies

I would like to ask you some more questions about how you think about the subjects that you study and teach.

— Based on your own experiences, what is a [e.g., mathematician, biologist, etc., i.e., disciplinary practitioner *or* scholar of _____]? What does a _____ work on or think about?

— To you, what is [subject/discipline]?

— Where do you find the [problems, questions, projects] on which you work? What makes a particular [problem, question, project] engaging enough for you to commit to working on it?

— How do you know when you've encountered a really good idea, let's say, in your reading about [subject]? For example, let's say that you're reading something in [your subject area]—you are moving along, and all of a sudden you say, "Gosh, that's a really good idea." What is the feel of a good idea in the subject matter that you study? (How do you know a good idea when you see one?)

— We all have high points and low points in our research or creative endeavor. In other words, there are times when things are going great, and other times, when that's not the case. Can you tell me what it's like for you when things are, in fact, going great? What is the experience of that?

— Now something of the converse: Sometimes professors talk about boredom in aspects of their work. Has boredom ever been an issue for you in your work? Can you tell me about that.

Learning

Learning is often talked about in reference to students, but professors also learn. The following questions focus on *your* experiences of learning in your subject matter.

— What kinds of situations help you to learn best about those subjects in [field] that you study or teach?

— Where do [disciplinary, e.g., mathematical, literary, biological, scientific, etc.] ideas that are new to you come from?

— Sometimes an encounter with a new or different idea (or a new method, approach, or simply, way of thinking) shapes the direction of our work for years to come. The idea (or method or perspective) may represent a turning point in our work. Have you encountered any ideas in your work, recently or in the past, that served as turning points for you?

— Some professors have told me that during their years at a particular university, they have taken on certain research or teaching that they probably would not have taken on if they were at a different university, or if they were in a different part of the world or the country. To what extent have you taken on certain research or teaching projects that reflect the uniqueness of this locale, and that you probably would not have taken on if you were elsewhere?

Scholarly identity

We often come to be known in certain ways by our colleagues in our fields. That is, our colleagues may see us as having certain "scholarly identities."

— How do you think that your colleagues in your field see you? In other words, what is your scholarly identity in their eyes? How does this compare to how you see yourself?
— You have been making a career for yourself in [name of field]. Why do you think you became attracted to this area of study in the first place?
— Do you consider yourself to have been mentored? [Focus follow-up questions on what the subject of the mentoring was.]

Relationships

— Who do you talk to most often about what's going on substantively in your research—for example, about the kinds of things you are learning, or the questions and issues that are giving you trouble?
— Who do you talk to most often about what's going on in your teaching— for example, about new lessons you are trying to put together, or about challenges you're facing in teaching difficult ideas or techniques?

Institutional issues and experiences

— How involved are you in institutional (campus-related) activities and issues at this time? What are these? Does this feel like the right level or kind of involvement to you? Would you say that this is more or less or about the same level of involvement in campus activities as you've had over the past two or three years?
— Professional activity that's not teaching or research [or creative endeavor] often is defined as service, whether for the university, discipline [field of study], practitioner audiences, or community groups. Usually the service component of professors' work involves citizenship activity for the good of the whole, or the giving to others of one's own knowledge. Yet every once in a while, a professor may gain something for him- or herself while doing such service—for example, identifying an interesting or important idea, or coming to see something in the field in a different way. Has any of the service that you've done through the years—whether in the university, the discipline [field], or the community—led you to a new idea or to a different way of thinking about some aspect of your work? Could you tell me about that.

— It has been a while now since you were granted tenure. What has changed most for you since you were awarded tenure?

Well-being in the workplace

— What do you worry about in your work?
— Academia is sometimes referred to as a stressful place in which to work, and some academics find themselves worrying about their health or their general well-being.
— What do you most look forward to in your work?

A professorial career in a life

— Years from now, what do you think you will remember about your work as a scholar and teacher at this time and in this place?
— How do you think about the place of your scholarly work in your life?
— Do you ever talk to members of your family about things that you are reading or thinking about in your scholarly work?
— Do you have any hobbies or avocational interests that you pursue?
— To what extent has living in this [community/city/region] affected your job and career as a professor?
— What is your personal ideal of what it means to be a professor? What should a professor be? What should a professor do?

Remaining questions

Specific to the interviewee

Informed Consent, Part I: Research Description
[completed before the interview]

In signing this form, you are agreeing to participate in the year-3 interview as part of the study of recently tenured professors' learning and scholarly identity development directed by Anna Neumann, Professor of Higher Education at Teachers College, Columbia University. The interview, which focuses on your learning and scholarly identity development, will last approximately two hours. Anna Neumann has sent you a letter redescribing the project and summarizing research procedures. With this consent form, she is also providing you with an abstract describing the study overall.

In order to create a complete and accurate record of your account, Anna is requesting permission to tape-record your interview. You will have the opportunity to designate your preference with regard to audiotaping in Part II of this form. If you agree to be tape-recorded, you may request that the tape-recorder be turned off at any point in time. You also have the right to decline to be tape-recorded. If you prefer not to be tape-recorded, Anna will take notes as you speak. Audiotapes will be destroyed once all project work, including final publication, has been completed.

Your interview and any documentary materials you share with Anna will be treated confidentially. For example, in all public reports of the study, pseudonyms will replace your own, others', and the university's names. In addition, as you proceed through the interview today, you are free, and encouraged, to point out to Anna any issues you wish to keep "off the record"—that is, issues you would prefer be omitted from published research reports, or described only in general terms. Anna Neumann and all other persons associated with the project will make every effort to safeguard your privacy. Data will be stored in the hard drives of designated project computers accessible only to Anna Neumann and research team members working under her supervision. All other project information will be kept in locked filing cabinets in secured work spaces.

Although Anna and any co-researchers working with her will make strenuous efforts to mask identifying information in published reports and presentations stemming from this research, it may not be possible to disguise your identity completely to those who know you, and your work, extremely well—for instance, institutional and disciplinary colleagues. For example, the text of a case study featuring your learning experiences may represent certain features of your work, background, or interests in ways that might lead a colleague on your campus or in your field to guess your identity. Although Anna and co-researchers plan to mask your identity in multiple ways (e.g., by involving approximately 40 professors, spread across four institutions, as participants, and by carefully selecting and editing quotations and other potentially identifying information), some aspects of who you are will inevitably remain in research reports based on your experiences. Anna and her co-researchers will make every effort to craft research reports that will not permit readers to associate you or other study participants with specific responses, and they will treat all materials so as to minimize the possibility of your own or others' inadvertent identification.

Furthermore, when you complete your interview today, Anna will discuss with you two different ways in which data about you might be presented in public reports of the study: one whereby editorial masking would retain some features of your intellectual and personal identity (for example, your discipline/field, your subjects of study or teaching, relevant biographical and contemporary data), and another whereby editorial masking would blur or exclude such features. At that time, you will have the opportunity to indicate your preference as regards presentation of data that you provide through this study.

Your participation in this interview, and the study of which it is a part, is completely free and voluntary. You may choose not to participate in the interview at all. You may refuse to respond to certain questions or to provide any documents requested. You may discontinue your participation in the interview and the study at any time without penalty or loss of benefits to which you are otherwise entitled.

Results of the study, to be reported as analyses that draw broadly but selectively from multiple interviews, or as individual or clustered case studies of professors, will be prepared for publication in academic/professional journals and books, and for presentation at professional conferences and meetings.

Informed Consent, Part II: Statement of Preference for Data Presentation
[completed after the interview]

Anna Neumann has explained her responsibility to safeguard your privacy, and the ways in which she and any co-researchers will use pseudonyms and other masking techniques to shield your identity in public reports of the study. She has also discussed with you two ways in which masked data about you could be presented in such reports: (A) a presentation that would reveal some features of your identity (e.g., your discipline/field, your subjects of study and teaching, and relevant biographical or other background information), (B) a presentation that would blur or exclude completely such features of your identity.

Please check only one of the following:

_____ (A) I permit Anna Neumann and researchers working with her to present data about me that retain fundamental features of my intellectual and personal identity. This option provides that my identity will be masked through pseudonyms and other masking techniques, and that public reports of the study may reflect the name(s) of my discipline(s) or field(s) of study, descriptions of my subjects of study and teaching, and biographical or other background information relevant to the research. The researchers will not make public any information that I have indicated is "off the record."

_____ (B) I do not permit Anna Neumann and researchers working with her to present data about me that retain fundamental features of my intellectual and personal identity. This option provides that my identity will be masked through pseudonyms and other masking techniques, and that public reports of the study will not include the name(s) of my discipline(s) or field(s) of study, descriptions of my subjects of study and teaching, and biographical or other background information relevant to the research. Such information will be reported only in broad, general terms or will be excluded. The researchers will not make public any information that I have indicated is "off the record."

Framework: University Professors' Scholarly Learning

Five propositions summarize the assumptions, ideas, and perspectives that frame this volume. Those propositions guided the *People's State University* and *Four Universities Projects* yet evolved substantially throughout them.[1]

> *Proposition 1. Professors' learning as part of professors' work:* Professors' work requires that they learn.

The work in which professors engage—teaching, research, outreach, and service—involves acts of cognition, of knowing, for to do the work is to get to know the work. And to get to know something is to learn it.[2] How a professor knows that work can change over time. The professor may come to see and think about it in new ways. Such learning may be intentional, for example, as the professor struggles purposefully to understand a substantive idea. Or it may be incidental, as when she learns, through informal conversation, about new ways to think about a theory, lab technique, or study finding. Over time a professor's substantive expertise may expand. She may gain new skills in research, teaching, and service and come to think of herself as a teacher, researcher, and college citizen in new ways, leading her to carry out her work in different ways. Thus, from a cognitive perspective professors' work implies the possibility of professors' learning, intentionally or incidentally, about research, teaching, outreach, or service as they engage in these activities, prepare to do so, or look back reflectively on completed projects. That is, professors learn "on the job" and within their work and careers.[3] The more conventional converse, however, cannot be ruled out: that professors' learning can shape their work.

Further, learning, as changed cognition, involves the personal and shared construction of knowledge. Learning involves coming to know something familiar in new or different ways. Learning may also entail a person's awakening to something about which she was not previously aware. Such learning may occur within one's own thoughts, for example, as a person reflects on an idea, or openly among others, as in conversation, or in engagement with a text (a book, movie, or poem). To learn is personal because it involves unique experiences of mind, limited in their transferability to others. Yet this work of mind is also interactive in that it draws on and produces cognitive connection among individuals who come to know related things, at times in unusual, even startlingly creative new ways. Professors' learning is complex because it may occur in different ways within any type of professorial work (research, teaching, outreach, service), in reference to diverse aspects of that work (subject matter, technical processes, social and cultural features), at any time, and whether the professor is alone or among others.[4] Professors' work and learning are thus entwined; one may shape the other.

> *Proposition 2. Learning as someone learning something:* To say that someone learns implies that some*one* is learning some*thing*. To understand a professor's learning requires knowing who the professor-as-learner is and what she learns at a certain point in time.

The second proposition follows from the first: that learning—whether in reference to professors' work or anybody else's work—implies *someone* learning *something*. To talk about learning, in and of itself, is vague and insubstantial: learning requires a learner and something to be learned.[5]

Learning cannot stand alone. Its connectedness to who is learning and what is learned—and also to who is thinking about the learning at issue and with what questions in mind—complicates efforts to understand it.[6] One reason for this complexity is that what is being learned, along with who is learning (including what a learner knows already or is open to knowing and what is being learned), help constitute how it is learned. How a student learns the chemistry of photosynthesis depends a great deal, for example, on who that student is as a learner of such natural processes: what she brings to class from prior exposure and related learning and simply curiosity about or openness to exploring the unique terrains of knowledge about (and ways of knowing) photosynthesis as a particular scientific idea. That photosynthesis is in fact a scientific idea, unique in its meaning to scientists who share an epistemic frame for its consideration, matters greatly, but how a student absorbs that idea, emphasizing some of its features over others, may vary.

Learning viewed this way does not generalize well: it happens differently, depending on the learners and on the material being learned. To understand learning, for example, one must note that learners bring unique ways of knowing and learning, from their homes and prior schooling, to their college communities and that they change in their learning over time and as they move from space to space.[7] This does not necessarily mean that in a learning situation one learner thinks about *X* while another thinks about *Y*. They may both think about *X* (or *Y*, for that matter), but in different ways, in light of the unique scaffoldings and interpretations they bring from their pasts to the learning situation. They may even use the same words to refer to *X* (or *Y*), but in their minds they see and think very different things. Learning entails a learner's bridging of such differences between her own and another person's (i.e., the teacher's, an author's, a peer's) knowing or among different instances of her own knowing across time and/or space.

Learning requires appreciation of differences among learners. Equally important, it requires appreciation of difference across the "stuff" they learn. What it takes to learn in one subject matter—to see and understand it—will probably differ from what it takes to learn in another subject matter because of *the differences in the substance and form of the subject matter itself*. Consider a student, Jon, who claims, as many students, do that "learning is hard." Jon makes this claim in reference to his learning of mathematics. Yet Jon later repeats the claim as he struggles to learn a challenging concept in psychology. He may say these words ("learning is hard") again as he reflects on his efforts to learn how to be a leader, a parent, a friend, or a gourmet chef. These words cannot be taken at face value. How hard it is for a certain person to learn any subject, topic, or skill depends in part on the learner (e.g., Jon's proclivity to learn one thing, like history, as opposed to another, like math). It also depends on the thing being learned (the differences in the epistemic structure of the mathematics and psychology, both of which, though different, Jon may find "hard" to learn). For Jon learning in mathematics will differ from learning in, say, history, not only because he happens to like history and is able to access it better than math but also because history and mathematics, as forms of knowledge, are, in the words of the curriculum theorist Joseph Schwab, "syntactically" different knowledge domains for anyone to learn, regardless of personal likes and dislikes.[8]

Learning does not happen in and of itself. For learning to occur, other entities must be present: there must be one or more learner, and there must be *something* to be learned. Without "something to be learned," it is quite unclear what learning entails or even whether it happens. And similarly, without the learner, it is unclear where the learning is and who is doing it. Thus, the phrase *to learn* in and of itself is an abstraction. To give meaning and form to learning—to understand where learning exists and indeed what goes on through it—calls for knowing who is doing the learning and what it is they are learning.

Whereas it is customary to talk about learning relative to students, like Jon, I aver that it applies equally to professors: learning requires a learner engaged in learning something in particular. The professor has a subject with which she is engaging—making and remaking it—by way of learning. Professors, like students, have many such subjects to learn: they learn the substantive concepts and skills they teach (disciplinary subject matter). They learn deeply and often in previously untried ways about their subjects as they conduct research or create scholarship. They learn how to engage in new or different research approaches or methods. They learn to teach, advise, mentor, and otherwise work with students in increasingly complex ways. They learn about their colleagues and how to relate to them. They learn about university organization and campus life. They learn about their scholarly communities beyond the university and how to engage in diverse forms of professional service. The list of what professors' learn, on and off the job, goes on. Each of these things that professors learn represents different kinds of knowledge. Learning one thing may differ from learning others by virtue of their appeal to a particular professor and also by virtue of their differing epistemic structures. Individual professors, like their students, vary in the ease and enjoyment they derive in learning some things as opposed to others.

> *Proposition 3. Professors' scholarly learning:* To understand a professor's scholarly learning is to understand how she learns *what* she professes through her practices of research, teaching, and service: her subject matter knowledge and ways of knowing unique to it.

A practicing lawyer works with the law. Although she has learned her professional community's practices of the law through approved law school study, she learns those practices still more deeply and creates her own unique enactments of them on the job, case by case. The same is true of doctors, architects, librarians, engineers, and a host of others whose work, in practice, requires expert knowledge and skill. Over years of professional work these practitioners come to understand and create their practices ever more deeply, within their communities' changing constraints and guidelines. This is true especially of those who reflect on their actions, looking again and again at what they have done and thought on the job, even as they keep up with developments "in the literatures" of their professions.[9]

To understand how professionals grow at the substantive core of their work, or not, requires understanding, as Lee Shulman has said, what specifically they profess in their distinctive practices, thus their knowledge of medicine, law, architectural design, information technology, and so on.[10] The same is true of professors. To understand professors' growth at the substantive core of their teaching, research, and service requires attention to changes in what they profess: in their subjects of study, in their ways of knowing and getting to know their subjects of study, in their ways of sharing all this with others, notably members of their disciplinary or professional communities and, significantly, their students. Because these activities involve professors' construction and reconstruction of their subjects of study and teaching, they entail scholarly learning.

To illustrate scholarly learning, I return to the example of Jon, the student learning mathematics. One might cast Jon's learning of mathematics as his construction of mathematical knowledge. But this view says little about where that mathematical knowledge comes from, to whom it may have meaning, and with whom Jon shares it. One might also cast Jon's learning of mathematics as his gaining of proficiency in the ways of thinking, about mathematics, that a community of mathematicians shares. In this view Jon immerses himself in the concerns and focus, structure, and patterns of flexibility and boundedness of mathematical knowledge. If Jon has learned mathematics in the past, one might also view him as elaborating, and in some cases refining, his understanding of the mathematical ways of thought that a community of mathematicians espouses and that he seeks to join.

A comparison helps make the point. A person who knows mathematics deeply can work with mathematical subject matter knowledge in mathematical ways, and this may be very different from his working deeply with history (in historical ways), sociology (in sociological ways), and psychology (in psychological ways). The learner of mathematics may thereby engage in mathematical thinking, in contrast to historical, sociological, psychological, or other subject matter thinking. Such thinking, in and through mathematics, may even lapse into inquiry as it moves onto ground not well plowed by the larger community of mathematicians at issue. Given the unique meanings that mathematical subject matter knowledge offers and constrains, the mathematics at issue interacts as well with the learner—for example, responding in mathematical terms to the learner's mathematical actions. In other words, the subject matter of mathematics, as a product of a mathematical community, interacts with the learner's mathematical knowledge as he constructs it. Given the unique substance and "syntax" of mathematics, the learner of mathematics and the mathematical knowledge at issue interact within the terms of what is mathematically possible. What is possible, mathematically, is likely to be quite different from what is possible historically, sociologically, psychologically, and so on (i.e., with regard to the historical knowledge of a community of historians, the sociological knowledge of a community of sociologists, or the psychological knowledge of a community of psychologists).[11]

Given this view of "what's learned" as a subject matter and as ways of thinking and inquiring that respond to the unique substantive and epistemic contours of that subject matter, I propose that what professors learn about their subjects of study and teaching is not static, lifeless subject matter knowledge. Rather, professors learn ways of interacting with subject matter knowledge that in a sense "talks back" to them, in a voice of its own, distinct by virtue of what it offers to learners and what it shuts off from their view. Professors, as scholars, pursue such knowledge, manipulating its content and boundaries, even as that knowledge, by virtue of its form, pushes back.[12] In this view what a professor learns is a community's ways of working with and thinking about a shared subject of study. A professor may also advance that community's repertoire of subject matter thought, enhancing the community's capacities to learn.

What might this idea of scholarly learning—as the construction of a subject matter and of ways of working with it—look like in the context of professors' work? When a professor of sociology learns something new about sociology, for example, extending her knowledge of sociology, whether in the context of research or teaching, she is in effect extending her competence as a worker with and extender of sociological knowledge. She is also extending her competence as a member of a community of sociological workers to which she holds herself accountable and with whom she shares her sociological learning, especially so if that learning is new or different from what the sociological community has held to in the past or if the sociological learning at issue is contestable. In this view what the professor of sociology is learning (namely, an aspect of sociology) is not a static thing taken in uncritically, with no vision or voice of its own. Rather, it is a fluid, live experience of knowing, made and remade, reflecting back on its maker through the minds of others who participate in its community-based making and testing out. A professor's subject of study thus has a "voice" that carries through the minds and voices of those who, through community, participate in its creation.[13]

Yet if subject matter knowledge and ways of subject matter knowing have voice, then such voice may vary considerably within a broad-ranging discipline or field—for example, across all who belong to the scholarly (disciplinary/professional) community of history, anthropology, education, sociology, engineering, physics, or psychology. That is, the subject matter knowledge and the ways of subject matter knowing and inquiring of any one disciplinary community will vary from subcommunity to subcommunity, from constituent group to constituent group, possibly even from person to person, and certainly from one moment in time to another. Thus within the larger community of sociologists, smaller communities of specialized forms of sociological knowing and inquiry may arise, differentiating themselves from each other by virtue of the unique meanings and aims of what they are "up to" sociologically. In this view of communities (and the meanings they represent) embedded within communities, the mega-community converts into "a constellation," while its constituent communities, sometimes yielding newer communities from within themselves, emerge as loci of local knowledge construction.[14]

Thus, in learning subject matters pertinent to their interests, scholars learn the ways of knowing of those subject matters and inquiring into them that respond to those subjects' unique content and form as constructed (or reconstructed) by communities and subcommunities of scholars who study related questions, problems, and topics. Because these ways of knowing and inquiring vary by community, and often by subcommunity, and because the knowledge at issue may vary, movement from the study of one topic to the study of another topic is hard work. Among other things it takes learning.

Learning, as a central feature of professors' work, is invisible and meaningless without considering what professors learn, who they are as learners, and where, when, and why their learning occurs. Further, I have emphasized that what is learned is complex: it includes subject matter knowledge and ways of knowing and inquiring about it. It also includes knowledge about many other things professors do as part of their jobs, related to subject matter and not. But no discussion of what is learned is complete without considering why learners learn it. I turn now to that discussion as it applies to university professors' scholarly learning.

Proposition 4. Professors' scholarly learning as personal and emotional experience: For many professors scholarly learning holds personal meaning. It may be intensely emotional.

The substantive understandings that professors pursue in their scholarly learning may be central to their lives as much as to their careers. The pursuit of such learning may matter personally to professors, some of whom experience their scholarly learning on a deeply emotional level. A professor's subject of study may represent a lifetime (albeit changing) endeavor, and the professor may weave its content into a life story. A professor's subject of study may reflect personal and autobiographical content: personally anchored questions or puzzles that a scholar projects onto a subject, rendering it meaningful for study. Sometimes as a scholar explores her subject, she gains insight that is personally relevant and that helps her understand herself while helping her understand a subject of study beyond herself. Alternatively, a scholar may reach into her personal understandings of self—for example, into childhood memories or other long-past, personal learnings—for previously untried ways to think through a scholarly problem or question. A scholar's life may both give to, and gain from, her scholarly learning, thereby infusing scholarly work with personal meaning.[15]

To understand what a scholar's substantive learning means to her requires knowing why she pursues a particular academic project, including how that project relates to her personal life experiences.[16] But this is not how educational researchers have traditionally thought about college and university professors' development. Research on higher education rarely refers to the personal meanings and sources of professors' intellectual work as researchers or teachers. Beyond isolated efforts, largely in the arts and humanities, most academic research portrays scholarly effort as objective investigation that strives to remove scholars' personal interests from what they study. As such, the academic cultures of most contemporary American universities, and of academe generally, divide the personal from the intellectual, the subjective from the presumed scientific, the emotional from the assumed objective. That division also pervades the content of the university as a workplace, deeming its workers' professional roles as distinct from their personal and family lives.[17] Professors themselves contribute to that divide as, in public university talk, they highlight the social or organizational utility of their work while avoiding discussing their personal reasons for taking it on. In doing so, they position the professional as apersonal and the personal as largely nonexistent. Examining the personal bases of professional endeavors thus remains a challenging subject, typically regarded as controversial and even taboo.[18]

Despite normative restrictions on personal thought and talk about academic matters, professors participating in my two studies struck a very different chord. Asked to describe what they love about their intellectual work, they talked about intense emotion—feelings of elation and despair, exuberance and distress, delight and sorrow, calm and frustration—that their being in the moment of an idea, or in its loss, stirs up in them. They also described what it is like to work and wait between such extremes of feeling: to remain patiently alert through the tedium built into research; to persist through long stretches of ambiguity; to call on resilience amid loss; to step back and try anew when thinking reaches an impasse. Professors' experiences of learning were intricately laced with a diverse range of emotions. (For detailed images, see chap. 2.) Yet as I suggested in proposition 2, professors' attention in learning was not open to anything and everything that appeared before them; their attention was trained on some things, less so on others. In the case of scholarly learning it was trained on subject matter that held special meaning for them.

Given the premise that professors' subjects of study are central to their career-long learning and work, one might wonder where those subjects come from or how scholars find them and claim them as their own. I suggest that those subjects derive from scholars' personal desires to make meaning of phenomena they find beautiful, puzzling, or troubling—in delightful or painful ways. Their learning then entails their striving to discern or create those subjects, to understand and express them.

Most subjects of study in the university are cast in terms of their meaning to others or the good they offer to society at large: art that enlightens its viewers' understandings, science that improves health and extends the lifespans of people around the globe, social science that improves work and living conditions in our own and other societies, and applied and professional studies that make daily existence safer or more enjoyable than it otherwise would be. I suggest that there is more to say: that in order to create a subject of study that holds meaning for others or that brings some good into the world (thereby generalizing the value of a study), a scholar must craft it first as meaningful to the scholar's own self, if only by virtue of wanting to share it with others. In this sense, scholarly learning is not fully self-less, for it requires the scholar's deep attentiveness to her own intellectual and creative impulses, responses, and aspirations, admittedly in relation to those of her scholarly and professional community. Thus, the personal core of scholarship cannot be ignored; it is part of that which is given to others.

Although a scholar's life matters to scholarship, it is but one context, of many, within which scholarly learning may occur. I turn next to a broader view of the multiple contexts of professors' scholarly learning.

> *Proposition 5. Contexts, in part, as the contents of learning:* Professors' learning happens in contexts that shape *what* they learn (content). Yet they can also learn new ways to think about those contexts, thereby influencing what they learn in them.

So far, I have proposed that professors' scholarly learning yields subject matter knowledge, including knowledge of subject matter practices such as disciplinary inquiry. Their broader learning (beyond the scholarly realm) yields additional knowledge: about subject matters other than their favored topics; about teaching, research, service, and outreach practices; about their university, field, or academe at large; and about self as scholar, and so on. Where does all this learning come from? In one sense or another it comes from context, realizing that context can be many different things for professors (see chap. 4). But what *is* context, and how does learning in it happen?

Sociocultural studies of how human beings know—and how they come to know what they know, or learn—use the term *context* to refer to the patterns of knowledge and ways of knowing that constitute the diverse environments in which individuals, relationships, and communities grow and in which identities evolve. The meanings inherent in these uniquely patterned environments frame the realities of individuals living and thinking in them. These environmentally embedded meanings are the *resources,* for thought, on which people draw for their knowing and learning. Contexts in this view offer unique knowledge resources—and thereby, meanings—to the people who enter and comprise them. Although they might resemble each other in key ways, contexts of a certain type (e.g., two universities) might differ from each other by virtue of the knowledge resources of which each is uniquely comprised and also by virtue of those knowledge resources that are absent but to which members may wish access. Knowledge resources, both those afforded and constrained, constitute a context for learning.[19]

But what is it about context, defined as an environment of unique knowledge offerings and constraints, that makes it matter in its members' learning, especially their scholarly learning? Consider that a certain way of knowing (e.g., critical judgment) dominates thought in a certain context (e.g., a community of teacher educators). We might ask how that way of knowing gets into the mind of a newcomer to that context so that it becomes the stuff of her learning, of her day-to-day knowing? Figuratively, how do features of context get under that person's skin? Borrowing from John Dewey, I'll simply say that this process happens through experience. It happens as selected elements of context, compelling to a learner (so that she sees and grasps them), enter her experience, constituting it in some part. What mediates an individual's learning—affording and constraining it in particular ways—are those features of her context that are available for her to explore or otherwise take in; and which she is open and prepared to pursue and to see, feel, and think about. Those features of context may then enter her consciousness. I refer to this combination of *contextual availability* and *learner receptivity* as the ingredients of an "experienced context" that sets the stage for an individual's learning, or her coming to consciousness about context.

What counts as context in a professor's learning? I suggest that context materializes at "macro," "mid," and "micro" levels of social reality. Examples of macro-level contexts of professors' learning include a national or cross-national culture, an economy, national and state politics, or a nation's or region's history. Examples of mid-level contexts include the cultures, structures, politics, and economies of organizations and communities, such as universities and disciplines. Examples of micro-level contexts include relationships, groups, and communities and networks within which meaning is made day by day; in universities these may include the academic programs, departments, institutes and centers, colleague networks, and colleague relationships that situate professors' day-to-day work. This framework assumes that micro-level contexts mediate the effects of macro- and mid-level contexts, in part by absorbing and concretizing their contents, then availing those contents locally to learners. That said, some features of a local context are likely to be unique, not reflecting at all some larger (macro- or mid-level) content. Yet not all features of a local (micro) context are subject to learning, and not all persons in them learn the same things. Further, although some learning occurs from that which is definitely there to be learned (resources), other learning derives from what is lacking, from members' awakenings to need or desire.[20] Although learning depends a great deal on contextual availability—at macro, mid-, and micro levels—it also depends on learners' receptivity to the range of what is there to be learned in the form of experienced context.

Professors' learning may also be shaped by the particularities of their life histories—their autobiographical pasts lodged in larger social structures and historical events, all as elements of personal experience. Their life histories may, by way of memory, offer questions and puzzles for their long-term academic learning, including their research. Thus, individuals' relationships with their own selves—their memories and self-understandings or patterns of their memories that have been suppressed—might well substantiate the subjects, questions, and passions that guide their subjects of study and of their teaching and learning.[21]

The experienced context, as a site for professors' learning, is clearly complex, combining social, cultural, historical, relational, remembered, interactive, and personal elements. It enters cognition by virtue of its experienced content.[22] Much like content, context represents knowledge, and it is thereby also a subject of individuals' knowing and learning. Viewed as knowledge, context can be formed and re-formed, for example, as learners devise—or learn—new ways to construe it and, subsequently, to act on or use it. Doing this thoughtfully (I prefer the term *strategically*) may help these individuals to assume agency for some portion of their learning—taking charge of their learning to the extent they can. In converting the context of their learning into a portion of the content they learn, they heighten their own powers to direct their learning overall.[23]

Scholarly Learning as Content and Context, Formed and Re-Formed

We see that professors' learning relates to their work (proposition 1) through the particular content (e.g., subject matters) to which they put their minds (propositions 2 and 3). Professors' learning of the subjects that they choose to explore or create can be deeply emotional and personally revealing to those professors. That learning may impel professors to extraordinary effort (proposition 4). Yet such learning does not occur in a vacuum. Rather, the learning takes its content from the multiple contexts of professors' work lives—their teaching, research, service, and outreach. These are contexts that professors experience. Such work contexts convert into content, for professors' learning, through channels of experience. Yet professors' experiencing, and thereby learning, need not be cast in passive terms (professors do not merely "land in" their work contexts, passively receiving the content of the learning that those contexts require). Professors can, in many cases, shape the contexts of their work and thus the content of the learning that those contexts require; they may thereby exert some agency over their learning (proposition 5). That power, and prerogative, must be viewed as a professional resource to be cultivated and preserved.

Notes

1. See Schatzman and Strauss, *Field Research,* for further discussion of how theory may help advance inductive research; and Lareau, "Common Problems in Field Work," for discussion of how such theory may shift through the course of a study.

2. The conceptual bases for propositions 1 and 2 draw heavily on literatures reviewed in Bransford, Brown, and Cocking, *How People Learn.* See also Greeno,

Collins, and Resnick, "Cognition and Learning"; Shulman, *Teaching as Community Property;* and Shulman, *Wisdom of Practice.*

3. Lin and Schwartz, "Reflections at the Crossroads of Culture"; Marsick and Watkins, "Informal and Incidental Learning"; Schon, *Reflective Practitioner;* Schon, *Educating the Reflective Practitioner.*

4. Learning is both social and of self. For discussion of learning as social, see Baltes and Staudinger, *Interactive Minds;* and Wertsch, del Río, and Alvarez, *Sociocultural Studies of Mind.* For discussion of learning as of self, see Krieger, *Social Science and the Self;* and Neumann, "On Experience, Memory, and Knowing."

5. Shulman, *Teaching as Community Property;* and *Wisdom of Practice.*

6. See Shulman, "Knowledge and Teaching"; and "Those Who Understand," for discussion of continuities between subject and subject matter learning. See Bransford and others, "Teaching Thinking," for discussion of dangers of dichotomizing content and learning.

7. Bronfenbrenner, *Ecology of Human Development;* Gergen, *Saturated Self;* and Ladson-Billings, "Toward a Theory of Culturally Relevant Pedagogy."

8. Schwab, "Education and the Structure of Disciplines." In clarifying "syntactic" differences among subject matters taught in schools, Joseph Schwab set the stage for understanding how human learning emerges distinctively across disciplinary domains, in response to the unique substantive and structural forms of academic knowledge. Schwab's writings built on core ideas about learning and teaching, in subjects, as presented by John Dewey; Schwab's ideas further influenced Lee Shulman's conceptions of knowledge and teaching as herein discussed. See Dewey, *How We Think;* and *On Education;* and Shulman, "Knowledge and Teaching"; and "Those Who Understand."

9. Schon, *Reflective Practitioner;* and *Educating the Reflective Practitioner.*

10. Shulman, "Students and Teachers."

11. Lave and Wenger, *Situated Learning;* Schwab, "Structure of the Disciplines"; Wenger, *Communities of Practice;* and Wenger, McDermott, and Snyder, *Cultivating Communities of Practice.*

12. Greeno, "Situativity"; and Neumann, "Professing Passion."

13. Dewey, *How We Think;* Palmer, *Courage to Teach;* and Wenger, *Communities of Practice.*

14. Becher and Trowler, *Academic Tribes;* Clark, *Academic Life;* Pallas, "Preparing Education Doctoral Students"; and Wenger, *Communities of Practice.*

15. For elaboration, see Neumann and Peterson, *Learning from Our Lives.*

16. This view draws from writings in a variety of fields: life span psychology (including Erikson, *Childhood and Society;* and McAdams, *Stories We Live By*); the sociology of the life course (Baltes and Baltes, *Successful Aging;* Clausen,

"Adolescent Competence"; Elder, "Time, Human Agency"; Lerner and Busch-Rossnagel, "Individuals as Producers"; and Marshall, "Agency"); the interpretive social sciences (Erickson, "Qualitative Methods"; Krieger, *Social Science and the Self;* Mead, *Mind, Self, and Society;* Rabinow and Sullivan, *Interpretive Social Science;* and Schutz, *Phenomenology*); and aesthetic studies of life and learning—perspectives on work as a personal life experience interacting with other such experiences, including struggles to speak, connect, know oneself or become known as a self (Greene, "Exclusions and Awakenings"; and *Releasing the Imagination;* Krieger, *Social Science and the Self;* and Scarry, *On Beauty*). I rely also on my learning through a lifetime of exposure to fiction and autobiography that probe emotion, in the present and in memory, in pursuits of beauty and understanding and in falls to anguish and loss. With few exceptions (see Behar, *Translated Woman;* and Gumport, "Fired Faculty"), however, researchers in education and the social sciences rarely analyze the emotional meanings of their own or others' studies. Such talk is largely nonexistent, even discouraged, in higher education (Boler, *Feeling Power*).

17. Women's entrance into the professoriate has induced change, however, in this way of doing business in the university. Key writings documenting such change include Astin, *Woman Doctorate;* Austin and Pilat, "Tension, Stress"; Bensimon, "Feminist's Reinterpretation"; Dickens and Sagaria, "Feminists at Work"; Glazer-Raymo, *Shattering the Myths;* Glazer-Raymo, *Unfinished Agendas;* and Ward and Wolf-Wendel, "Academic Motherhood"; and Wolf-Wendel and Ward, "Academic Life and Motherhood."

18. Neumann, "Professing Passion."

19. Related theory includes Bronfenbrenner, *Ecology of Human Development;* Greeno, "Situativity"; Greeno, Collins, and Resnick, "Cognition and Learning"; and Wenger, *Communities of Practice.* See esp. the overview provided in Bransford, Brown, and Cocking, *How People Learn.* Recent applications to the study of faculty in higher education include Creamer and Lattuca, *Advancing Faculty Learning.*

20. For examples of professors learning of their identities in micro-level contexts, see Bensimon, "Lesbian Existence"; Creamer, "Knowledge Production"; Creamer, *Working Equal;* and Gumport, "Fired Faculty." For discussions of mid-level contexts that may be subject to learning, see Birnbaum, *How Colleges Work;* for examples, see Creamer and Lattuca, *Advancing Faculty Learning;* and Gumport, "Feminist Scholarship." For discussion and illustration of individuals' learning in macro-level contexts, though mediated through mid- and micro-level settings, see Bronfenbrenner, *Ecology of Human Development;* and Wortham, *Learning Identity.*

21. Behar, *Vulnerable Observer;* and Myerhoff, *Number Our Days.*

22. For a discussion of the multiple contexts that may frame the learning of academics, see Creamer and Latucca, *Advancing Faculty Learning*. See also Neumann and Peterson, *Learning from Our Lives,* esp. the concluding chapter, "Learning from Research and Everyday Life," 228–48.

23. But the context may also be viewed as learning and as changing over time; see Bronfenbrenner, *Ecology of Human Development.* That contextual learning and change differ from—but may influence—the learning and change of a person in that context. A state college that reconstructs itself into a major research university over two decades is learning how to be a different kind of institution. That learning, as a collective act, will doubtless influence the learning of individual professors working within the collective during this institutional transformation. Because of study design limitations, I was not able to hone in on this kind of institutional change and its implications for individual professors. For further discussion of this conundrum, see Hermanowicz, *Stars.*

Introduction

1. See, e.g., Tierney and Bensimon, *Promotion and Tenure.*

2. For an overview of the full post-tenure career, see Baldwin, Lunceford, and Vanderlinden, "Faculty in the Middle Years." That study does not address learning specifically, however, nor does it hone in on the early post-tenure years. Further, Baldwin, Lunceford, and Vanderlinden aggregate the experiences of professors in diverse types of institutions, whereas I focus only on the experiences of professors in major research universities on the assumption that scholarly learning may differ by institutional type, much like professors' work generally. For further discussion of differences in the aims, definitions, and designs of their study and mine, see Neumann and Terosky, "To Give and to Receive."

3. For examples, see Chait, *Questions of Tenure;* Immerwahr, "Taking Responsibility"; Kennedy, *Academic Duty.*

4. I present the theoretical bases of these views in app. C. I borrow the phrase *inner experience* from Krieger, *Social Science and the Self.*

5. Schuster and Finkelstein, *American Faculty.*

6. Schuster and Finkelstein, *American Faculty.*

7. Gappa, Austin, and Trice, *Rethinking Faculty Work.*

8. Schuster and Finkelstein, *American Faculty.*

9. See Birnbaum, *How Colleges Work;* Kast and Rosenzweig, *Organization and Management;* Katz and Kahn, *Social Psychology of Organizations;* Meyer and Rowan, "Institutionalized Organizations"; Pfeffer and Salancik, *External Control of Organizations;* Scott, *Organizations.*

10. This may help explain differences in conceptions of scholarship on campuses differing by mission and thereby "institutional type" (e.g., major research university, private liberal arts college, community college). For discussion of application to selective liberal arts colleges, see Ruscio, "Distinctive Scholarship." For discussion of contextual constraints on learning, see Greeno, "Situativity"; Greeno, Collins, and Resnick, "Cognition and Learning." Although variation in institutional type accounts for distinctions in what it means to be a faculty member and to work as one (including what it means to engage in scholarly learning), it must be noted that institutions also vary within type. Such was the case among the universities I studied (see chap. 6 and app. A).

11. Parker Palmer discusses uses of the "grain of sand" and "microcosm of knowledge" concept in classroom-based teaching of ideas central to a discipline. I make use of it here as a research and representational tool. See Palmer, *Courage to Teach,* esp. chap. 5, "Teaching in Community: A Subject-Centered Education," 115–40.

12. I must add that almost fifteen years later, I remain as intrigued by scholarly learning as I was years ago, though now in ways that span a far broader time frame and program of professorial endeavor.

13. For thoughtful analysis of this distinction, see Hansen, *Exploring the Moral Heart.*

14. To access the meaning of career requires the assumption of a more personal stance, from within a context, including from within a life, a point I take up in several chapters. For examples of writings that speak from "within a life," exploring the personal contexts that give rise to scholarly endeavor, see Behar, *Translated Woman;* and *Vulnerable Observer;* Kondo, *Crafting Selves;* Neumann and Peterson, *Learning from Our Lives;* Rose, *Lives on the Boundary;* and Tompkins, *Life in School.* It is noteworthy that these texts are autobiographical in content and viewpoint; the autobiographical voice may be a key point of access to personal meaning (and its contexts) in research and scholarship; for further discussion, see Neumann and Peterson, *Learning from Our Lives.*

Chapter One: Into the Middle

1. I frequently refer to professors' "subjects," "subject matters," or "subject matter knowledge," defined as the disciplinary, or field-based, knowledge that instructors shape through their teaching and learning. For full discussion of this view of classroom-based teaching and learning, see Shulman, *Teaching as Community Property;* and Shulman, *Wisdom of Practice.* Here I adapt this view in order to investigate academic careers in higher education, viewing them as subject matter constructions as well. Although useful for thinking about classroom teaching, the terms *subjects, subject matters,* and *subject matter knowledge* may also signify a scholar's intentional selection and shaping of certain ideas within larger disciplines and fields, the full range of whose knowledge cannot be represented by any one person in any one work, research agenda, or career. Much as a teacher selects certain ideas and topics for a course syllabus, so does a scholar select certain concepts, perspectives, topics—hence, subjects—for her or his study in the near or long-term future. The scholar, like the teacher, never "studies it all." The broader term *disciplinary knowledge,* though applicable, does not adequately capture the selectivity of professors' subject matter work. Because I focus on individual professors' learning (as opposed to the learning of their fields), the terms *subject* and *subject matter* apply.

2. For many years researchers and writers have explored faculty workload concerns, and their efforts have yielded numerous recommendations for improved administrative practice and university policy: enhanced accountability schemes, post-tenure reviews, incentive systems, among others. See Baldwin, Lunceford, and Vanderlinden, "Faculty in the Middle Years," for discussion of changes in professors' work through the post-tenure career. For discussion of the management of faculty work in twenty-first-century American higher education, see Colbeck, *Evaluating Faculty Performance;* Fairweather and Beach, "Variations in Faculty Work"; O'Meara, "Beliefs about Post-Tenure Review"; Tierney, "Academic Community"; and Tierney, *Faculty Productivity.* For substantial reviews of research and data compilations on the faculty role and faculty work in American higher education, see esp. Austin and Gamson, *Academic Workplace;* Blackburn and Lawrence, *Faculty at Work;* Bowen and Schuster, *American Professors;* Finkelstein, Seal, and Schuster, *New Academic Generation;* Menges and Austin, "Teaching in Higher Education"; and Schuster and Finkelstein, *American Faculty.* Other helpful sources on professors' careers include Baldwin and Blackburn, "Academic Career"; and Finkelstein and LaCelle-Peterson, *Developing Senior Faculty.* For discussion of impending harsh career realities and responses, see Altbach, "Harsh Realities."

Yet this literature indicates significant gaps. First, these writings are rarely intended for college and university professors and instructors; they are directed, rather, at higher education researchers, policy makers, and administrators whose interests in the faculty career usually differ from those of faculty members themselves—focusing more on policy, e.g., than on day-to-day practice. Second, virtually none of the extant research on faculty considers the learning side of professors' work—e.g., what it is like for a professor to "get up to speed" with new responsibilities while keeping up with those already in place. And third, none of this writing addresses scholarly learning, defined as professors' work with the subject matters that they study, teach, and create.

3. For related research on professors' greater workload after earning tenure, see Baldwin and Blackburn, "Academic Career"; Baldwin, Lunceford, and Vanderlinden, "Faculty in the Middle Years"; Becher and Trowler, *Academic Tribes;* and Neumann and Terosky, "To Give and to Receive." For examples of practice-based comments, see Midler, "Plight"; and Midler, "Service Masochists." These sources speak to the full length of the post-tenure career, though implications for its earliest years may be inferred. Others present implications for professors' work and development in more advanced phases of the post-tenure career. See, e.g., Bland and Bergquist, *Vitality of Senior Faculty;* Clark and Lewis, "Faculty Vitality"; and Licata, *Post-Tenure Faculty Evaluation.* For more generalizing treatments, see Baldwin, "Faculty Career Stages"; and *Incentives for Faculty Vitality.*

4. Professors' learning of instrumental work—occasionally referred to as "instrumental learning"—addresses a broader and more varied array of "stuff to be learned" than does scholarly learning. As I use it, *instrumental learning* serves to bracket off scholarly learning analytically, rather than to designate a distinctive form of learning. As such, it may be defined as all the professional learning in which professors engage other than the scholarly. The *Oxford English Dictionary* defines *instrumental* as "contributing to the accomplishment of a purpose or result" (*Oxford English Dictionary Online,* s.v. *Instrumental,* definition entry A. *adj.* 1a; italics added) and thus as secondary to but necessary for that accomplishment. Following on this definition, I purposefully position scholarly learning in the foreground (a focal "result") and instrumental learning as providing background that may, in part, shape or direct a professor's scholarly pursuits ("contributing"). I strive, however, to keep instrumental learning in view, even if in the background, and thus I discuss it in relation to scholarly learning (see chaps. 3–5). I adopt the phrasing *instrumental learning* at the risk of possible confusion with the eminent psychologist Edward L. Thorndike's writings about "the type of learning where a particular response is the instrument by which the organism is taught to alter its environment" (*Oxford English Dictionary Online,* s.v. *Instrumental,* definition entry A. *adj.* 7.) My use of the term bears no relation to Thorndike's view.

5. All names of individuals (including unique titles), institutions, locations, titled events or processes, and the like are pseudonyms. To comply with promises of confidentiality made to study participants, I have also altered other features of identity, including subjects of study for a small number of interviewees. Some study participants allowed me to name their disciplines and fields, and specific topics of study, but others requested that I denote their fields only in terms of a broader disciplinary sector (arts, humanities, sciences, social sciences, professional or applied fields). For discussion of confidentiality protocols, see app. A; for confidentiality provisions in consent forms, see app. B.

6. For broader representation of Sandra Covington's early post-tenure experiences, among those of others at People's State University, see Neumann, "Between the Work I Love and the Work I Do."

7. For a profile of People's State University at the time of the study and a detailed discussion of the study's design and method, see app. A. For the final study report, see Neumann, "Between the Work I Love and the Work I Do."

8. For profiles of the four study institutions, see chap. 6. For details of study design and method, see app. A.

9. With few exceptions (see, e.g., Huber, *Balancing Acts*) current research does not portray faculty careers explicitly as trajectories of subject matter learning but, rather, as paths of progression through or stasis within "rank" (assis-

tant, associate, full professor; from junior to senior faculty status). Research on professors' movement through rank has not attended to what professors learn substantively along the way but, instead, to what they have produced (whether learned or not) toward institutional promotion reviews. Similar critique applies to the other topics listed.

10. Myth is part of the stuff of oral tradition in a culture—here in the culture of higher education. Higher education's post-tenure myth has also been codified in numerous popular texts (see, e.g., Smith, *Killing the Spirit;* and Sykes, *Profscam*). Given its public exposure, this academic myth is now also a public myth.

11. Be it academic, public, or both, the myth underlies many critiques of the American tenure system, as voiced by business leaders, legislators, academic administrators, and even some professors (see Chait, *Questions of Tenure;* Chait, "Employment Options"; Immerwahr, "Taking Responsibility"; and Kennedy, *Academic Duty*). Some writers have gone so far as to describe tenured professors as "slothful . . . 'incompetents,'" constituting a "'deadwood problem' . . . receiv[ing] tenure and then proceed[ing] to do no research, no writing, and mediocre teaching for decades thereafter" (Karabell, *What's College For?* 122, 136), yet supported by a "lifelong meal ticket" from the public purse (Smith, *Killing the Spirit,* 14). Anne Matthews offers perhaps the most severe caricature of post-tenure professors as "deadwood . . . estivating faculty, turtles sunk deep in mud." "After tenure," says Matthews, "a campus asks only one thing of its professors: keep your brain alive," yet in her view, "many do not, will not, cannot" (*Bright College Years,* 151). In both public and professional discourses few questions are as contentious as those about academic tenure and the tenured career.

12. That said, a number of helpful, organizationally anchored (not directly learning oriented, in the substantive sense to which I refer) considerations have appeared through the years, either in the form of policy recommendations or analyses thereof. See "Culture of Tenure," theme issue of *Academe,* esp. Finkin, "Assault on Faculty Independence"; Bess, "Contract Systems, Bureaucracies"; and Bland and others, "Impact of Appointment Type." For a helpful review of the long-term consequences to the faculty, collectively, of changes in appointment type in the wake of the tenure controversy, see Gappa, Austin, and Trice, *Rethinking Faculty Work.*

13. See Shulman, *Teaching as Community Property;* and Shulman, *Wisdom of Practice.*

14. Schon, *Reflective Practitioner;* and Schon, *Educating the Reflective Practitioner.*

15. These propositions are taken, with slight revision, from Neumann, "Observations." I explain them in app. C. For research-based references to the literature that these propositions summarize, I refer readers to a thoughtful, highly

readable compendium of writings by key scholars of teaching and learning and of human cognition, aptly entitled *How People Learn: Brain, Mind, Experience, and School,* edited by John D. Bransford, Ann L. Brown, and Rodney R. Cocking, for the Committee on Developments in the Science of Learning, Commission on Behavioral and Social Sciences and Education of the National Research Council. For the electronic version, see www.nap.edu/html/howpeople1/notice.html. Other useful sources include Greeno, Collins, and Resnick, "Cognition and Learning"; Krieger, *Social Science and the Self;* Shulman, *Teaching as Community Property;* Shulman, *Wisdom of Practice;* and others cited in app. C.

16. As often occurs in social science research, these questions evolved through the course of the two studies (see, e.g., Lareau, "Common Problems in Field Work").

17. Neumann and Peterson, *Learning from Our Lives.*

Chapter Two: The Heart of the Matter

1. Campbell, *Handbook for the Strong-Campbell Interest Inventory;* Holland, *Making Vocational Choices: A Theory of Careers;* Holland, *Making Vocational Choices: A Theory of Vocational Personalities;* Holland and Gottfredson, "Using a Typology"; Kohn, "Unresolved Issues"; Perlmutter and Hall, *Adult Development and Aging;* Super, "Coming of Age in Middletown"; Super, "Life Span, Life Space"; Super, *Psychology of Careers.*

2. Wenger, *Communities of Practice.*

3. Career decision making is usually less linear than shown here.

4. Scarry, *On Beauty.*

5. For examples of writings that elaborate each of these contrasting views, see Kerlinger, *Behavioral Research,* for a "distanced science" perspective on educational research; and Krieger, *Social Science and the Self,* on self and emotion in social science research.

6. Csikszentmihalyi, *Evolving Self,* 176. See also Csikszentmihalyi, *Creativity; Finding Flow;* and *Flow;* and Csikszentmihalyi and Csikszentmihalyi, *Optimal Experience.*

Of the forty participants in the *Four Universities Project* only two dissociated emotional experience from their subject matter–based work. One of them linked emotion (love) only to experiences of professional freedom and (nonsubstantive) colleague relations. The other relegated emotion to a personal life that this participant defined as separate from intellectual endeavor. Thus, these two participants' responses to questions on love of work include no references to "passionate thought" as herein defined. The remaining thirty-eight openly referred to emotion in subject matter work, often in research and occasionally in teaching.

7. For related discussion of academic women creating "alternative realities"

through departures (often momentary, sometimes clandestine) from "everyday life," see Greene, "Exclusions and Awakenings"; with expanded discussion throughout Neumann and Peterson, *Learning from Our Lives*.

8. Although they portray the high (and positive) experience of passionate thought as being interactive, the three scholars indicate that these experiences include some less than positive moments—e.g., a scholar stumbling, perhaps for extended periods, through processes that yield little insight. As the scholar of literary studies describes it, in classrooms creative insight "often doesn't happen," and in personal conversations ("dialogue") you must travel a distance before "certain energy gets exchanged." The professor of romance languages also points out that classroom-situated passionate thought is exceptional, that "sometimes it happens . . . [in] talking . . . with a reasonably . . . receptive class." The earlier case of the business professor working on a statistical package with a collaborator also echoes this two-sided view of interactively created passionate thought—e.g., as these colleagues quickly shift from euphoria (having "a really great day") to disappointment (having "a disastrous day") in their work.

Chapter Three: Mindwork

1. Seeking to naturalize professors' representations of their scholarly mindwork as much as possible, I used indirect means to identify activities of mind. I posed a series of questions to professors about their research, teaching, service, careers, and lives—about their subjects of study and how they came to claim them and work with them, especially their experiences of so doing. I tape-recorded the open flow of interview talk that ensued, had that talk fully transcribed, and later culled, from within the complete transcripts, professors' references to mindful, substantive activity. I used the previously presented analytic question to guide my selections.

The approach reflects multiple limitations. First, the generalized activities of mind herein presented derive from professors' experiences of their scholarly learning, and I did not attempt to confirm them. Nevertheless, I trust those professors' views to the extent that I can trust any expert practitioner's reflections on practice as *part* of her enactment of her practice-based expertise, especially so when multiple and diverse practitioners' reflections are subjected to comparative review. (For more analytic assessments of learning, including experimental approaches, see the extensive review presented in Bransford, Brown, and Cocking, *How People Learn*.) Second, those activities of mind do not and cannot distinguish among substantive intra-discipline issues. I did not attempt to bring subject matter specialists into the study as co-researchers of their colleagues' substantive learning, which is what that would have required (see, e.g., Ball, Hill, and Bass, "Knowing Mathematics"). Third, I could not assess, and therefore cannot speak to, the consequences of professors' different approaches to learning through the early post-tenure career.

A fair amount of the scholarly learning described in this section is closely associated with professors' teaching. This is not irrelevant, a point I take up in the next chapter.

2. For a far more palpable and tragic comparison of thirst, as feeling and being, in times of safety and horror, see Lawrence Langer, *Holocaust Testimonies*. Langer interprets Charlotte Delbo's representations of concentration camp survivors' existence as between knowing and being in and of two worlds; see Delbo, *Mémoire*. Holocaust survivors may represent capacities to know dualities of sensation, such as thirst, between two spaces in which it is experienced.

3. It is conceivable that over time some professors may strive to avoid scholarly and instrumental work and learning, yet I found no such cases in the *Four Universities* and *People's State* study samples. I say more about this finding, relative to the myth of post-tenure decline, later in this chapter.

4. Table 3.2 presents professors' responses to two kinds of interview questions: directly targeting an interviewee's learning; and targeting other topics yet indirectly revealing the interviewee's learning. For the interview questions, see app. B.

Chapter Four: Location

1. My theoretical warrant for this claim is summarized in proposition 5 in chap. 1 (see also app. C). Here I emphasize the immediate (micro-level) contexts of learning but assume they grow out of, and within, broader (embedding) contexts: social, historical, cultural, political, economic, and so on. For further discussion of contextual embedding and its implications for human learning and development, see Bronfenbrenner, *Ecology of Human Development*.

2. See Becher and Trowler, *Academic Tribes*.

3. Professors who take brief leaves to learn in other fields may serve as "knowledge brokers"; for discussion of the roles of knowledge brokers in communities of practice, see Wenger, *Communities of Practice;* for analysis of knowledge brokers' contributions to learning in schools of education, see Pallas, "Preparing Education Doctoral Students." For images of interdisciplinarity in higher education, see Lattuca, *Creating Interdisciplinarity*. Although *interdisciplinarity* is more widely used, I prefer *cross-disciplinarity* in that it does not connote a particular form of cross-field connection, allowing for abundant possibilities. Because the term *interdisciplinarity* (e.g., interdisciplinary activity or effort) was widely in use in participating institutions, I retained it when quoting study participants. I use *cross-disciplinarity* in referring to my own study findings.

4. The question of what counts as a field, and thereby what counts as a

"within-field" and "cross-field" endeavor, is sometimes challenging. I would have had to code Sharan's move as "within field" had I associated her only with a broad area of study (e.g., literature). I chose, instead, to view literary study as a conglomerate of multiple, sometimes overlapping fields and subfields. In doing so, I cast Sharan (and at least one other study participant) as moving between fields of literary study. Sharan spoke of her work in relation to one or another "field" within literary study cast broadly. Given the indistinct boundaries around and within literary study as a large "field of many fields," Sharan's cross-field movement is more diffuse than is Velez's movement out of psychology, which is, indeed, a more distinctly bounded discipline. That said, Velez retains a foothold in the community of psychologists, given her formulation of a new research agenda—female corporate officers' midlife transitions—that spans two fields, business and psychology.

5. For related cases in the *People's State University Project,* see Neumann, "Between the Work I Love and the Work I Do"; and "Inventing a Labor of Love."

6. Higher education leaders and researchers have traditionally conceived of faculty as being pulled between campus obligations and disciplinary commitments (see Alpert, "Performance and Paralysis"; Clark, "Organizational Conception"); writers and leaders in higher education portray the campus and the discipline as in tension over the course of professors' careers. What this view misses is that each of these "spaces" requires the other: disciplinary commitment is enacted on campus in a faculty role that exists because the campus exists. Campus obligation is rooted in the university's social role as producer and provider of specialized academic learning rooted in disciplines and fields.

7. I analyze *Four Universities Project* data from the perspective of the institutional collectivity (higher education organization) in chap. 6, in which I discuss universities' responses to professors' efforts to strengthen their scholarly learning. For discussion of collectivity as a feature of the contexts of human development, see Bronfenbrenner, *Ecology of Human Development.* I have already discussed professors' personal lives as contexts of their scholarly learning (see chap. 2); for background, see Neumann, "Professing Passion"; and Neumann and Peterson, *Learning from Our Lives.*

8. Given the prominence of emotion in professors' scholarly learning (see chap. 2), I suggest that scholars' lives must be viewed as contexts of their scholarly learning much as their campuses and disciplines or fields are. For further discussion, see Neumann and Peterson, *Learning from Our Lives.*

9. It is conceivable, e.g., that professors' learning in their teaching provides students with otherwise inaccessible models of expert subject matter learning. Yet widespread attention to teaching that highlights the teachers' subject matter

learning alongside that of the students could be problematic in the present-day reality of heightened accountability and public watchfulness over faculty work; see Altbach, "Harsh Realities." My own writing about professors' subject matter learning in their teaching might usefully be linked to others' presentations of integration and separation of teaching and research; see Colbeck, "Merging in a Seamless Blend"; and Cuban, *How Scholars Trumped Teachers*. These writings, though related, have different focuses: Colbeck and Cuban, e.g., look at the ways in which two activities—teaching and research—merge and separate, without explicit reference to professors' learning in them. My work on scholarly learning in teaching focuses explicitly on professors' learning.

10. Lave and Wenger, *Situated Learning;* Wenger, *Communities of Practice.*

11. For writing on the conceptual bases of this view, see Shulman, *Teaching as Community Property;* and Shulman, *Wisdom of Practice.* See esp. Shulman, "Knowledge and Teaching"; and Shulman, "Those Who Understand."

12. See Prawat and Peterson, "Social Constructivist Views." See also Bransford, Brown, and Cocking, *How People Learn;* Shulman, *Wisdom of Practice;* Wertsch, Del Río, and Alvarez, *Sociocultural Studies of Mind.*

13. Neumann and Terosky, "To Give and to Receive," 282.

14. Neumann and Terosky, "To Give and to Receive."

15. I limit discussion to institutional service (such as committee work, program coordination, and administration) and public service (such as outreach, community service), both of which are campus based. It is widely known that professional service also opens doors to scholarly learning; one might serve one's discipline and field, e.g., by acting as an officer of one's professional association or editing a journal. Due to space limitations and a desire to focus on learning in surprising places, I forgo discussion of professors' scholarly learning in the context of professional service. See Neumann and Terosky, "To Give and to Receive," for the full report of the analysis that I present here in condensed form.

16. Becher and Trowler, *Academic Tribes.*

Chapter Five: Becoming Strategic

1. Neumann, Terosky, and Schell, "Agents of Learning."

2. Hitlin and Elder, "Agency."

3. Elder and Johnson, "Life Course and Aging," 61.

4. Pallas, "Subjective Approach to Schooling."

5. Marshall, "Agency," 4.

6. Key sources for this definition of agency derived from the sociology of the life course include Clausen, "Adolescent Competence"; Lerner and Busch-Rossnagel, "Individuals as Producers"; Marshall, "Agency"; and Pallas, "Subjective

Approach to Schooling." Sources from developmental psychology include Erikson, *Childhood and Society;* and McAdams, *Stories We Live By.* Anthropological sources include Behar, *Translated Woman;* Behar, *Vulnerable Observer;* and Kondo, *Crafting Selves.* A key source from social psychology is Bronfenbrenner, *Ecology of Human Development.* Contributions from philosophy of education include Dewey, *How We Think;* and Hansen, *Exploring the Moral Heart.* For discussion of obstacles to agentic action, see Clausen, "Adolescent Competence." Higher education studies that portray obstacles to the enactment of agency include Rose, *Lives on the Boundary;* Tierney and Bensimon, *Promotion and Tenure;* Tierney and Rhoads, *Faculty Socialization;* Tompkins, *Life in School;* and Tokarczyk and Fay, *Working-Class Women.*

7. Schon, *Reflective Practitioner;* and Schon, *Educating the Reflective Practitioner.*

8. For definitions of organizational strategy broadly, see Mintzberg, "Crafting Strategy"; Mintzberg, "Strategy-Making"; and Mintzberg and Waters, "Mind of the Strategist(s)." For definitions of organizational strategy in higher education, see esp. Chaffee, "Successful Strategic Management"; see also Bensimon, Neumann, and Birnbaum, *Making Sense of Administrative Leadership.* Drawing on professors' interviews, we adopted the following definition of *strategy:* "personal and self-directed meaning-making amid an otherwise disordered, even chaotic informational setting (Schutz, *Phenomenology of the Social World;* and Weick, *Social Psychology of Organizing*)—one's efforts to interpret and arrange one's reality (the setting of work and/or life) to render it sensible to one's self" (Neumann, Terosky, and Schell, "Agents of Learning," 92). To render one's reality as "sensible to one's self" is to render it as amenable to one's pursuits.

9. Anderson, Neumann, and Schell, "Academic Life."

10. Seven of the forty participants indicated no strategies in use. Three of them stated desires to take strategic action yet felt blocked from so doing (due to service commitments or challenging personal or family issues). Another three offered strategies directed at goals other than scholarly learning (e.g., to move into administration). A seventh participant, indicating no strategies in use, reflected no clear motivations.

11. For an extended case study of Carmen Elias-Jones, see Neumann, Terosky, and Schell, "Agents of Learning."

12. Wenger, *Communities of Practice.* What makes a group a community of practice is sustained engagement that facilitates significant learning. Wenger says, "Communities of practice can be thought of as shared histories of learning" (86).

13. For an extended case study of Benjamin Lucas, see Neumann, Terosky, and Schell, "Agents of Learning."

14. Details of this analysis are reported in Neumann and Terosky, "To Give and to Receive."

15. It is conceivable that women involved in caregiving are less open about their so doing then are men. Because it is widely believed that women value caregiving or that it falls to them (see Gilligan, *In a Different Voice;* see also Montero-Sieburth, "Weaving of Personal Origins"; and Noddings, "Accident, Awareness, and Actualization"), they may fear that extended talk about their caretaking responsibilities will lead others to define them as being family, rather than professionally, oriented. In contrast, men may relish public talk about their own involvement in caregiving: men who contribute to the care of children or elderly parents give the impression of breaking through traditional gender roles. This topic, and its implications for women's positioning in the academic workplace, is deserving of further study. For related discussion, see Terosky, Phifer, and Neumann, "Shattering Plexiglas."

16. For an extended case study of Elizabeth Ferrara, see Neumann, Terosky, and Schell, "Agents of Learning."

17. Boyer, *Scholarship Reconsidered.* Professional service, defined as work for disciplinary or professional associations and communities, is an exception. Professors may use it to advance their scholarly learning, given proximity to disciplinary activity. See Neumann and Terosky, "To Give and to Receive." Yet professional learning also may entail significant instrumental effort.

18. See also Neumann and Terosky, "To Give and to Receive."

19. Hochschild, *Time Bind.*

20. Neumann and Peterson, *Learning from Our Lives.*

Chapter Six: Organizing to Learn

1. Rather than using *outside* and *inside,* I use *outside in* and *inside out* in order to highlight a couple of points. One, neither view is purely in or out; each incorporates features of the other. And two, just as the first term of a hyphenated pair primes that pair's meaning, so does a researcher's *conceptual start point* prime her or his meaning making within complex social realities (such as professors' work lives). I suggest that most of the extant research on professors' work and careers reflects an outside-in perspective. Discussion of professors' passionate thought, scholarly learning and its contexts, and agency and strategy toward its accession are heavily anchored in an inside-out perspective. The latter perspective is not well represented in the study of faculty careers in higher education, nor is it used enough by university leaders and policy makers. I employ both views in this chapter though favoring the latter. For further discussion of these views and a thoughtful case example, see Larson, "Organizational change from the 'inside.'"

Given higher education's topical scope and conceptual complexity, I suggest that future research take close account of the researchers' guiding views.

2. This classic open systems view derives from core images of organization presented in Katz and Kahn, *Social Psychology of Organization;* Pfeffer and Salancik, *External Control of Organizations;* Scott, *Organizations;* and related social-psychological writings on contemporary social organization. For higher education applications, see Bensimon, Neumann, and Birnbaum, *Making Sense of Administrative Leadership;* Birnbaum, *How Academic Leadership Works;* Birnbaum, *How Colleges Work;* Chaffee, "Successful Strategic Management"; Jedamus and Peterson, *Improving Academic Management;* and Peterson, Dill, and Mets, *Planning and Management.*

3. Boler, *Feeling Power;* and Neumann, "Professing Passion." An inside-out view can do even more. It can reveal how people work together, engage in conflict, form groups, exercise power, and more.

4. My point here is that neither view need cancel out the other. The inside-out view need not block the outside-in perspective; the two can be made to work together. An inside-out view that draws university leaders' attention to professors' scholarly learning could anchor and direct those leaders' outside-in analysis of environmental events bearing specifically on professors' scholarly learning—for example, a growing scarcity of well trained scholars in a promising field of study central to the university's mission, a sudden decline in grant monies in a well-entrenched field represented by a large and expensive program faculty, or growing student markets in another field. These three environmental events, typically viewed from outside in, can bear on certain professors' scholarly learning, providing opportunities for its enhancement or posing constraints. If administrators care about professors' scholarly learning, then they will attend specifically to those environmental issues that threaten that learning or promise to build it up, as opposed to other matters "out there." Administrators who are attentive to professors' scholarly learning may rethink how they recruit faculty into a promising field; they may redirect their fund-raising efforts to help professors acquire new monies; they may assess the university's interests in exploiting new student markets. They will take such actions but with their minds trained on implications for their faculties' scholarly learning.

Here is a point of contrast: administrators who begin their thought with attention to the larger environmental issues, rather than to scholarly learning (or another valued internal issue), may have no clear internal anchor as they analyze external environments, or they may latch onto one uncritically, possibly after the fact. Administrative actions of this sort may well improve faculty recruitment procedures, fund-raising, or marketing but ignore what these actions imply, specifically, for the faculty's scholarly learning. I suggest that beginning, conceptually, with professors' scholarly learning—making it a topic of driving concern—can (and should) push administrators to direct environmental action in relation to that learning.

All this assumes, of course, a core commitment, by university leaders, to enhancing opportunities for professors' scholarly learning. Although adapted for use in higher education organizations, this conceptualization assumes that an individual's "standpoint" has much to say about where she will anchor her thought (external to faculty life, viewing it from a distance; or internal to faculty life, striving to extend it outward) and thus the kinds of sense that that person will make of a particular reality. For theoretical discussion of standpoint, see Harding, *Science Question;* and *Whose Science?* and Smith, *Everyday World.* For a useful critique, see Haraway, "Situated Knowledges." For application to college and university presidential leadership, see Neumann and Bensimon, "Constructing the Presidency."

5. More specifically, the analysis reported in this chapter relied on five kinds of data gathered through the *Four Universities Project*: (1) campus documentary data collected on site or from public sources (university Web sites, viewbooks, major newspapers, campus and other local news briefs, books and articles about the universities, and so on; strategic plans, annual reports, and other institutional documents); (2) a central university administrator's and senior faculty leader's representations of the university, its performance, and values (two such interviews per campus, conducted in project year 1); (3) the newly tenured professors' (focal participants') responses to direct questions about features of campus life that supported or detracted from scholarly learning (nine to eleven interviews per campus, conducted in project years 1 and 3); (4) professors' incidental allusions to their experiences of scholarly learning; and (5) supplementary data, including professors' publications, curriculum vitae, tenure narratives, and site observations. As indicated in app. A, in year 1 of the study all forty focal participants (newly tenured professors) were interviewed; in year 3 of the study thirty-nine were interviewed. Items 1 and 2 and limited features of items 3, 4, and 5 contributed to university profiles in an outside-in view; items 3, 4, and 5 contributed to inside-out views of professors' experiences of their scholarly learning and institutional support toward it.

6. I include a similar profile for People's State University in app. A. I did not factor People's State University data into the analysis reported in this chapter, however, given differences in the aims and perspectives of the two research projects. On initiating the *People's State University Project,* I did not have the anchor of scholarly learning to guide data collection from within professors' experiences. As such, the *People's State* study looked more broadly at participants' organiza-

tional experiences rather than deeply into their scholarly learning, as does the *Four Universities Project*. The existence (and potential import of scholarly learning) was an outcome of the *People's State University Project*.

7. The Carnegie Foundation for the Advancement of Teaching, "Basic Classification Description," www.carnegiefoundation.org/classifications/index.asp?key =791 (accessed December 28, 2007).

8. I refer to measures popularized by *U.S. News and World Report, America's Best Graduate Schools* and *America's Best Colleges,* and by the National Research Council. The study universities relied on other less formal measures as well.

9. For discussion of organizational cultures and human cognition in American higher education, see Bensimon, Neumann, and Birnbaum, *Making Sense of Administrative Leadership;* and Birnbaum, *How Colleges Work*.

10. Like all research perspectives, the inside-out view has its shortcomings. Given the constraints of language to convey experience, individuals can but rarely articulate their "felt experiences" in full. See, e.g., Neumann, "On Experience, Memory, and Knowing."

11. None of these facets is fully independent of the others, and any one feature of university functioning may represent one or more facet at a time. Professors' long-term working relationships on campus may be viewed, for instance, as contributing, simultaneously, to (1) organizational norms around local colleagueship; (2) cross-disciplinary endeavor; and (3) externalization of academic work (e.g., public outreach). The distinctive contributions of these three facets of academic organization to professors' scholarly learning are less obvious from an outside-in perspective than from a "lived" inside-out perspective.

12. Although I rely most heavily on interviewees' terminology, *colleagueship* is an analytic construct that I developed in reviewing their words.

13. Terosky, Phifer, and Neumann, "Shattering Plexiglas," 71.

14. Bronfenbrenner, *Ecology of Human Development*.

15. Neumann, "Helping to Foster Collegiality for Newcomers"; Neumann, Kadar, and Terosky, "I Get By with a Little Help."

16. Erickson, "Qualitative Methods," provides useful insights on within-sample generalization in qualitative educational research.

17. When discussing their colleagueship, women in the arts and humanities portrayed their careers as more precariously situated than did women in other fields. In talking about workload or work content, however, women in the sciences described careers as more precarious than did women in other fields (see Terosky, Phifer, and Neumann, "Shattering Plexiglas"). Emanating from the same body of data, these finding are not contradictory. Rather, they suggest that for academic women, career risks are multifaceted; they may show up in different ways across the disciplines. For discussion of related risks, see Neumann, "Be-

tween the Work I Love and the Work I Do"; Neumann, "Inventing a Labor of Love"; and Terosky, Phifer, and Neumann, "Shattering Plexiglas." Researchers in higher education have described the instability that many academic women associate with their careers (see, e.g., Glazer-Raymo, *Shattering the Myths;* and Glazer-Raymo, *Unfinished Agendas*); researchers also have analyzed gender-differentiated patterns of work (Schuster and Finkelstein, *American Faculty*). Yet none have studied the conditions of women's scholarly learning specifically and from a cross-disciplinary perspective.

18. O'Meara, "Striving for What?"

19. This two-part representation parallels the definition of *discipline* as (1) an area of knowledge and (2) a community of knowledge practitioners. See Becher and Trowler, *Academic Tribes;* Wenger, *Communities of Practice.*

20. Only two professors who spoke of their scholarly learning in relation to cross-disciplinarity did so without reference to colleagueship.

21. Lattuca, *Creating Interdisciplinarity;* Lattuca, "Learning Interdisciplinarity."

22. Schuster and Finkelstein, *American Faculty.*

23. See Wenger, *Communities of Practice.* These observations follow from Wenger's distinctions between *participation* and *reification* as forms of social relationship within community, with implications for the flow and freezing, as well as unfreezing, of knowledge constituting those relationships.

24. See, e.g., Lynton and Elman, *New Priorities.*

25. Italicized emphases are added to help clarify the vision of externalization that Acker experiences, the external environment (city) entering the classroom (as an aspect of organization), versus the more conventional converse.

26. See, e.g., Boyer, *Scholarship Reconsidered;* Glassick, Huber, and Maeroff, *Scholarship Assessed;* and O'Meara, *Scholarship Unbound.* For background on outreach or public service as a form of professors' work, see Lynton and Elman, *New Priorities.*

Chapter Seven: The Middle Remapped

1. Emily Lifton, David Mora, and Richard Marin speak to select portions of this overall narrative; George Bellanov, Serena Mandell, and Nina Altman, to the whole. For other whole-life autobiographical representations of the shifting contexts of professors' scholarly learning, based on study data, see the case of Elizabeth Ferrara (Neumann, Terosky, and Schell, "Agents of Learning"); and of Rachel Teller (Neumann, "Inventing a Labor of Love"). For related images outside this study, see Neumann and Peterson, *Learning from Our Lives.*

2. Women's struggles for epistemic legitimacy must be viewed as part of the "unfinished agenda" of higher education; see Glazer-Raymo, *Unfinished Agendas.* Yet epistemic legitimacy is an issue for other diverse segments of the higher

education community as well. Sadly, study design limitations curbed my analysis of professors' scholarly learning experiences by racial and ethnic background, immigrant and refugee status, sexual orientation, religious background, age and life stage, health and (dis)ability, and socioeconomic origins. Because scholarly learning draws on personal knowledge derived from personal experience, such differences warrant attention in future studies. For other rationales for advancing research on diverse professors' experiences of their work and learning, see Antonio, "Diverse Student Bodies"; Bensimon, "Lesbian Existence"; Miller and Skeen, "POSSLQs and PSSSLQs"; Turner, Myers, and Creswell, "Exploring Underrepresentation."

Alpert, Daniel. "Performance and Paralysis: The Organizational Context of the American Research University." *Journal of Higher Education* 56, no. 3 (1986): 241–81.

Altbach, Philip G. "Harsh Realities: The Professoriate Faces a New Century." In *American Higher Education in the Twenty-first Century,* edited by Philip G. Altbach, Robert O. Berdahl, and Patricia J. Gumport, 271–98. Baltimore: Johns Hopkins University Press, 1999.

Anderson, Gregory M., Anna Neumann, and Julie Schell. "Academic Life and Higher Education as a Field of Struggle." Research paper presented at the annual meeting of the American Sociological Association, Atlanta, August 2003.

Antonio, Anthony Lising. "Diverse Student Bodies, Diverse Faculties." *Academe* 89, no. 6 (2003): 14–17.

Astin, Helen S. *The Woman Doctorate in America: Origins, Career, and Family.* New York: Russell Sage, 1969.

Austin, Ann E., and Zelda F. Gamson. *Academic Workplace: New Demands, Heightened Tensions.* Washington, D.C.: Association for the Study of Higher Education, 1984.

Austin, Ann E., and Mary Pilat. "Tension, Stress, and the Tapestry of Faculty Lives." *Academe* 76, no. 1 (1990): 38–42.

Baldwin, Roger, G. "Faculty Career Stages and Implications for Professional Development." In *Enhancing Faculty Careers: Strategies for Development and Renewal,* edited by Jack H. Schuster and Daniel W. Wheeler, 20–40. San Francisco: Jossey-Bass, 1990.

———, ed. *Incentives for Faculty Vitality.* San Francisco: Jossey-Bass, 1985.

Baldwin, Roger G., and Robert T. Blackburn. "The Academic Career as a Developmental Process: Implications for Higher Education." *Journal of Higher Education* 52, no. 6 (1981): 598–614.

Baldwin, Roger G., Christina Lunceford, and Kim E. Vanderlinden. "Faculty in the Middle Years: Illuminating an Overlooked Phase of Academic Life." *Review of Higher Education* 29, no. 1 (2005): 97–118.

Ball, Deborah Lowenberg, Heather C. Hill, and Hyman Bass. "Knowing Mathematics for Teaching." *American Educator* 29, no. 3 (2005): 14–46.

Baltes, Paul B., and Margaret M. Baltes. *Successful Aging: Perspectives from the Behavioral Sciences*. New York: Cambridge University Press, 1990.

Baltes, Paul B., and Ursula M. Staudinger. *Interactive Minds: Life-Span Perspectives on the Social Foundation of Cognition*. Cambridge: Cambridge University Press, 1996.

Becher, Tony, and Paul R. Trowler. *Academic Tribes and Territories: Intellectual Enquiry and the Culture of Disciplines*. 2nd ed. Buckingham, UK: Society for Research into Higher Education and Open University Press, 2001.

Behar, Ruth. *Translated Woman: Crossing the Border with Esperanza's Story*. Boston: Beacon, 1993.

———. *The Vulnerable Observer*. Boston: Beacon, 1996.

Bensimon, Estela M. "A Feminist's Reinterpretation of Presidents' Definitions of Leadership." In *Women in Higher Education: A Feminist Perspective*, edited by Judith S. Glazer, Estela M. Bensimon, and Barbara K. Townsend, 465–74. Needham Heights, Mass.: Ginn Press, 1993.

———. "Lesbian Existence and the Challenge to Normative Constructions of the Academy." *Journal of Education* 174, no. 3 (1992): 98–113.

Bensimon, Estela M., Anna Neumann, and Robert Birnbaum. *Making Sense of Administrative Leadership: The "L" Word in Higher Education*. Vol. 1: *ASHE-ERIC Higher Education Reports*. Washington, D.C.: School of Education and Human Development, George Washington University, 1989.

Bess, James L. "Contract Systems, Bureaucracies, and Faculty Motivation: The Probable Effects of a No-Tenure Policy." *Journal of Higher Education* 69, no. 1 (1998): 1–22.

Birnbaum, Robert. *How Academic Leadership Works: Understanding Success and Failure in the College Presidency*. San Francisco: Jossey-Bass, 1992.

———. *How Colleges Work: The Cybernetics of Academic Organization and Leadership*. San Francisco: Jossey-Bass, 1988.

Blackburn, Robert, and Janet Lawrence. *Faculty at Work: Motivation, Expectation, Satisfaction*. Baltimore: Johns Hopkins University Press, 1995.

Bland, Carole J., and William H. Bergquist. *The Vitality of Senior Faculty Members: Snow on the Roof, Fire in the Furnace*. Vol. 25, no. 7: *ASHE-ERIC Higher Education Research Reports*. Washington, D.C.: George Washington University Graduate School of Education and Human Development, 1997.

Bland, Carole J., Bruce A. Center, Deborah A. Finstad, Kelly R. Risbey, and Justin Staples. "The Impact of Appointment Type on the Productivity and Commitment of Full-Time Faculty in Research and Doctoral Institutions." *Journal of Higher Education* 77, no. 1 (2006): 89–123.

Boler, Megan. *Feeling Power: Emotions and Education*. New York: Routledge, 1999.

Bowen, Howard R., and Jack H. Schuster. *American Professors: A National Resource Imperiled*. New York: Oxford University Press, 1986.

Boyer, Ernest L. *Scholarship Reconsidered: Priorities of the Professoriate*. Princeton, N.J.: Carnegie Foundation for the Advancement of Teaching, 1990.

Bransford, John D., Ann L. Brown, and Rodney R. Cocking, eds. Committee on Developments in the Science of Learning, Commission on Behavioral and Social Sciences and Education, National Research Council. *How People Learn: Brain, Mind, Experience, and School*. Washington, D.C.: National Academy Press, 1999.

Bransford, John D., Nancy Vye, Charles Kinser, and Victoria Risko. "Teaching Thinking and Content Knowledge: Toward an Integrated Approach." In *Dimensions of Thinking and Cognitive Instruction*, edited by Beau Fly Jones and Lorna Idol, 381–414. Mahwah, N.J.: Erlbaum, 1990.

Bronfenbrenner, Urie. 1979. *The Ecology of Human Development*. Cambridge: Harvard University Press, 1979.

Campbell, David P. *Handbook for the Strong-Campbell Interest Inventory*. Stanford: Stanford University Press, 1974.

Chaffee, Ellen Earle. "Successful Strategic Management in Small Private Colleges." *Journal of Higher Education* 55, no. 2 (1984): 212–41.

Chait, Richard, ed. *The Questions of Tenure*. Cambridge: Harvard University Press, 2002.

———. "Thawing the Cold War over Tenure: Why Academe Needs More Employment Options." *Chronicle of Higher Education*, February 7, 1997, B4, http://chronicle.com/che-data/articles.dir/art-43.dir/issue-22.dir/22b00401.htm (accessed May 15, 2005).

"Characteristics of Full-Time Faculty Members with Teaching Duties, Fall 1992." *Chronicle of Higher Education: Almanac, 1997–98* (Fall 1997), http://chronicle.com/che-data/infobank.dir/almanac.dir/97alm.dir/facts.dir/fac4.htm (accessed December 31, 2007).

Clark, Burton R. *The Academic Life: Small Worlds, Different Worlds*. Princeton: Carnegie Foundation for the Advancement of Teaching and Princeton University Press, 1987.

———. "The Organizational Conception." In *Perspectives on Higher Education: Eight Disciplinary Perspectives*, edited by Burton R. Clark, 106–31. Berkeley: University of California Press, 1984.

Clark, Shirley M., and Darrell R. Lewis. "Faculty Vitality: Context, Concerns, and Prospects." In *Higher Education: Handbook of Theory and Research*, edited by John C. Smart, 282–318. New York: Agathon, 1988.

Clausen, John. "Adolescent Competence and the Shaping of the Life Course." *American Journal of Sociology* 96, no. 4 (1991): 805–42.

Colbeck, Carol L., ed. *Evaluating Faculty Performance*. San Francisco: Jossey-Bass, 2002.

———. "Merging in a Seamless Blend: How Faculty Integrate Teaching and Research." *Journal of Higher Education* 69, no. 6 (1998): 647–71.

Creamer, Elizabeth G. "Knowledge Production, Publication Productivity, and Intimate Academic Partnerships." *Journal of Higher Education* 70, no. 3 (1999): 261–77.

———. *Working Equal: Academic Couples as Collaborators*. New York: Routledge Press, 2001.

Creamer, Elizabeth G., and Lisa R. Lattuca, eds. *Advancing Faculty Learning through Interdisciplinary Collaboration*. San Francisco: Jossey-Bass, 2005.

Csikszentmihalyi, Mihalyi. *Creativity: Flow and the Psychology of Discovery and Invention*. New York: HarperCollins, 1996.

———. *The Evolving Self: A Psychology for the Third Millennium*. New York: HarperCollins, 1993.

———. *Finding Flow: The Psychology of Engagement with Everyday Life*. New York: Basic Books, 1997.

———. *Flow: The Psychology of Optimal Experience*. New York: Harper and Row, 1990.

Csikszentmihalyi, Mihalyi, and Isabella Selega Csikszentmihalyi, eds. *Optimal Experience: Psychological Studies of Flow in Consciousness*. Cambridge: Cambridge University Press, 1988.

Cuban, Larry. *How Scholars Trumped Teachers: Change without Reform in University Curriculum, Teaching, and Research, 1890–1990*. New York: Teachers College Press, 1999.

"The Culture of Tenure: The Responsibilities of the Community of Scholars." Theme issue. *Academe* 83, no. 3 (1997).

Delbo, Charlotte. *La Mémoire et les jours*. Paris: Berg International, 1985.

Dewey, John. *How We Think*. 1910. Reprint. Mineola, N.Y.: Dover, 1997.

———. *On Education*. Chicago: University of Chicago Press, 1964.

Dickens, Cynthia Sullivan, and Mary Ann D. Sagaria. "Feminists at Work: Collaborative Relationships among Women Faculty." *Review of Higher Education* 21, no. 1 (1997): 79–101.

Elder, Glen H., Jr. "Time, Human Agency, and Social Change: Perspectives on the Life Course." *Social Psychology Quarterly* 57, no. 1 (1994): 4–15.

Elder, Glen H., Jr., and Monica Kirkpatrick Johnson. "The Life Course and Aging: Challenges, Lessons, and New Directions." In *Invitation to the Life Course: Toward New Understandings of Later Life*, pt. 2, edited by Richard A. Settersten Jr., 49–81. Amityville, N.Y.: Baywood, 2002.

Erickson, Frederick. "Qualitative Methods in Research on Teaching." In *Hand-

book of Research on Teaching, edited by Merlin C. Wittrock, 119–61. 3rd ed. New York: Macmillan, 1986.

Erikson, Erik H. 1950. *Childhood and Society.* New York: Norton, 1950.

Fairweather, James S., and Andrea L. Beach. "Variations in Faculty Work at Research Universities: Implications for State and Institutional Policy." *Review of Higher Education* 26, no. 1 (2002): 97–115.

Finkelstein, Martin J., and Mark W. LaCelle-Peterson, eds. *Developing Senior Faculty as Teachers.* San Francisco: Jossey-Bass, 1993.

Finkelstein, Martin J., Robert K. Seal, and Jack H. Schuster. *The New Academic Generation: A Profession in Transformation.* Baltimore: Johns Hopkins University Press, 1998.

Finkin, Matthew W. "The Assault on Faculty Independence." *Academe* 83, no. 4 (1997): 16–21.

Gappa, Judith M., Ann E. Austin, and Andrea G. Trice. *Rethinking Faculty Work: Higher Education's Strategic Imperative.* San Francisco: John Wiley and Sons, 2007.

Gergen, Kenneth. *The Saturated Self: Dilemmas of Identity in Contemporary Life.* New York: Basic Books / HarperCollins, 1991.

Gilligan, Carol. *In a Different Voice: Psychological Theory and Women's Development.* Cambridge: Harvard University Press, 1992.

Glaser, Barney, and Anselm L. Strauss. *The Discovery of Grounded Theory: Strategies for Qualitative Research.* Chicago: Aldine, 1967.

Glassick, Charles E., Mary Taylor Huber, and Gene I. Maeroff. *Scholarship Assessed: Evaluation of the Professoriate.* San Francisco: Jossey-Bass, 1997.

Glazer-Raymo, Judith. *Shattering the Myths: Women in Academe.* Baltimore: Johns Hopkins University Press, 1999.

——, ed. *Unfinished Agendas: New and Continuing Gender Challenges in Higher Education.* Baltimore: Johns Hopkins University Press, 2008.

Greene, Maxine. "Exclusions and Awakenings." In *Learning from Our Lives: Women, Research, and Autobiography in Education,* edited by Anna Neumann and Penelope L. Peterson, 18–36. New York: Teachers College Press, 1997.

——. *Releasing the Imagination: Essays on Education, the Arts, and Social Change.* San Francisco: Jossey-Bass, 1995.

Greeno, James G. "The Situativity of Knowing, Learning, and Research." *American Psychologist* 53, no. 1 (1998): 5–26.

Greeno, James G., Alan M. Collins, and Lauren B. Resnick. "Cognition and Learning." In *Handbook of Educational Psychology,* edited by David C. Berliner and Robert C. Calfee, 15–46. New York: Macmillan, 1996.

Gumport, Patricia J. "Feminist Scholarship as a Vocation." *Higher Education* 20, no. 3 (1990): 231–43.

———. "Fired Faculty: Reflections on Marginalization and Academic Identity." In *Naming Silenced Lives: Personal Narratives and the Process of Educational Change,* edited by Daniel McLaughlin and William G. Tierney, 135–54. New York: Routledge, 1993.

Hansen, David T. *Exploring the Moral Heart of Teaching: Toward a Teacher's Creed.* New York: Teachers College Press, 2001.

Haraway, Donna. "Situated Knowledges: The Science Question in Feminism as a Site of Discourse on the Privilege of Partial Perspective." *Feminist Studies* 14, no. 3 (1988): 575–99.

Harding, Sandra. *The Science Question in Feminism.* Ithaca, N.Y.: Cornell University Press, 1986.

———. *Whose Science? Whose Knowledge? Thinking from Women's Lives.* Ithaca, N.Y.: Cornell University Press, 1991.

Hermanowicz, Joseph C. *The Stars Are Not Enough: Scientists—Their Passions and Professions.* Chicago: University of Chicago Press, 1998.

Hitlin, Steven, and Glen H. Elder Jr. "Agency: An Empirical Model of an Abstract Concept." In *Constructing Adulthood: Agency and Subjectivity in Adolescence and Adulthood,* edited by Ross Macmillan, 33–68. Amsterdam: Elsevier, JAI, 2007.

Hochschild, Arlie Russell. *The Time Bind: When Work Becomes Home and Home Becomes Work.* New York: Metropolitan Books, 1997.

Holland, John L. *Making Vocational Choices: A Theory of Careers.* Englewood Cliffs, N.J.: Prentice Hall, 1973.

———. *Making Vocational Choices: A Theory of Vocational Personalities and Work Environments.* Englewood Cliffs, N.J.: Prentice Hall, 1985.

Holland, John L., and Gary D. Gottfredson. "Using a Typology of Persons and Environments to Explain Careers: Some Extensions and Clarifications." *Counseling Psychologist* 6, no. 3 (1976): 20–29.

Huber, Mary Taylor. *Balancing Acts: The Scholarship of Teaching and Learning in Academic Careers.* Washington, D.C.: American Association for Higher Education and the Carnegie Foundation for the Advancement of Teaching, 2004.

Immerwahr, John. "Taking Responsibility: Leaders' Expectations of Higher Education." National Center for Public Policy and Higher Education, Public Agenda Foundation, New York City, 1999. ED 437863.

Jedamus, Paul, and Marvin W. Peterson, eds. *Improving Academic Management: A Handbook of Planning and Institutional Research.* San Francisco: Jossey-Bass, 1980.

Karabell, Zachary. *What's College For? The Struggle to Define American Higher Education.* New York: Basic Books, 1998.

Kast, Fremont E., and James E. Rosenzweig. *Organization and Management: A Systems and Contingency Approach.* 4th ed. New York: McGraw-Hill, 1985.

Katz, Daniel, and Robert L. Kahn. *The Social Psychology of Organizations.* 2nd ed. New York: Wiley, 1978.

Kennedy, Donald. *Academic Duty.* Cambridge: Harvard University Press, 1997.

Kerlinger, Fred N. *Behavioral Research: A Conceptual Approach.* New York: Holt, Rinehart, and Winston, 1979.

Kohn, Melvin L. "Unresolved Issues in the Relationship between Work and Personality." In *The Nature of Work, Sociological Perspectives,* edited by Kai Erikson and Steven Peter Vallas, 36–68. New Haven, Conn.: Yale University Press, 1990.

Kondo, Dorinne K. *Crafting Selves: Power, Gender, and Discourses of Identity in a Japanese Workplace.* Chicago: University of Chicago Press, 1990.

Krieger, Susan. *Social Science and the Self: Personal Essays on an Art Form.* New Brunswick, N.J.: Rutgers University Press, 1991.

Kvale, Steinar. *Interviews: An Introduction to Qualitative Research Interviewing.* Thousand Oaks, Calif.: Sage, 1996.

Ladson-Billings, Gloria. "Toward a Theory of Culturally Relevant Pedagogy." *American Educational Research Journal* 32, no. 3 (1995): 465–91.

Langer, Lawrence L. *Holocaust Testimonies: The Ruins of Memory.* New Haven, Conn.: Yale University Press, 1991.

Lareau, Annette. "Common Problems in Field Work: A Personal Essay." Appendix to *Home Advantage: Social Class and Parental Intervention in Elementary Education,* 187–223. London: Falmer Press, 1989.

Larson, R. Sam. "Organizational Change from the 'Inside': A Study of University Outreach." Ph.D. diss., Michigan State University, 1997.

Lattuca, Lisa R. *Creating Interdisciplinarity: Interdisciplinary Research and Teaching among College and University Faculty.* Nashville: Vanderbilt University Press, 2001.

———. "Learning Interdisciplinarity." *Journal of Higher Education* 73, no. 6 (2002): 711–39.

Lave, Jean, and Etienne Wenger. *Situated Learning: Legitimate Peripheral Participation.* Cambridge: Cambridge University Press, 1991.

Lerner, Richard M., and Nancy A. Busch-Rossnagel. "Individuals as Producers of Their Development: Conceptual and Empirical Bases." In *Individuals as Producers of Their Development: A Life-Span Perspective,* edited by Richard M. Lerner and Nancy A. Busch-Rossnagel, 1–36. New York: Cambridge University Press, 1981.

Licata, Christine M. *Post-Tenure Faculty Evaluation: Threat or Opportunity.* Vol. 1: *ASHE-ERIC Higher Education Reports.* Washington, D.C.: George

Washington University and the Association for the Study of Higher Education, 1986.

Lin, Xiaodong, and Daniel L. Schwartz. "Reflections at the Crossroads of Cultures." *Mind, Culture, and Activity* 10, no. 1 (2003): 9–25.

Lynton, Ernest A., and Sandra E. Elman. *New Priorities for the University: Meeting Society's Needs for Applied Knowledge and Competent Individuals.* San Francisco: Jossey-Bass, 1987.

Marshall, Victor W. "Agency, Structure and the Life Course in the Era of Reflexive Modernization." Research paper presented at the annual meeting of the American Sociological Association, Washington, D.C., August 2000.

Marsick, Victoria, and Karen E. Watkins. "Informal and Incidental Learning." In *The New Update on Adult Learning Theory,* edited by Sharan B. Merriam, 25–34. San Francisco: Jossey-Bass, 2001.

Matthews, Anne. *Bright College Years: Inside the American Campus Today.* New York: Simon and Schuster, 1997.

Maxwell, Joseph A. *Qualitative Research Design.* Thousand Oaks, Calif.: Sage, 1996.

McAdams, Dan P. *The Stories We Live By: Personal Myths and the Making of the Self.* New York: Guilford Press, 1993.

Mead, George Herbert. *Mind, Self, and Society, from the Standpoint of a Social Behaviorist,* edited by Charles W. Morris. Chicago: University of Chicago Press, 1962.

Menges, Robert J., and Ann E. Austin. "Teaching in Higher Education." In *Handbook of Research on Teaching,* edited by Virginia Richardson, 1122–56. 4th ed. Washington, D.C.: American Educational Research Association, 2001.

Meyer, John W., and Brian Rowan. "Institutionalized Organizations: Formal Structure as Myth and Ceremony." *American Journal of Sociology* 83, no. 2 (1977): 340–63.

Midler, Frank. "The Plight of the Newly Tenured." *Chronicle of Higher Education,* April 5, 2004, http://chronicle.com/jobs/2004/04/2004040501c.htm (accessed May 15, 2005).

———. "Service Masochists. *Chronicle of Higher Education,* January 27, 2006, http://chronicle.com/jobs/2006/01/2006012701c.htm (accessed February 1, 2006).

Miller, Dorothy C., and Anita Skeen. "POSSLQs and PSSSLQs: Unmarried Academic Couples." In *Academic Couples: Problems and Promises,* edited by Marianne A. Ferber and Jane W. Loeb, 106–27. Urbana: University of Illinois Press, 1997.

Mintzberg, Henry. "Crafting Strategy." *Harvard Business Review* 65, no. 4 (1987): 66–75.

————. "Strategy-Making in Three Modes." *California Management Review* 16, no. 2 (1973): 44–53.

Mintzberg, Henry, and James A. Waters. "The Mind of the Strategist(s)." In *The Executive Mind*, edited by Suresh Srivasta, 58–83. San Francisco: Jossey-Bass, 1983.

Montero-Sieburth, Martha. "The Weaving of Personal Origins and Research: 'Reencuentro y Reflexión en la Investigación.'" In *Learning from Our Lives: Women, Research, and Autobiography in Education*, edited by Anna Neumann and Penelope L. Peterson, 124–49. New York: Teachers College Press, 1997.

Myerhoff, Barbara. *Number Our Days*. New York: Touchstone / Simon and Schuster, 1978.

Neumann, Anna. "Between the Work I Love and the Work I Do: Creating Professors and Scholars in the Early Post-Tenure Career." MS, Occasional Paper Series, Center for the Education of Women and Institute for Research on Women and Gender, University of Michigan, Ann Arbor, 1999.

————. "On Experience, Memory, and Knowing: A Post-Holocaust (Auto)biography." *Curriculum Inquiry* 28, no. 4 (1998): 425–42.

————. "Helping to Foster Collegiality for Newcomers." In *The Department Chair's Role in Developing New Faculty into Teachers and Scholars*, by Estela Mara Bensimon, Kelly Ward, and Karla Sanders, 123–25. Bolton, Mass.: Anker, 2000.

————. "Inventing a Labor of Love: Scholarship as a Woman's Work." In *Women's Untold Stories: Breaking Silence, Talking Back, Voicing Complexity*, edited by Mary Romero and Abigail J. Stewart, 243–55. New York: Routledge, 1999.

————. "Observations: Taking Seriously the Topic of Learning in Studies of Faculty Work and Careers." In *Advancing Faculty Learning through Interdisciplinary Collaboration*, edited by Elizabeth G. Creamer and Lisa Lattuca, 63–83. New Directions for Teaching and Learning series, no. 102, Marilla D. Svinicki, editor-in-chief, and R. Eugene Rice, consulting editor. San Francisco: Jossey-Bass, 2005.

————. "Professing Passion: Emotion in the Scholarship of Professors in Research Universities." *American Educational Research Journal* 43, no. 3 (2006): 381–424.

Neumann, Anna, and Estela M. Bensimon. "Constructing the Presidency: College Presidents' Images of Their Leadership Roles, A Comparative Study." *Journal of Higher Education* 61, no. 6 (1990): 678–701.

Neumann, Anna, Riva Kadar, and Aimee LaPointe Terosky. "'I Get By with a Little Help from My Friends': Exploring Recently Tenured University Professors' Experiences of Colleagueship." Research paper presented at the annual meeting of the American Educational Research Association, San Diego, Calif., April 2004.

Neumann, Anna, and Penelope L. Peterson, eds. *Learning from Our Lives: Women, Research, and Autobiography.* New York: Teachers College Press, 1997.

Neumann, Anna, and Aimee LaPointe Terosky. "To Give and to Receive: Recently Tenured Professors' Experiences of Service in Major Research Universities." *Journal of Higher Education* 78, no. 3 (2007): 282–310.

Neumann, Anna, Aimee LaPointe Terosky, and Julie Schell. "Agents of Learning: Strategies for Assuming Agency, for Learning, in Tenured Faculty Careers." In *The Balancing Act: Gendered Perspectives in Faculty Roles and Work Lives,* edited by Susan J. Bracken, Jeanie K. Allen, and Diane R. Dean, 91–120. Sterling, Va.: Stylus, 2006.

Noddings, Nel. "Accident, Awareness, and Actualization." In *Learning from Our Lives: Women, Research, and Autobiography in Education,* edited by Anna Neumann and Penelope L. Peterson, 166–82. New York: Teachers College Press, 1997.

"Number of Full-Time Faculty Members by Sex, Rank, and Racial and Ethnic Group, Fall 2005." *Chronicle of Higher Education: Almanac, 2007–8* (Fall 2007), http://chronicle.com/weekly/almanac/2007/nation/0102402.htm (accessed December 31, 2007).

O'Meara, KerryAnn. "Beliefs about Post-Tenure Review: The Influence of Autonomy, Collegiality, Career Stage, and Institutional Context." *Journal of Higher Education* 75, no. 2 (2004): 178–202.

———. *Scholarship Unbound.* New York: RoutledgeFalmer, 2001.

———. "Striving for What? Exploring the Pursuit of Prestige." In *Higher Education: Handbook of Theory and Research,* edited by John C. Smart, 121–79. Dordrecht: Springer Netherlands, 2007.

Oxford English Dictionary Online, edited by John Simpson and others. Oxford: Oxford University Press, 2000, http://dictionary.oed.com.greenleaf.cc.columbia.edu:2048/entrance.dtl (accessed April 5, 2006).

Pallas, Aaron M. "A Subjective Approach to Schooling and the Transition to Adulthood." In *Constructing Adulthood: Agency and Subjectivity in Adolescence and Adulthood,* edited by Ross Macmillan, 173–98. Amsterdam: Elsevier, JAI, 2007.

———. "Preparing Education Doctoral Students for Epistemological Diversity." *Educational Researcher* 30, no. 5 (2001): 6–11.

Palmer, Parker. *The Courage to Teach: Exploring the Inner Landscape of a Teacher's Life.* San Francisco: Jossey-Bass, 1998.

Perlmutter, Marion, and Elizabeth Hall. *Adult Development and Aging*. New York: John Wiley and Sons, 1992.

Peterson, Marvin, David D. Dill, and Lisa Mets, eds. *Planning and Management for a Changing Environment: A Handbook on Redesigning Postsecondary Institutions*. San Francisco: Jossey-Bass, 1997.

Pfeffer, Jeffrey, and Gerald R. Salancik. *The External Control of Organizations: A Resource Dependence Perspective*. New York: Harper and Row, 1978.

Prawat, Richard S., and Penelope L. Peterson. "Social Constructivist Views of Learning." In *Handbook of Research on Educational Administration,* edited by Joseph Murphy and Karen Seashore Louis, 203–26. 2nd ed. San Francisco: Jossey-Bass, 1999.

Rabinow, Paul, and William M. Sullivan, eds. *Interpretive Social Science: A Reader*. Berkeley: University of California Press, 1979.

Rhodes, Susan R., and Mildred Doering. "An Integrated Model of Career Change." *Academy of Management Review* 8, no. 4 (1983): 631–39.

Rose, Mike. *Lives on the Boundary*. New York: Penguin, 1989.

Ruscio, Kenneth P. "The Distinctive Scholarship of the Selective Liberal Arts College." *Journal of Higher Education* 58, no. 2 (1987): 205–22.

Scarry, Elaine. *On Beauty and Being Just*. Princeton: Princeton University Press, 1999,

Schatzman, Leonard, and Anselm L. Strauss. *Field Research: Strategies for a Natural Sociology*. Englewood Cliffs, N.J.: Prentice Hall, 1973.

Schon, Donald A. *Educating the Reflective Practitioner: Toward a New Design for Teaching and Learning in the Professions*. San Francisco: Jossey-Bass, 1987.

———. *The Reflective Practitioner: How Professionals Think in Action*. New York: Basic Books, 1983.

Schuster, Jack H., and Martin J. Finkelstein, in collaboration with Jesus Francisco Galaz-Fontes and Mandy Liu. *The American Faculty: The Restructuring of Academic Work and Careers*. Baltimore: Johns Hopkins University Press, 2006.

Schutz, Alfred. *The Phenomenology of the Social World*. Translated by George Walsh and Frederick Lehnert. Evanston, Ill.: Northwestern University Press, 1967.

Schwab, Joseph. "Education and the Structure of Disciplines." In *Science, Curriculum, and Liberal Education,* edited by Ian Westbury and Neil J. Wilkof, 229–69. Chicago: University of Chicago Press, 1978.

Scott, Richard W. *Organizations: Rational, Natural, and Open*. 2nd ed. Englewood Cliffs, N.J.: Prentice Hall, 1987.

Shulman, Lee S. 1987. "Knowledge and Teaching: Foundation of the New Reform." *Harvard Educational Review* 57, no. 1 (1987): 1–22.

———. "Students and Teachers: What Should They Know?" Keynote address given at Conference on the Future of Education, Northwestern University, Evanston, Ill., May 2000.

———. *Teaching as Community Property: Essays on Higher Education*. San Francisco: Jossey-Bass/Wiley, 2004.

———. "Those Who Understand: Knowledge Growth in Teaching." *Educational Researcher* 15, no. 2 (1986): 4–14.

———. *The Wisdom of Practice: Essays on Teaching, Learning, and Learning to Teach*. San Francisco: Jossey-Bass, 2004.

Smith, Dorothy E. *The Everyday World as Problematic: A Feminist Sociology*. Boston: Northeastern University Press, 1987.

Smith, Page. *Killing the Spirit: Higher Education in America*. New York: Penguin Books, 1991.

Super, Donald E. "Coming of Age in Middletown: Careers in the Making." *American Psychologist* 40, no. 4 (1985): 405–14.

———. "A Life Span, Life Space Approach to Career Development." *Journal of Vocational Behavior* 16, no. 3 (1980): 282–98.

———. *The Psychology of Careers*. New York: Harper and Row, 1957.

Sykes, Charles J. *Profscam: Professors and the Demise of Higher Education*. New York: St. Martin's Press, 1988.

Terosky, Aimee LaPointe, Tamsyn Phifer, and Anna Neumann. "Shattering Plexiglas: Continuing Challenges for Women Professors in Research Universities." In *Unfinished Agendas: New and Continuing Gender Challenges in Higher Education*, edited by Judith Glazer-Raymo, 52–79. Baltimore: Johns Hopkins University Press, 2008.

Tierney, William G. "Academic Community and Post-Tenure Review." *Academe* 83, no. 3 (1997): 23–25.

———, ed. *Faculty Productivity: Facts, Fictions, and Issues*. New York: Falmer Press, 1999.

Tierney, William G., and Estela M. Bensimon. *Promotion and Tenure: Community and Socialization in Academe*. Albany: State University of New York Press, 1996.

Tierney, William G., and Robert A. Rhoads. *Faculty Socialization as Cultural Process: A Mirror of Institutional Commitment*. Washington, D.C.: ERIC Clearinghouse on Higher Education, George Washington University, in cooperation with the Association for the Study of Higher Education, 1994.

Tokarczyk, Michelle M., and Elizabeth A. Fay, eds. *Working-Class Women in the Academy: Laborers in the Knowledge Factory*. Amherst: University of Massachusetts Press, 1993.

Tompkins, Jane. *A Life in School: What the Teacher Learned*. Reading, Mass.: Perseus Books, 1996.

Turner, Caroline Sotello Viernes, Samuel L. Myers Jr., and John W. Creswell. "Exploring Underrepresentation: The Case of Faculty of Color in the Midwest." *Journal of Higher Education* 70, no. 1 (1999): 27–59.

Ward, Kelly, and Lisa Wolf-Wendel. "Academic Motherhood: Managing Complex Roles in Research Universities." *Review of Higher Education* 27, no. 2 (2004): 233–57.

Weick, Karl E. *The Social Psychology of Organizing*. 2nd ed. New York: Random House, 1979.

Wenger, Etienne. *Communities of Practice: Learning, Meaning, and Identity*. Cambridge: Cambridge University Press, 1998.

Wenger, Etienne, Richard McDermott, and William M. Snyder. *Cultivating Communities of Practice: A Guide to Managing Knowledge*. Boston: Harvard Business School Press, 2002.

Wertsch, James V., Pablo del Río, and Amelia Alvarez, eds. *Sociocultural Studies of Mind*. Cambridge: Cambridge University Press, 1995.

Wolf-Wendel, Lisa, and Kelly Ward. "Academic Life and Motherhood: Variations by Institutional Type." *Higher Education* 52, no. 3 (2006): 487–521.

Wortham, Stanton. *Learning Identity: The Joint Emergence of Social Identification and Academic Learning*. Cambridge: Cambridge University Press, 2006.

Page numbers in *italics* refer to tables.

engendering opportunities for interchange, 148–49

environments, learning in varied, 97–98. *See also* contexts for scholarly learning; location

expressive space, search for, 68–70

extension of subject matter knowledge, 75–78

externalization: definition of, 206; experiences of, 215–17; as feature of university organization, 214–15; images of, 209–11; internalization and, 211–14; scholarly learning and, 206–9

faculty: appointment status, 8–9; implications of study for, 227–28; return on social investment in, 5–6; workload increases for, 16–18; work of, 1–2; work options for, 9

faculty service. *See* service

family commitments, 157–59

Ferrara, Elizabeth, 160

field of study: Altman on, 25–26; colleagueship and, 194; Covington on, 30–33; cross-disciplinary, scholarly learning in, 106–15; externalization and, 215–16; home, scholarly learning in, 104–6; knowledge extension within, 75–78; Marin on, 21–23; passionate thought and, 58–61, 70. *See also* subject matter knowledge

Finkelstein, Martin, 9

"flow" of optimal experience, 54, 55

Four Universities Project: campus descriptions, 175–76; data gathered through, 282n5; description of, 35–36, 236–37; passionate thought and, 72–73; post-tenure learning, range of, 95, 96, 97–99; propositions guiding, 255–65; study design, 237–40

Galina, Iris, colleagueship and, 190–92

gender comparisons: colleagueship, 185–86, 193–94; disengagement, 99–100; early post-tenure career, 221–22; externalization, 215; family commitments, 159

global confidentiality, 242n8

group interaction, 150–52

high point/thought. *See* passionate thought

Hitlin, Steven, 138

Hope State University, 179–80

Horizon University, 178–79

identity masking, 238, 253–54, 272n5

implications of study: for professors, 227–28; for researchers, 229–30; for university leaders and policy makers, 228–29

informed consent: research description, 251–53; statement of preference for data presentation, 253–54

inside-out view: of cross-disciplinary opportunities, 195–205; of externalizing opportunities, 206–17; of faculty colleagueship, 184–95; overview of, 173–75, 183

institutional type, 9–12

instrumental learning, 17–18, 93–95

interviews: data analysis and, 275–76n1; *Four Universities Project,* 239; *People's State University Project,* 234; project year one guide, 243–47; project year three guide, 247–51

Johnson, Monica Kirkpatrick, 138

Keishin, Regina, on cross-disciplinarity, 203

knowledge: contextualizing, 81–82; crystallization of, 204, 205. *See also* subject matter knowledge

leadership, 228–29

learning: broad range of, 221; as central experience of early post-tenure career, 222–23; changes in, over career, 223–24; definition of, 6, 39, 42; instrumental, 17–18, 93–95; in-the-moment, and service, 130–33; as part of work, 255–56; as personal and emotional, 53–54, 55, 261–63; post-tenure, range of, 95, 96, 97–99; practices of, 258–61; promise of higher education and, 231; propositions of, 39–42, 255–65; as someone learning something, 256–58. *See also* cross-disciplinary learning opportunities

learning load increases, 16–18
leaves: longer-term, 108–14; temporary and focused, 107–8
Lessard, Belinda, 156–57
Libra State University, 180–82
life cycle of institution, and cross-disciplinarity, 205
life experience: Altman on, 27–28; connecting with scholarly activity, 165–69; Elias-Jones on, 52–53; Marin on, 23; Mora on, 47–49; recontextualizing knowledge and, 88–89; search for expressive space and, 69–70
Lifton, Emily: connecting contexts strategy and, 161–63; on connective work, 80; on cross-disciplinarity, 200–202, 203; externalized opportunity and, 210; on recontextualizing knowledge, 83–85; on rethinking ideas or perspectives, 80–81; service and, 130–32
local confidentiality, 241–42n8
location: recontextualizing knowledge and, 83–85; of scholarly learning, 115–18, 117. See also contexts for scholarly learning; externalization
Lucas, Benjamin, 153–54
Lunceford, Christina J., 4

Mandell, Serena: connecting contexts strategy and, 161, 162–63; on connective work, 79–80; on groups, 150–51; service and, 155–56
Marco, Anthony, on cross-disciplinarity, 196–97
Marin, Richard: cross-disciplinary efforts of, 108, 197–98; on engaging in scholarly learning, 18–25; on sensation, 56–57
Marshall, Victor W., 139
mastery of subject matter, striving for, 119–20
mentoring: connecting with scholarly activity, 160–63; Elias-Jones on, 52; Marin on, 24–25; passionate thought and, 71–72
midcareer, early. See early post-tenure career
mindwork, 220. See also activities of mind

mission: differences in institutional, 10–12; scholarly learning and, 15
Mora, David: on absorption, 55–56; connecting contexts strategy and, 166; containment strategy and, 153, 154–55; on engaging in scholarly learning, 45–50; on family commitments, 158; on intensified awareness, 57–58; on passionate thought, 67; on sensation, 56
myths of post-tenure career, 1, 36–39, 100–101, 206–7

newspapers and popular press, learning from, 210–11
norms of scholarly engagement, and cross-disciplinarity, 200–202

occupational choice, branching of, 43–45
Oldak, Jennifer: on connective work, 79; on externalized opportunity, 207–9
O'Meara, Kerry Ann, 195
On Beauty and Being Just (Scarry), 49–50
open-systems model, 173, 175
optimal experience, 54, 55
organizational context, 13–14
organizational theory, 10–11
organizational views: overview of, 172–75, 217; research and, 230. See also inside-out view; outside-in view
outreach. See externalization
outside-in view: of externalizing opportunities, 208–9; overview of, 173, 174; universities as social organizations, 175–83

Pallas, Aaron M., 138
Parsons, Jeannette, on colleagueship, 185–86
passionate thought: absorption and, 55–56; Altman on, 26–27, 28–29; creation and, 60–61; definition of, 43, 220; discernment and, 59–60; Elias-Jones on, 51–52; experience of, 61; false starts, false hopes, and, 62–63, 65–66; field of study and, 70; "flow" and, 54; high points of, 55–58; inten-

sified awareness and, 57–58; Marin on, 19–20; Mora on, 46–47; peak emotion and, 55; as rare and fleeting, 63–64, 66–68; scholarly learning surrounding, 62–64; search for expressive space and, 68–70; sensation and, 56–57; sharing experiences and, 71–72; significance of, 58–61; through time, 64–68; varieties of, 68–72

peak emotion, and passionate thought, 55

People's State University Project: campus background information, 235–36; description of, 34–35; propositions guiding, 255–65; study design, 233–35

Pereira, Kimberley B., 137–38, 139, 141

personal existence, learning located in, 115–18, *117*, 219. *See also* life experience

post-tenure career: myths of, 1, 36–39, 100–101, 206; range of learning in, 95, *96*, 97–99. *See also* early post-tenure career

practice: definition of, 206; moving substantive ideas into, 85–87. *See also* externalization

pre-tenure career, mission of university and, 11–12

priming service for scholarly learning, 163–65

professional service, 280n17

puzzle solving, and discernment, 59–60

real-world perspective, 85–87

recontextualization of subject matter knowledge, 81–90, 106–15

Redrick, Jack, on interdisciplinary work, 202, 203

re-formation of subject matter knowledge, 78–81

representation of subject matter knowledge, 90–93, 121–26

research: academic, and scholarly learning, 41; containment in, 153–55; implications of study for, 229–30; knowledge extension within, 78; questions guiding, 40–41; scholarly learning and, 36, 116

rethinking established ideas or perspectives, 80–81

return on social investment, 5–6

revision of subject matter knowledge, 126–28

Scarry, Elaine, 49–50

Schell, Julie, 137

scholarly learning: academic research and, 41; as bidirectional, 225–26; commitment to advancement of, 224–26; conceptions of, 74–75; content of, 41–42, 135–36, 138–39, 263–65; definition of, 6, 224–25; in early post-tenure career, 3–4; focus on, 12–14; importance of, 7, 224; instrumental learning compared to, 17–18; propositions of, 39–42, 255–65; reality of, 219–20; research on, 36; as spreading out, 218–19. *See also* activities of mind; agency for scholarly learning; contexts for scholarly learning; cross-disciplinary learning opportunities; strategy

Schon, Donald, 140

Schuster, Jack, 9

sciences, definition of, 240n1

self-identity, learning, 98–99

sensation, and passionate thought, 56–57, 219

service: community resources and, 133–34; connecting with scholarly activity, 163–65; definition of, 129; in-the-moment learning and, 130–33; scholarly learning and, 102, 115–18, 134; selecting projects for, 155–57; strategy and, 169–70. *See also* externalization

settings. *See* contexts for scholarly learning; location

Sharan, Esther: on colleagueship, 186–87; cross-disciplinary efforts of, 111–14; on rethinking ideas or perspectives, 81

sharing experiences, and passionate thought, 71–72

Signal University, 176–77

social costs of faculty preparation, 5

social organizations, universities as, 175–83